Canon Law
and the
Archpriest of Hita

medieval & renaissance texts & studies

VOLUME 27

Canon Law
and the
Archpriest of Hita

BY

Henry Ansgar Kelly

medieval & renaissance texts & studies
Center for Medieval & Early Renaissance Studies
Binghamton, New York
1984

Library of Congress Cataloging in Publication Data

Kelly, Henry Ansgar, 1934–
  Canon law and the Archpriest of Hita.

  (Medieval & Renaissance texts & studies; v. 27)
  Includes bibliographical references.
  1. Ruiz, Juan, fl. 1343. Libro de buen amor. 2. Ruiz, Juan, fl. 1343 –
Knowledge – Law. 3. Canon law. 4. Canon law in literature. I. Title.
II. Series.

PQ6430.K44 1984   861'.1   83–774
ISBN 0-86698-058-X

For

Rudolf Borchert

Contents

Preface

The *Libro de buen amor*, or "Book of True Love," is the greatest work of literature produced in fourteenth-century Spain. Its author, who identifies himself as Juan Ruiz, Archpriest of Hita, can be favorably compared with another poet of the fourteenth century, Geoffrey Chaucer. But we can observe Chaucer's skills in working with a wide range of genres and themes in numerous works, whereas Juan Ruiz's extensive powers are on display in only one composition. And whereas Chaucer's historical character is firmly established – he is named in, or associated with, something like five hundred contemporary documents – we know nothing whatsoever about Juan Ruiz except what can be gleaned from the *Libro de buen amor*.

Like Chaucer, Juan Ruiz invariably uses the autobiographical mode. But we are able to distinguish grains of truth in Chaucer's self-portraits, whereas with Juan Ruiz we are totally at sea. We cannot even be sure that his real name was Juan Ruiz, or that he was the archpriest of Hita. Furthermore, we cannot be sure of what his purposes were in composing the work. Whether or not we accept as authentic, and truthful, his statement at the end of the prose Introduction, that he intended to provide a set of examples of various kinds of poetic forms, we must often remain puzzled about the structure of the parts and the whole, and uncertain of the logic behind some of his progressions, tangents, and transitions.

Nevertheless, we do know something about the author, and there is good hope of learning more. We can at least deduce what sort of man would be capable of writing the *Libro de buen amor*. For instance, he must have read, or heard of, the twelfth-century Latin "comedy," *Pamphilus*, for he draws on it in his work.

In this study, I address myself to one kind of "literary allusion" and to the corresponding area of implied accomplishment: namely, references to and knowledge of canon law. As narrator of the *Libro de buen amor*, Juan Ruiz claims an amateur's interest in canon law; he is a simple student of the subject, and not a master or a doctor. This, of course, may be a humble, or mock-humble, way of saying he knows a great deal about it. But because some of his citations have escaped verification, and because of various other deductions, some readers are inclined not only to take him at his word (that he is not expert in law), but also to conclude that he is sometimes "faking" his acquaintance with the authorities he alludes to.

In the first chapter below, I examine some of Juan Ruiz's specific references to canonistic compilations and commentaries, and find the weight of evidence in his favor: that he really does know the works he alludes to. Furthermore, I identify one of the works he cites as having been completed and published only in 1338, in Bologna. This new certainty about Juan Ruiz (if it is accepted as such) must call into question some hitherto accepted certainties: particularly the idea that one of the manuscripts of the *Libro de buen amor* fixes the year of composition as A.D. 1330. My general conclusion about the dating of the work is that the only certain date is the *terminus ante quem* of A.D. 1389. This opens the possibility that Juan Ruiz was an exact contemporary of Geoffrey Chaucer and perhaps even influenced by him (or vice versa), via the Spanish court of John of Gaunt and Constance of Castile.

In Chapter II, I take up Juan Ruiz's claim to be the archpriest of Hita. I give something of the history of the office of archpriest, and look into the expected duties and actual practices of archpriests of the diocese of Toledo in the fourteenth century. Archpriests of Hita, it turns out, were not pastors of the principal church of the town of Hita, and in fact were not pastors at all. They were instead ecclesiastical administrators and judges with power of correction over the entire archipresbyterate—a fairly large area surrounding the town of Hita. The proper exercise of the office naturally demanded some knowledge of canon law.

I also set forth some of the principles of the "beneficial" system of the Church in the fourteenth century, and show that as a *beneficium curatum* the archipresbyterate of Hita could not have gone unmentioned in papal documents dealing with holders of the post; and that therefore recent attempts to identify archpriests of Hita without sufficient documentation are fallacious.

In Chapter III, I continue my discussion of the office of archpriest by looking at another archipresbyteral capital, Talavera. I suggest that the *Cántica de los clérigos de Talavera*, which forms an appendix to the *Libro de buen amor* in one of the manuscripts, was written in the fifteenth century, and does not reflect the historical conditions of Talavera during the time when Gil de Albornoz was archbishop of Toledo, namely, from 1338 to 1350. The doubts raised in Chapter I about the connections of the original *Libro de buen amor* with Archbishop Albornoz are thereby further strengthened.

In the fourth chapter, I discuss the trial presided over by Don Ximio (Mr. Justice Monkey), in which a criminal accusation is brought by Wolf against Mrs. Fox. In it, Juan Ruiz shows a profound knowledge of the niceties of procedural law, including the requirements that canon law had imposed upon the secular courts. The upshot of this examination is that the author of the *Libro de buen amor* was very likely a judge or a practicing lawyer; and that, given his knowledge of canon law elsewhere in the work, particularly in connection with the sacrament of confession, he may well have been connected to an ecclesiastical court, say, the sort of court that an archpriest would preside over. But whether or not he actually was an archpriest must remain an open question.

This study represents my first venture into the fascinating fields of medieval Spanish literature and culture, and I apologize for any inaccuracies or misstatements to which my inexperience may have given rise. But I have some confidence that the work will prove to be a valuable contribution to those fields. My excuse for undertaking the project (apart from the fact that I enjoy the kind of research it entails) is my previous experience in the area of medieval canon law. I have, for instance, examined the bearing of canon law upon various works of literature in my *Love and Marriage in the Age of Chaucer* (1975), and have investigated procedural law in *The Matrimonial Trials of Henry VIII* (1976).

I wish to thank all of the scholars who have given me help and advice in my researches, especially Robert Burns, S.J., Daniel Eisenberg, Michael Gerli, Joaquín Gimeno, Stephan Kuttner, Carlos Otero, and Anthony Zahareas. I wish also to thank my family and friends for enduring patiently and cheerfully the various reports I have made to them about archpriests, benefices, exceptions, and excommunications.

Canon Law
and the
Archpriest of Hita

Chapter One

Canons, Canonists, and Dates in the *Libro de Buen Amor*

1. *Citations from Canon Law*

Juan Ruiz makes direct citation of canon law[1] in two sections of the *Libro de buen amor*:[2] the prose Introduction, and the episode of Don Carnal's confession. In the latter section, actual canonical doctrine and practice is at issue, while in the former it is largely a question of backing up proverbial or commonplace wisdom with a canonical authority. It is in the discourse on confession that Juan Ruiz states in effect his beginner's status as a canonist: "Escolar só mucho rudo, nin maestro nin dotor" (stanza 1135).[3]

When Juan Ruiz refers to the *Decreto*, he means, of course, the *Decretum* or *Concordantia discordantium canonum* compiled by Gratian of Bologna around 1140, which was received as the basic collection of early canon law. Félix Lecoy has identified a number of passages in Gratian that correspond to the citations in the discussion on confession, but notes that Juan Ruiz could have found some of the same material in earlier works.[4] We need not, I think, take this suggestion seriously, that Juan Ruiz drew upon Gratian's sources and only pretended to find them in Gratian. Apart from the fact that it would be a pointless mystification, it would entail an even higher degree of learning in him than would the straightforward use of the *Decretum*. More plausible is the possibility that he found the allusions in a later source, say, a confessor's manual; but this is a question that we can leave aside, at least for the moment.

In discussing the penance imposed by the Friar on Don Carnal, Juan

Ruiz alludes to the discussion in the *Decretum* on the necessity of auricular confession:

> En el santo *Decreto* ay grand disputaçión
> Si se faz penitençia por sola contriçión:
> Determina al cabo que es la confesión
> Mester de todo en todo con la satisfaçión. (1136)

The discussion in question occurs in the first distinction of Gratian's so-called *Tractatus de Poenitentia* (which takes up the whole of Question 3 in Case 33 of the Second Part of the *Decretum*).[5] The question posed is: "Utrum sola cordis contritione et secreta satisfactione, absque oris confessione, quisque possit Deo satisfacere?" Gratian's answer, which Juan Ruiz reports, comes after canon 60, and runs as follows: "Ex his itaque apparet quod sine confessione oris et satisfactione operis peccatum non remittitur."[6]

In stanza 1142, where Juan Ruiz speaks of the repentance of St. Peter, he seems clearly to be drawing on *Petrus doluit*, the first canon of Distinction 1 of the *De poenitentia*.[7] Earlier, in stanza 1130, which deals with the unacceptability of a written confession, he may be drawing on canon 88, *Quem poenitet*, taken from the eleventh-century pseudo-Augustinian treatise *De vera et falsa poenitentia*.[8] Lecoy also cites *Qui vult confiteri*, the first canon of Distinction 6, as a possible source for the example of two men falling into a ditch.[9] But in none of these cases does Juan Ruiz cite the *Decretum* by name.

Let us turn now to the sermon that serves as an introduction to the *Libro de buen amor*. Here the *Decretum* is mentioned several times by name, but without further specifics, and so far none of the references have been traced.

Juan Ruiz attributes to Gratian's work, first of all, the idea that human nature is more inclined to evil than to good:

> E viene otrosí esto por razón que la natura umana que más aparejada e inclinada es al mal que al bien, e a pecado que a bien: esto dize el *Decreto*.   (lines 76–79)

Perhaps he is thinking of the canon *Proclivis* from the Sixth Council of Toledo: "Proclivis autem cursus est ad voluptatem, et imitatrix natura vitiorum." In some texts of the *Decretum* the reading is *proclivior* or *proclivius* instead of *proclivis*.[10] Another canon says that every age is prone to evil from "adolescence" on.[11]

The next two citations deal with the fallibility of human memory and the need for making records in pictures and writing. Juan Ruiz attributes to Gratian first the idea that the memory of man is fleeting, and second the point that it is more the mark of divinity than of humanity to keep all things in the memory and to forget nothing. The text reads as follows:

> Otrosí fueron la pintura e la escriptura e las imágenes primeramente falladas, por razón que la memoria del omne desleznadera es; esto dize el *Decreto*. Ca tener todas las cosas en la memoria, e non olvidar algo, más es de la divinidat que de la umanidad; esto dize el *Decreto*.   (lines 81–87)

I have not been able to find anything exactly corresponding to these sentiments in Gratian. It would be a nice irony if Juan Ruiz was relying on his fallible memory at this point and went astray. He could, for example, have read about the fleeting memory of man in the constitutions of the diocesan synod of Toledo in 1323: "Cum hominis memoriam labilem experientia manifestet,"[12] and mistakenly remembered it as coming from Gratian. It is possible, however, that he found the idea in Gratian only by interpretation: by drawing, for instance, on concrete examples of the possibility of memory lapses. This is what John Andreae of Bologna does in his *Apparatus to the Clementine Constitutions* when commenting on the pope's insistence that proper records be kept in court cases. Andreae says, "Ratione memoriae, quae labilis est, 23 dist., *Praeterea*." He is referring to the twelfth canon, *Praeterea*, of Distinction 23 in the First Part of Gratian's *Decretum*, where Pope Nicholas I says he has not read of a certain practice, "nisi nos fallat oblivio."[13]

Alternatively, it may be that Juan Ruiz was drawing on a commentator like Andreae who alleged that the idea of memory as *labilis* was to be found in Gratian. It is likely, in fact, that Juan Ruiz was familiar with Andreae's *Apparatus*, which was published in 1322 and quickly became accepted as the *Glossa ordinaria* to the *Clementines*.[14] We shall see below that Juan Ruiz not only quotes from the *Clementines*, but also alludes to a later work by Andreae.

Other relevant passages on faulty memory can be found in the

Decretum. For instance, Pope Nicholas is quoted again as referring to cases which do not come to his memory,[15] and Pope Leo I, dealing with the subject of baptismal investigations, distinguishes between what can be remembered and what is foreign to memory.[16] According to St. Augustine, those who have died can be informed of events that occur later in this life by others who die after them, but the memories of these latter are restricted: they can tell only of what they are allowed to remember.[17]

As for the contrast between the divine and human memories, the sentiment appeared originally in the *Justinian Code*. In the title *De veteri iure enucleando*, law 2 (*Tanta circa nos*), paragraph 13 (*Si quid autem*), Justinian attributes man's faulty memory to the *imbecillitas humana quae naturaliter inest*, and observes:

> Omnium habere memoriam et penitus in nullo peccare divinitatis magis quam mortalitatis est.[18]

William Durantis refers to this paragraph, without quoting it, as the source for the sentiment that man's memory is *labilis*. We can add this to our examples given above of loose juristic citations. This example is particularly interesting, since Juan Ruiz would have had good opportunity to see it. It appears in the *Speculum iudiciale*, which must have been Juan Ruiz's constant companion (as will become abundantly clear in Chapter IV below). In the passage in question, Durantis is comparing the reliability of documentary and testimonial evidence; when something from the distant past is being proved, documents are far more reliable than witnesses:

> Sed et temporis consideratio habenda est. Nam cum res vel factum antiquum probatur, magis credendum est instrumento quam testibus. Hominum enim memoria labilis est, *Codex*, *De veteri iure enucleando*, lex i[i], *Si quid autem*. Longum secus in novo aut recenti, ubi testes sunt boni, discreti, et honesti.[19]

Justinian's dictum is not only cited but also quoted by Azzo of Bologna, the great "civilian" jurist (d. 1230), at the beginning of his *Summa Codicis*. But his version differs in several ways from the received text given above, most notably by the substitution of the more readily understandable *humanitas* for *mortalitas*:

Omnium habere memoriam et in nullo penitus peccare divinitatis est potius quam humanitatis.[20]

He follows the same wording later when he comes to comment on the law itself.[21]

Whether Azzo himself or some other commentator (or scribe, or series of scribes or commentators) was responsible for rephrasing the text, it is closer than the original version to the form used by two canonists of note, namely Cardinal Hostiensis and Bernard of Parma.

Hostiensis, who is referred to by name elsewhere in the *Libro de buen amor* (as we will see in the next section), speaks of the need for facts to be recorded in documents, and then quotes the *Justinian Code* as follows:

Omnium habere memoriam et in nullo peccare est potius divinitatis quam humanitatis.[22]

Bernard of Parma was the author of a commentary on the *Decretals of Gregory IX* which became accepted as the *Ordinary Gloss*. He worked on it for a generation, and the final version was completed shortly before his death in 1266. He quotes Justinian's dictum twice, in both instances referring to the possibility of the pope's forgetfulness. He uses the following wording:

Omnium habere memoriam et in nullo peccare potius est divinitatis quam humanitatis.[23]

Both Hostiensis and Bernard refer directly to the *Justinian Code*, though the quotation doubtless came to them through an intermediate source—unless we are to believe that they and Azzo were all using corrupt texts of the *Code*. And speaking of corrupt texts, it may be that our text of the *Libro de buen amor* is faulty at this point, and that for *decreto* we should read *derecho*: in which case Juan Ruiz would be saying that the dictum about divine and human memory is found in the "law." There seems to be a clear case of the opposite mistake later on, when Juan Ruiz speaks of the cruelty of a man who belittles his own reputation: "Ca mucho es cruel quien su fama menospreçia: el Derecho lo dize" (lines 117–18). In this instance, the manuscript reads *drho*, which most editors expand to *derecho*. But Giorgio Chiarini emends it to *decreto*, and I agree with him; for the sentiment can be found in Gratian, where he cites St. Augustine in the canon *Nolo*: "Qui fidens conscientiae negligit famam suam crudelis est."[24] In any case, one can easily see how the two words could be confused.

It is also possible, however, that Juan Ruiz, or some commentator that he draws upon, takes Justinian's dictum as summing various ideas in Gratian. In fact, in Bernard of Parma's first use of the quotation, when he is commenting on the chapter *Cum adeo*, he cites two instances of popes with faulty memories, namely Nicholas I in the canon *Praeterea* and Urban II in the canon *Quod autem uxor*, before giving Justinian's comment.[25] As for God's memory, St. Augustine indicates (in one of Gratian's canons) that it is not only total but preexistent: the sons of God even before the preaching of the Gospel were written ineradicably in the "memorial" of their Father.[26] In another canon by Pope Nicholas, the pontiff recommends that one implore God not to draw on His memory, that is, not to remember sins of ignorance.[27] Elsewhere, we find the assumption that God does indeed remember all things, but will sometimes act as if He does not: He promises not to remember the iniquities of the penitent.[28] Human beings, in contrast, can be truly forgetful of their sins, and when they do finally remember them it is sometimes too late.[29]

Pictorial representations of the saints are defended as serving to call the saints themselves to memory.[30] The purpose of writing, too, is to aid human memory. For instance, the time of manumission is to be recorded, lest the condition of origin be obscured by length of time.[31] The decrees of the Fathers are divinely inspired,[32] and teachings are memorialized in Holy Scripture.[33] When a man is ordained exorcist, the book containing the exorcisms is given to him to commit to memory.[34]

Let us move to Juan Ruiz's next citation of the *Decretum* in his Introduction. After appealing to the "law" on the point of the man who demeans his own reputation (see above), he goes on to say that his book will inspire men to love themselves more than sin, for ordered charity begins with oneself, as the *Decretum* says:

E querrán más amar a sí mesmos que al pecado; que la ordenada
caridad de sí mesmo comiença: el *Decreto* lo dize. (lines 118–20)

He may be referring to the long canon *Caritas* in Gratian's *De poenitentia*, which is taken from a treatise by Prosper of Aquitaine. Prosper says, for example:

> Ex ea enim parte quis peccat, ex qua minus diligit Deum; quem si ex toto corde diligamus nihil erit in nobis unde peccati desideriis serviamus. Et quid est diligere Deum, nisi illi occupari animo, concipiere fruendae visionis eius affectum, peccati odium, mundi fastidium, diligere etiam proximum, quem in se censuit diligendum, in ipso amore servare legitimum modum, nec pervertere dilectionis ordinem constitutum?

And again:

> Corpus nostrum, quia pars nostri est, ad hoc nobis diligendum est, ut saluti eius ac fragilitati naturaliter consulamus, et agamus quatinus spiritui ordinate subiectum ad aeternam salutem, accepta immortalitate et incorruptione, perveniat.

We are to love our neighbors because they are "naturae nostrae participes," and we must love them as ourselves.[35]

Earlier in his Introduction, Juan Ruiz may be drawing on the canon *Ille rex* of the *De poenitentia* when he says that sin does not come from right understanding or good will or good works but from the frailty of human nature that is in man, which cannot escape from sin:

> Este desacuerdo non viene del buen entendimiento, nin tal querer non viene de la buena voluntad, nin de la buena obra non viene tal obra; ante viene de la flaqueza de la natura humana que es en el omne, que se non puede escapar de pecado, (lines 57–67)

though he goes on to quote the *Distichs* of Pseudo-Cato. In *Ille rex*, St. Ambrose, speaking of King David, says that the saints sometimes fall, "naturae magis fragilitate quam peccandi libidine"; and he adds: "culpam itaque incidisse naturae est, diluisse virtutis."[36]

So far, we have concentrated on Juan Ruiz's citations of Gratian's *Decretum*, but he would also have been familiar with the *Decretals of Gregory IX*, the official collection of laws compiled by the Catalan Dominican St. Raymond of Peñafort and issued in 1234, and one can also assume that he knew Bernard of Parma's *Ordinary Gloss*, which

I cited above. It is doubtless Gregory IX's collection that Juan Ruiz
is primarily referring to when he recommends that his readers consult
las decretales on the matter of reserved sins (stanza 1148),[37] and when
he speaks of *los libros, las glosas, e los testos* (1151) he would naturally
be including the *glossae ordinariae* of all the canonical collections. In
his Introduction he may be remembering Celestine III's statement in
the decretal *Secundo requiris* when he attributes to "law" the idea that
words serve the intention, not vice versa: "Secund derecho, las palabras
sirven a la intençión e non la intençión a las palabras" (lines 139–40).
The pope says: "Secundum beatum Gregorium, verba intentioni deser-
vi[u]nt."[38]

At the end of his Introduction, Juan Ruiz cites the *Clementines*, the
decretal collection of Pope Clement V, completed in 1314 and published officially in 1317 by Pope John XXII.[39] In doing so, he gives,
for once, a full citation:

> E porque de toda buena obra es comienço e fundamento Dios
> e la fe cathólica, e dízelo la primera decretal de las *Clementinas*,
> que comiença "Fidei catholicae fundamento," e do éste non es
> çimiento, non se puede fazer obra firme nin firme hedifiçio, segund
> dize el Apóstol.   (lines 156–61)

The quotation from St. Paul, 1 Corinthians 3:11, is taken from the
decretal, which reads:

> Fidei catholicae fundamento, praeter quod, testante Apostolo,
> nemo potest aliud ponere, firmiter inhaerentes. . . .[40]

I wish to conclude this section by discussing Juan Ruiz's final citation
in his Introduction, which, though it has nothing to do with canon
law, may have confirmed the idea of his ignorance in the mind of
some readers, for he refers to the so-called Athanasian Creed as a psalm.
He says:

> Tomé el verso primero del salmo que es de la santa Trinidad e
> de la fe cathólica, que es "Quicumque vult," el verso que dice,
> "Ita Deus Pater, Deus Filius,"[41] e cetera.   (lines 162–66)

He is within his rights not to identify the piece as a creed or *sym-*

bolum; and in calling it a psalm he is following a recognizable tradition, not only in Spain but also in England. In Toledo in 1338 we hear of the office of Prime being sung on feastdays "usque ad psalmum de *Quicumque vult.*" In England, an example appears in the statutes of the synod of Exeter held in 1287 under Bishop Peter Quinel; reference is made to the simple understanding of the articles of the Christian faith, "prout in psalmo *Quicumque vult* et utroque symbolo continetur." Another typical formula refers to it as the *treatise* that is *psalmed* every day at Prime: "Sicut continetur in symbolo, tam maiori quam minori, et in tractatu qui dicitur *Quicumque vult*, qui quotidie ad Primam in ecclesia psallitur."[42]

Let me sum up what we have seen thus far of Juan Ruiz's use of canon law. He cites Gratian accurately on points of law or ecclesiastical discipline. He makes an accurate citation from the most recent official papal collection of decretals in his day, the *Clementine Constitutions*. He cites Gratian loosely on matters of proverbial wisdom: but whether one wishes to take the charitable view and justify his citations on grounds of general content, or instead prefers to accuse him of inaccuracy in his references, the juristic origin of the apophthegms is pretty evident—and even crystal clear in the case of Justinian's remark on memory.[43] It is a promising start.

II. *The List of Canonistic Authorities*

In the episode of Don Carnal's confession, Juan Ruiz refers to several commentaries on canon law which supposedly elaborate on questions of penitential jurisdiction:

> Lea en el *Espéculo* e en el su *Repertorio*;
> [*or*: Lea en el *Espéculo* o en el *Repertorio*;]
> Los libros de Ostiense, que son grand parlatorio;
> El Inoçençio Quarto, un sotil consistorio;
> El *Rosario* de Guido; *Novela*; e *Diratorio*.[44]   (1152)

The two versions of the first line can be interpreted as follows:

> Read in the *Speculum* and in its *Repertorium*.
> Read in the *Speculum* or in the *Repertorium*.

The works named here have been taken to be the *Speculum iudiciale* and the *Repertorium* by William Durantis the Elder, Bishop of Mende, who died in 1296. The *Repertorium* has a section on confession entitled *Aureum confessorium et memoriale sacerdotum*, in which there is a discussion of reserved sins.[45] The *Speculum*, however, which I cited earlier, has virtually nothing to do with confession, but rather deals with procedural law. Juan Ruiz must have been thoroughly familiar with it, as we will see in our examination of the episode of Don Ximio. Perhaps, then, he names the *Speculum* in the context of confession simply to identify the author of the *Repertorium* as the great "Speculator." Or it may be that he considered the *Repertorium* to be a supplement to the *Speculum*; each treatise has cross-references to the other for further information on various points, and the two works were sometimes bound together in the same manuscript.[46] This is true of two of the four fourteenth-century copies of the *Speculum* now in the Cathedral Library of Toledo.[47]

Hostiensis, that is, Henry of Suse or Segusia, was cardinal bishop of Ostia (hence "Hostiensis").[48] His best-known work was the comprehensive *Summa super titulis Decretalium Gregorii IX*, or *Summa aurea*, which I cited earlier. It was begun in 1239 and finished in 1253. It alone would merit Juan Ruiz's characterization of Hostiensis as a "great talker," but it fits him even more as the author of the enormous *Lectura* or *Commentaria in quinque libros Decretalium*. This work was also begun around 1239 and finished shortly before his death in 1271. Hostiensis was also the author of a *Lectura* on the *Novellae constitutiones* of Innocent IV, which he composed shortly after finishing the *Summa*.

Innocent IV, the former Sinibaldo Fieschi, was pope from 1243 to 1254. I will discuss his *Novellae constitutiones* below. Juan Ruiz's reference must be to his *Apparatus in quinque libros Decretalium*, which was composed after 1246 and before 1253, probably by 1251.[49] It is odd that Juan Ruiz calls him a "subtle consistory." Perhaps he means that his work contains a wealth of closely argued judgments.

In contrast to the decretalists Hostiensis and Innocent IV, Guido of Baysio, commonly known as "the Archdeacon," was best known as a decretist, or commentator on Gratian's *Decretum*. His *Rosarium* was finished at the beginning of 1300.[50]

The last two works named by Juan Ruiz have remained a puzzle. I identify them as John Andreae's *Novella* on the *Decretals of Gregory IX*, finished in 1338, and the *Directorium iuris* of Peter Quesnel, which he completed in 1322.

Let us take up the earlier work first. The three manuscripts of the *Libro de buen amor* give different readings. The Toledo text repeats *Repertorio* from the earlier line, and is easily rejected. The Gayoso reading of *Decretorio* has found favor with some editors, but it too must be eliminated, since it makes no sense: there is no such word as *decretorium*, and no work of canon law had a title resembling it. We are left with the Salamanca reading of *Diratorio*, which has rightly been taken to correspond to the Latin word *directorium*. The word became common later as a title for reference works, and its popularity holds to the present day, as is evidenced, for instance, by our telephone directories. But in Juan Ruiz's time it was not common, and it almost certainly refers to the *Directorium iuris*.[51] It is noteworthy that the fifteenth-century copy of the work now in the Burgos Cathedral Library has the title *Diritorium iuris*,[52] which is close to Juan Ruiz's vernacular form *Diratorio*.

The *Directorium iuris* was compiled by a Franciscan friar named Petrus, surnamed Quesnel (often interpreted as "Quesvel"). According to J. C. Russell, "the statement that Peter Quesnel was Franciscan warden of Norwich has probably no firmer basis than the early known fact of the existence of his book in the library of that house."[53] The *Dictionary of National Biography* puts the time of his death around 1299,[54] but historians of canon law have placed him in the first half of the fourteenth century,[55] and rightly so, since he draws on the *Clementines*.[56] Russell says that he may not have lived in England at all,[57] but the Yale manuscript of his work, which may be in his own hand, is English.[58]

In his Introduction, the author identifies himself as "Frater Petrus inter minores minimus."[59] There is no title provided for the work in the Yale text, but the Merton copy has the following:

Incipit summa que vocatur directoria iuris in foro conscientie et iudiciali composita a fratre petro quesnel de ordine fratrum minorum ex iuribus et doctorum sentencijs diuersorum.[60]

Elsewhere, Quesnel refers to his work not only as *Summa directoria* but also as *Directorium iuris*.[61]

Quesnel deals with the *Clementine Constitutions* under the name of *Liber septimus*.[62] He says he has not seen these new laws treated fully by any doctor.[63] Now, Quesnel could perhaps have been able to say this even if he had seen the *Apparatus to the Clementines* written in 1319 by the Gascon canonist William of Montlauzun, when he was professor at Toulouse.[64] (William is one of the authors that Quesnel names in his list of authorities; he may have known only his earlier *Lectura* on the *Liber sextus*.[65]) But he could hardly have said it of John Andreae's magisterial *Apparatus* of 1322. Quesnel does in fact cite Andreae's *Glossa ordinaria* on the *Liber sextus*, which Andreae completed in 1301.[66]

We should therefore take as authentic the note at the end of the Yale manuscript stating that the book was compiled by its author in the year 1322.[67] We can well imagine that it took Quesnel several years to complete the massive work.

Because of its practical nature as a guide to confessors and ecclesiastical lawyers, the *Directorium* seems to have been quite influential, and was widely disseminated.[68] A complete copy was possessed by the Franciscan house of Toledo in the seventeenth century.[69] Perhaps it was this volume that had come to the attention of Juan Ruiz. Quesnel deals with the sacrament of penance formally in title 15 of Book 1,[70] and treats of confessional jurisdiction in paragraphs 67–122.[71]

We move now to the citation of *Novela*. Giorgio Chiarini relates it to what he says is juridical terminology for an appendix to a codex.[72] Perhaps he is thinking of the *Novellae* of Justinian, which Joan Corominas explicitly names as intended by Juan Ruiz.[73] The *Justinian Novels*, however, have nothing whatsoever to do with the matter at hand (reserved sins in canon law), and the inappropriateness of this identification is pointed out by J. L. Bermejo Cabrero, who refers instead to some medieval uses of the term, for instance, the *Novellae* of Innocent IV, and the *Novellae super Decretalibus* of John Andreae.[74]

The decretals of Innocent IV were called *novellae decretales* or *novae constitutiones* in the thirteenth century, in contrast both to the *Decretales Gregorii IX* and the *decretales novissimae* of Gregory X (1274). But these "new" and "newest" decretals were incorporated with still newer decretals into Boniface VIII's *Liber sextus decretalium* in 1298; and more recent decretals and decretal collections followed in the fourteenth century. Consequently, the term *novellae* as referring to the decretals of Innocent IV would have been somewhat dated by that time, though, of course, it could still appear in manuscripts of the collection and commentaries on it. But it does not appear in the two copies of the collection, one of the thirteenth and the other of the fourteenth century, now in the Toledo Cathedral Library.[75] Furthermore, none of Innocent IV's "novels" deals with the sacrament of confession or with confessional jurisdiction. Finally, since Juan Ruiz has already mentioned Innocent IV as an authority, there would not be much point in referring to one of his constitutions later on.

Of course, any other recent (or comparatively recent) papal or even episcopal constitution could be called "new." For instance, Boniface VIII's successor Benedict XI refers to one of Boniface's decretals in the *Sext* as "quaedem novella constitutio super negotio haereticae pravitatis." He revokes another decretal of Boniface's, *Super cathedram*, which he calls a *nova constitutio*. In the *Clementines*, we find Clement V "innovating" Boniface's *Super cathedram*, and a few years later, in 1325, the Bishop of Rochester grants a Franciscan friar the right to preach and hear confessions in his diocese "iuxta formam constitutionis novellae quae incipit *Super cathedram*."[76]

It is possible, I suppose, that a new constitution dealing with confession, like *Super cathedram*, was so well known that Juan Ruiz could recommend it to his readers without further identification, not as *constitutio novella*, but simply as *novella*, but I do not think it likely. Apart from the grammatical problem, which would be the same in Spanish as in Latin, presumably, the context of the passage does not call for reference to a single papal decretal but to a commentary on papal decretals, just as the context of the next line shows that the Gayoso manuscript reading, "Dotores más de çiento, en libros e questiones," is to be preferred to the Salamanca reading, "Decretales más de çientos en libros e en questiones" (1153a). Finally, I know of no such well known recent papal decretal on confession.

If then we must reject Bermejo's suggestion of new papal constitutions, his suggestion of John Andreae is an entirely different matter. For if the reference is to his work, the requirements of both form and context would be satisfied, as well as the requirement of familiarity, for Andreae was the most authoritative canonist of his time. I wish to maintain that Juan Ruiz can *only* be referring to Andreae's commentary on the *Decretals of Gregory IX*. The commentary was not called *Novellae*, as Bermejo would have it, but *Novella*, which corresponds to the form used by Juan Ruiz. As we have seen, the word is basically an adjective meaning "new," and Andreae employs it as such in the preface of his work, which he characterizes as a *novella glossarum compilatio*. In some editions, the word is used as a neuter plural: *In quinque Decretalium libros novella commentaria*.[77] But the word was also regularly used, both by Andreae and by his readers, as a substantive or self-standing title for the commentary. Andreae had a strong precedent for this substantive use of the word, for his mother's name was Novella, and in fact he named his commentary after her, and he gave his daughter the same name. He refers to his commentary in this way as early as 1311, but only as a work in progress. It was not completed or promulgated as a whole until 1338.[78] Some time later, Andreae completed the *Novella* on the *Liber sextus*.

Portions of the *Novella*-in-progress were circulated before 1338, but there is no evidence that these published fragments were ever referred to as the *Novella* or as part of the *Novella*. Andreae himself does not refer to the *Novella* in his earlier published works, for instance, the *Apparatus to the Clementines*, which as we saw was finished in 1322. Andreae's students at Bologna would of course have heard him speak of the *Novella*, for their classroom notes were in effect part of it.

Since Andreae was the best known canon lawyer of his time, one can easily imagine that word of the forthcoming *Novella* spread all over Europe long before 1338. Spain would be no exception, since there were over 150 Spaniards studying at Bologna during the first three decades of the fourteenth century,[79] and in fact one of them was decapitated in 1321 for raping a kinswoman of John Andreae's.[80] But we can hardly imagine anyone in Spain recommending to others that they read the *Novella* on a certain point before the work was published and widely available.[81]

Therefore, if I am right that Juan Ruiz is citing Andreae's *Novella*, we have a dating problem. One of the accepted dates for the *Libro de buen amor*, A.D. 1330, is clearly out of the question. The other accepted date, 1343, is no doubt possible, but still very early. We will take up the question of the manuscript dates below. I will only note here that the Cathedral Library of Toledo possesses some dated copies of the *Novella*, which may give us some idea of the time and expense involved in reproducing the work. The scribe, Andrew of Modena, says that he spent two years and seven months working on the *Novella* on the five books of the *Decretals*, for which he received 274 pounds from his master John of Piacenza, apart from "goods and great provisions." The Cathedral has only Books III–V of this set: Book III was finished on 9 March 1359, Book IV (which is very short) on 16 May 1359, and Book V on 21 August 1359, a Wednesday (therefore his date, m.ccc.lviiiii, is a mistake for m.ccc.lviiii). He finished the *Additiones* and the *Novella* on the *Sext* for the same employer thirteen months later, 29 September 1360. A year and a half later, he finished the first part (Books I–II) of another set, on Wednesday, 30 March 1362 (his date of m.ccc.lxiii is a mistake for m.ccc.lxii).[82] Another Italian copy of the *Novella* on Books III–V of the *Decretals* was given to the Cathedral by Pedro Díaz de Tenorio, Archbishop of Toledo, in 1386.[83] Yet another copy of the *Novella* on Books IV–V, this one not said to be Italian in origin, was also given by Tenorio at the same time.[84]

It may be of interest for us to look at a typical passage or two from the *Novella*, as an illustration of the way in which Andreae draws on previous authorities. Let us see what he has to say on the subject of reserved sins in the case of an urban archpriest. Referring to the final gloss of the *Glossa ordinaria* on the chapter *Officium archipresbyteri de urbe*,[85] which interprets the text as saying that "omnes possunt recurrere ad archipresbyterum maioris ecclesiae," Andreae says that Innocent IV and the Abbot[86] seem to understand this to refer to serious sinners. But if it was their meaning to include sins reserved to the bishop, Hostiensis disagrees; he says that without a special licence from the bishop the archpriest cannot give absolution in such cases, and Andreae agrees with his opinion. He goes on to say that according to Hostiensis there are three levels of authority over souls: the pope and his vicars; the bishop and the archpriest of the city, who is his vicar in this matter; and the curate.[87]

The next chapter, *Ut singulae plebes*, deals with the office of rural archpriest, which as we shall see is the title that Juan Ruiz claims for himself. On the point that such archpriests are to refer all things to the bishop, the *Glossa ordinaria* says: "Praeter minora quae ipsi archipresbyteri determinare possunt, cum habeant ordinariam iurisdictionem." Hostiensis agrees, Andreae says, since otherwise the decretal would contradict itself; therefore, he goes on, Pope Innocent held that the archpriest was to determine minor matters according to the norms established by the bishop.[88]

Andreae referred to the chapter *Officium archipresbyteri* in his early *Ordinary Gloss* on the *Sext*, when discussing Boniface VIII's decretal on reserved sins, *Si episcopus*. He also gave here a list of such sins, and referred to other chapters in the *Decretals of Gregory IX*; in due course he dealt specifically with each each of these sins as he came to the cited chapters in the *Novella*. In the *Novella* on the *Sext*, he gives a bibliography on the subject somewhat like Juan Ruiz's reading list. After mentioning Guido da Baysio's commentary on the *Sext*, he refers us for further reading to the *Summas* of Hostiensis and Raymond of Peñafort, Durantis's *Repertorium*, John Monachus's commentary on Boniface VIII's *Super cathedram*, and his own treatment of *Super cathedram* in the *Clementines*.[89]

From these samples, it should be clear that Juan Ruiz knew the right authorities to cite on the subject of confession. On the subject of archpriests, however, as I shall try to show in Chapter II, these authorities seem to have had little knowledge of, or interest in, archpriests as they existed in various forms in the real world.

III. *The Stated Dates of the Manuscripts*

We come now to the question of the date of the *Libro de buen amor*, in the light of what we have seen. First of all, we must review the explicit statements to be found in the manuscripts.

Of the three extant manuscripts, only the one named after the seventeenth-century collector Benito Martínez Gayoso has a dated colophon, which comes after the two extraneous *Cantares de ciegos*. It reads:

> fenito libro, graçias a domino nostro jesu xpisto. este libro fue acabado jueues xx iij dias de jullio del año del Nasçimiento del nuestro saluador jesu xpisto de mill e tresientos e ochenta e Nueue años.[90]

There is something wrong with this date, since July 23 fell on Friday in 1389; July 23 came on Thursday during the 1380s only in 1383 and 1388. But it is more likely that the scribe got the Roman numerals of the day wrong than that he was mistaken in writing out the year. The manuscript is thought to belong to the last years of the fourteenth century, and therefore the date, A.D. 1389, can be taken as an authentic indication by the copyist of the time that he finished his work.

The Toledo manuscript, which belonged to the cathedral of that city, is likewise in a hand of the end of the fourteenth century. The Salamanca manuscript, which before 1807 was in the possession of the Colegio Major de San Bartolomé in Salamanca, is dated by Giorgio Chiarini to the end of the fourteenth century or the beginning of the fifteenth century, whereas Jacques Joset and others place it firmly in the beginning years or decades of the fifteenth century. Perhaps the late dating has been influenced by Ramón Menéndez Pidal's identification of the scribe, who signs himself "Alffon*sus* perati*nensis*" (or "*p*aratine*nsis*"), as Alfonso de Paradinas, an attribution that Chiarini himself seems to accept.[91] Menéndez takes the scribe to be the Alfonso de Paradinas who became bishop of Ciudad Rodrigo in 1463 and died in 1485, having lived, according to his epitaph, for ninety years (and therefore having been born in 1395). He was the founder of the church and hospice of San Giacomo dei Spagnoli at Rome in the 1450s; and, according to the *Historia del Colegio viejo de San Bartolomé* published in 1776, he was a student at San Bartolomé in 1417 and 1418, and later on was archdeacon of Ledesma in the cathedral chapter of Salamanca.[92]

The identification is suggestive, of course, but so far no evidence has been offered to show that Paradinas (or "Paladinas," as it appears in the *Historia*)[93] took the adjectival form *paratinensis* in Latin. In the bishop's Latin epitaph, he is named simply Alfonsus de Paradinas,[94] and the same is true of the Alfonsus de Paradinas who was litigating for the cantorship of Salamanca in 1445.[95] A. D. Deyermond has noticed "occasional comments" in recent years that reveal some skepticism about Menéndez Pidal's identification, but he does not cite them.[96]

The Toledo manuscript ends with stanza 1634, which is clearly the end of the original *Libro*. The Salamanca manuscript contains the same original ending but with a different date in stanza 1634; it also contains after stanza 1634 some extraneous poems, shared in part with the Gayoso manuscript; the final poem, the *Cantica de los clérigos de Talavera*, is unique to the Salamanca manuscript.

The Salamanca version of the date in stanza 1634 reads:

Era de mill E tresientos E ochenta E vn años
fue conpuesto el rromançe.

The Toledo text has instead:

Era de mill & tresyentos & sesenta & ocho años
fue acabado este lybro.[97]

The word *era* has always been taken to indicate in both cases the "Era of Spain," according to which the year was computed from 1 January 38 B.C.[98] The Salamanca date would therefore be 1381 E.S., which would yield A.D. 1343, whereas the Toledo date would be 1368 E.S., that is, A.D. 1330.

But since Ruiz's citation of Andreae's *Novella*, which appears in both the Salamanca and Toledo manuscripts, indicates that he must have been writing after 1338, we must look for a hypothesis that would eliminate the date of 1330.

The simplest solution would seem to be one offered by Chiarini, but taken in reverse, since he holds for the authenticity of the 1330 date over that of 1343. He suggests that the original date of 1368 was written in roman numerals and confused as 1381 in transcription.[99] If so, the "ands" must have been left out in the original number (which for the present we assume to have been 1381); thus it would have been written not as:

Era de .m. e .ccc. e .lxxx. e .j. años,

but rather as:

Era de .m.ccc.lxxxj. años.

This authentic date of 1381 E.S. (= A.D. 1343) would then have been confused thus:

Era de .m.ccc.lxviij. años,

a simple mistake of reading *xx* as *vii*, to produce the erroneous date of 1368 E.S. (= A.D 1330).

By accepting A.D. 1343 as the date of the body of the *Libro* we would be able to date the appendix on the clergy of Talavera to roughly the same time, if we take the mandate from Archbishop Gil to refer to Gil de Albornoz, Archbishop of Toledo from 1338 to 1350. Talavera fell within the diocese of Toledo, and Albornoz was the only archbishop of that see named Gil (except for Cardinal Gil Torres, archbishop-elect in 1247).[100] Chiarini, however, since he accepts the authenticity of the 1330 date as well as the reference to Archbishop Albornoz, must date the Talavera appendix at least eight years later.

Our elimination of the 1330 dating on the basis of the citation of Andreae's *Novella* does not touch the question of whether there was a double redaction of the body of the *Libro*, a short edition represented by the Gayoso manuscript and a longer one represented by the other two manuscripts; but we can at least put to rest the idea of "thirteen years" separating two different versions of the poem, if the Salamanca date is accepted as meaning A.D. 1343. But convincing attacks have been made on the double-redaction theory, especially by Chiarini, who argues that all three manuscripts depend on a single archetype. The gaps and other differences in the Gayoso text would therefore have to be explained otherwise.[101]

Joset accepts Chiarini's demonstration as convincing; but unlike him he accepts the 1343 dating, because he finds the phraseology of the Salamanca reading of stanza 1634 to be more authentic than that of the Toledo text. In the former, it is a question of the *composition* of a *romance* (a term that can refer to any vernacular writing), whereas in the latter a *libro* is said to have been *acabado*. This is the same terminology as that used by the scribe of the Gayoso manuscript in his colophon of A.D. 1389. Joset concludes that it is better to take the reading of the Toledo manuscript with its date of 1368 E.S. as a copyist's error.[102]

Joset does not speculate on the reasons for the error, which he says could have been committed either by the scribe of the Toledo manuscript or by the scribe of the copy from which he was working. However, it would seem to make little sense for a scribe to change Juan Ruiz's statement that he "composed the romance" in A.D. 1343 to say that he "finished the book" in A.D. 1330. It may be, then, that whoever made the change understood 1381 to refer to the Dominical rather than to the Caesarian year, perhaps because the latter usage had become obsolete in his time and place of writing.[103] Such a date, A.D. 1381, would no doubt have struck him as very late—and it may even have been later than his time of writing—so that he decided to change the date to the more plausible year of A.D. 1368.

On the other hand, perhaps the scribe in question did understand Ruiz's reference to mean 1381 E.S. (= A.D. 1343), and wished for some reason to say that the book was finished in A.D. 1368, but did not choose to change *era* to *año*, perhaps because of the unpleasant redundancy that would result: "*año* de mill e tresyentos e sesenta e ocho *años*"; and therefore he intended *era* to be interpreted as the Christian Era rather than as the Spanish Era.

It was not until the decree of King Juan I in 1383 making the Dominical dating mandatory that the awkward formula *año de (x) años* came into general use in Castile and León,[104] though earlier examples can be found (I have seen two cases from 1381 in the diocese of Burgos).[105] We have observed its use by the scribe of the Gayoso manuscript: *año de 1389 años*. There seems to have been little reluctance about abandoning the Spanish Era (though it is surprising to see King Enrique III using it at one point in A.D. 1392).[106] But there are occasional signs of a resistance to or neglect of the tautological aspect of King Juan's formula, even in legal instruments. For instance, a document of 1391 leaves out the *años*:

> En la villa de Talavera martes once dias de abril deste año del nascimiento de Nuestro Señor Jesu-Christo de mil e trecientos e noventa e uno, ante las puertas de la Iglesia Colegial de Sancta Maria, que es dentro de la dicha villa. . . .[107]

This style, of course, would be in conformity with the Latin practice of dating by the *annus Domini*, which was current in Spain long before the style of the Spanish Era was abolished. It was sometimes employed even in letters otherwise written in Spanish.[108]

Another variation can be seen at times, in which only *años* appears. For example a testament made at the town of Tordómar on August 19, 1387, is dated: "Lunes, diez e nueve dias de agosto de mill e tresientos e ochenta e siete annos."[109] One might suppose that since the usual *año* is missing in such cases, only *año* could be understood. But Joaquín Gimeno Casalduero has adduced a clear instance where it is *era* that is not only understood but used, in conjunction with the Dominical year of 1408. It comes in the first lines of a poem by Ruy Páez de Ribera:

> Andando la era del Nuestro Señor
> En doss seteçientos e ocho viniendo
> A çinco del mess, el alva rronpiendo. . . .[110]

He argues for a similar interpretation of the opening lines of the *Disputa del alma y el cuerpo*:

> Después de la prima la hora pasada
> En el mes de enero la noche primera
> En cccc e veynte, durante la era,

to yield the date of A.D. 1420, not 1420 E.S. (= A.D. 1382).[111]

If it is true that the word *año* or *annus* was not used by itself to designate the Era of Spain, *era* was not used exclusively for the Era of Spain but was sometimes employed for other systems, including the Christian Era. For example, in the third-redaction prologue to the *Siete partidas* Alfonso el Sabio (or Pseudo-Alfonso, if the collection postdates Alfonso's reign) says that it was begun when the Era of Adam was proceeding in 5011 Hebrew years, the Era of the Deluge in 4353 Roman years, the Era of Nebuchadnezzar in 1998 Roman years, the Era of Philip the Great of Greece in 1574 Roman years, the Era of Alexander the Great of Macedon in 1562 Roman years, the Era of Caesar in 1289 Roman years, the Era of the Incarnation in 1251 Roman years, the Era of Diocletian the Egyptian in 967 Roman years, the Era of the Arabs in 629 Roman years (or, according to their years, 649), and the Era of Yazdegerd the Persian in 620 Roman years (or, according to the years of the Persians, 620).[112]

When only one *era* is mentioned for a single date, it is admittedly the Era of Spain that is normally meant; but not always. An exception can be seen in the exchange of letters in 1356 between Pedro the Cruel of Castile and Pedro IV of Aragon, as recorded in a memorandum made by the latter. The first letter, written by the scribe Juan Fernández at the command of Pedro the Cruel, is dated: "Era de m.ccclvi. annos."[113] Pedro IV's response of September 4 is dated, in contrast, "en el anyo de la Natividad de Nuestro Senyor m.ccc.lvi."[114] Pedro the Cruel dictated an answer to Juan Fernández on October 18, "era de mil e trecientos e cinquenta e quatro" [sic]. Pedro IV responded on December 6, "en el anyo de la Natividad de Nostro Senyor Mil ccc lvi."[115]

The fact that Fernández got the date wrong in his second letter and wrote 1354 rather than 1356 may indicate that he made a faulty subtraction from the Spanish Era year of 1394, which may in turn indicate that he was not used to the Dominical dating style but was simply accommodating himself to the Aragonese usage. We note that Pedro the Cruel dated his will, made in A.D. 1362, by the Spanish Era: "Era de mil e quatrocientos años."[116]

Nevertheless, if the dates are authentically recorded, we have a definite precedent on the official level for *era* by itself to signify the Christian Era. Perhaps a similar freedom was enjoyed in unofficial or poetic writings of the time. The prologue to the *Libro de cavallero Zifar* is a pertinent example, if the text as we have it accurately passes on the original phrasing; for the same formula is used for both the Christian and Spanish Eras. The author refers to the century beginning in the *era de 1300 años* and ending in the *era de 1400 años* (that is, 1300 to 1400 A.D.), and then relates an event that occurred in the *era de 1339 años* (that is, 1339 E.S. = A.D. 1301).[117]

It seems to me that we must not only consider the possibility that the phrases *era de 1368 años* and *era de 1381 años* could have been wrongly interpreted as A.D. 1368 and A.D. 1381, respectively, by the copyists of the work; but we must also ask whether this is in fact the right interpretation and whether Juan Ruiz himself could have been writing in one or other of these years.

There is no internal or external evidence, apart from stanza 1634 (however interpreted), that requires us to date the *Libro* much before A.D. 1389, the year named by the scribe of the Gayoso manuscript. There is nothing in the poem to connect the author with Gil de Albornoz. This connection is made only in the final rubric of the Salamanca manuscript, which, however, errs in stating that Albornoz, who is said to have imprisoned the author, was a cardinal when he held the see of Toledo. In actual fact, he became a cardinal only when he was transferred from Toledo to the papal curia at the end of 1350. The rubric, therefore, shows late authorship, and may be nothing more than a scribal flight of fancy, perhaps the work of the latest scribe, Alfonsus Peratinensis.

The appendix of the Salamanca manuscript, especially the *Cántica de los clérigos de Talavera*, must also come under suspicion. As far as its date is concerned, all that we have been able to say so far is that it was written after 1338, the year in which Albornoz became archbishop of Toledo, if "arçobispo don Gil" refers to Albornoz. But it could have been written much later, say in A.D. 1368, the year after Cardinal Albornoz's death. It could also have been written in the 1380s or even later, since the Gayoso *terminus ante quem* of 1389 does not apply to the extraneous material of the Salamanca manuscript.

If there is any truth to the story that Juan Ruiz was jailed by order of Archbishop Albornoz, he may have stayed in prison even after Albornoz departed for his duties in France and Italy, for he retained powerful interests in Spain.[118] Juan Ruiz may have composed most of his book while in prison, may have been released on the cardinal's death in 1367, and may have completed the book a year later, hence the date: *era de 1368 años*; as an afterthought, he may have added the *Cántica de los clérigos de Talavera*. The Salamanca copyist, or a predecessor, may have known about Juan Ruiz's imprisonment but not about its duration; he may have found the date of 1368 to be either too early (if interpreted as A.D. 1330) or too late (if read as A.D. 1368) for the reign of Archbishop Albornoz, and so changed it to 1381, which he intended to be interpreted as A.D. 1343.

Another possible scenario: The Salamanca scribe may have found the date of 1381 in his received copy and interpreted it, rightly or wrongly, as A.D. 1343. This date, and the reference to Albornoz in the *Cántica*, may have inspired him to invent the story of the archpriest's imprisonment. Or the scribe himself may have composed the *Cántica*. If the date of A.D. 1343 is authentic for the composition of the *Libro* through stanza 1634, there is reason to doubt that the *Cántica* is by the same author or at least written at the same time. For in 1343 there was not as yet an archpriest in the collegiate church of Talavera. We shall discuss this point in Chapter III, after we look at archpriests in general.

Chapter Two

Archpriests,
and the Archpriest of Hita

1. *Obsolete Laws, Rulings from Afar*

I wish now to pose the question of what Juan Ruiz supposed himself to be, or portrayed himself as being, from the canonical or ecclesiastical point of view, when he called himself an archpriest. Much of what has been written on the point is not helpful. Joset, for example, simply refers to Aguado's *Glosario* for the function of the archpriest in general, and Aguado merely indulges in some Isidorian guesswork: in the "diocesan chapter," the archpriest represented the priests, and the archdeacon the deacons![1] Others are well enough informed to draw on the chapter on archpriests contained in the *Siete partidas*, which will be taken up below. But for the most part, discussion is restricted to "literary" evidence of evil-living archpriests. Let us instead look at what historical evidence we can find.

When St. Raymond of Peñafort[2] compiled the *Decretals of Gregory IX* he imitated his predecessors in including not only recent papal decretals, but also earlier materials supposedly not present in Gratian. Sometimes he took over whole blocks of previously collected canons without inquiring as to whether they corresponded to contemporary reality. Such was the case with the titles on minor diocesan functionaries that he inserted in Book I, including the title *De officio archipresbyteri*. Under this rubric, he passed on four chapters. The first, *Ut archipresbyter*, which is ascribed to a Council of Toledo, was in fact already present in Gratian; it appears as an insert in a letter ascribed to Isidore of Seville.[3] The next two chapters, *Ministerium archipresbyteri* and *Officium archipresbyteri de urbe*, come from Pope Leo III (795–816) and seem to deal with the city of Rome; and the fourth chapter, *Ut singulae plebes*, appears to derive from a constitution of the emperor Lambert of Spoleto (A.D. 898).[4] However, in the previous title, *De officio archidiaconi*, which is more up-to-date, the decretal *Ad haec* of Innocent III (1198–1216) acknowledges that archpriests are commonly called deans and states that rural deans with limited terms are to be appointed and dismissed by both archdeacon and bishop.[5]

Even in Gratian the identification of archpriests as deans is made, in the canon *In capite quadragesimae*. Originally, the text read that public penitents at the beginning of Lent were to present themselves to the bishop of the city, accompanied by archpriests of the parishes, that is, the priests of the penitents.[6] But in Gratian it is said that deans, that is, archpriests of parishes, are to be present, along with the priests of the penitents.[7] In the *Glossa ordinaria* to the *Decretum*, prepared in its final form by Bartholomew of Brescia around 1245, a possible contradiction is noticed between this canon and *Nullus episcopus*, where a distinction seems to be made between deans and archpriests.[8] Two solutions are suggested: one is that the *aut* of *Nullus* is not used with disjunctive force; the other is that *In capite* refers to rural deans (and that therefore in this case archpriests and deans are identical).[9]

However, in the title on archpriests in the *Decretals of Gregory IX*, the chapters of which we have listed above, there is no reference to the equivalency between archpriests and deans; the same is true of Bernard of Parma's *Ordinary Gloss* on the *Decretals* and of Andreae's *Novella*. Bernard does make the equation between archpriests and rural deans elsewhere, however, as does Innocent IV, at least by implication.[10] Hostiensis, too, is clear at times that rural archpriests can be called *decani*, but he is is not always clear about whether the same holds true of urban archpriests. Perhaps some of the confusion arose from the fact that there existed city deans, or "deans of Christianity," who did not correspond to the urban archpriests of the *Decretals* (that is, cathedral functionaries with spiritual jurisdiction over all residents of the diocese) but rather to rural archpriests, with correctional jurisdiction over their respective districts; but the districts of the city deans consisted of the parishes of the cathedral city and its immediate environs.[11] In any case, he never identifies urban archpriests with the deans of cathedral chapters, who he says are the ranking members of the chapters.[12] Rather, in accord with the decretal *Ut archipresbyter*, he considers urban archpriests to be of a rank inferior to that of archdeacon, and subject to the archdeacon—though he admits that legitimate local custom might dictate otherwise; and he goes on at great length about the supposed duties of such persons.

It would be truer to say that the ranks and duties of archpriests and archdeacons and their equivalents were *entirely* governed by local custom, and were not at all (or negligibly) influenced by the archaic provisions of the *Decretals of Gregory IX*. Usually, there was no archpriest at all in the cathedral chapter; but where a cathedral archpriest did exist he was sometimes the ranking dignitary of the chapter—this was the case at Milan and Cremona.[13] In the cathedral of Carcassonne, there were two archpriests, a major and a minor.[14]

In speaking of rural archpriests, Hostiensis touches on Spanish custom indirectly at one point. He says in the *Summa aurea* that sometimes archpriests are improperly called abbots, and refers to the decretal *Ex transmissa*. In his *Commentary* on that decretal, however, he is not speaking of archpriests but of rectors of collegiate churches: there are may such "secular abbots," he says, in Spain.[15] There are many references in the next century to Spanish secular abbacies. For instance, in 1353 Juan Rodríguez de Cisneros held the *abbatia curata* and a canonry and prebend in the church of Santa Leocadia in the city of Toledo, and a quarter portion in the church of Santa Maria in Valladolid, which is elsewhere identified as a secular and collegiate abbey.[16] But this does not mean that the rector or ranking cleric of such a church had jurisdiction over anything except his parish and the clergy of his "college." If, then, such rectors were improperly called abbots in Spain, Hostiensis is mistaken in implying that they would properly be called archpriests, for they corresponded neither to the rural nor to the urban archpriests of the *Decretals* (nor, for that matter, to city deans); they would be archpriests only in the etymological sense of "head priests."[17] We shall see below that the chief dignitary in the secular collegiate church of Talavera was the dean, and that when the rural archpriest of Talavera became a member of the chapter he did not replace the dean but rather the subdean.

The office of archpriest is dealt with in the *Siete partidas*, which, though attributed to Alfonso X, may have been compiled, or at least modified, after his death in 1284.[18] The section on the archpriest comes only after sections on the dean and other dignitaries of the cathedral chapter (namely, the archdeacon, cantor, treasurer, and master of the school).[19] An attempt has clearly been made to reconcile what the *Decretals* says about archpriests with the realities of the Church in Spain. It is stated that there are three kinds of archpriests: 1) those in cathedral churches who function as deans; 2) those in other cathedral churches who do not hold so high a rank, but are subordinate to the archdeacons; and 3) minor archpriests situated in the towns of the episcopate. The first two categories were probably included only out of deference to the *Decretals*. Gregorio López in his edition of 1555 does not seem to know of archpriests who are dignitaries of cathedral chapters in Spain, though he covers himself by saying that they are not to be seen except in a few instances.[20]

The *Partidas* says that the rural archpriest is under obedience to his archdeacon, which was certainly the custom in Spain, but it also says that he is to be appointed and removed by both bishop and archdeacon.[21] This regulation may not reflect previous usage, but may be an attempt to impose Innocent III's ruling for temporary archpriests on the permanent archpriests of Castile.[22] It was in fact a stipulation that Cardinal Gil Torres made for the diocese of Burgos in 1250.[23]

According to the *Partidas*, the rural archpriest must visit all the churches of his archipresbyterate, to see how the clergy are performing their duties and how the laity are living. If any of them have erred, he is to seek their amendment and chastise them so that they will not repeat the offenses in the future. If the faults are such that he cannot chastise and reform them, he is to report them to the archdeacon or the bishop, who will see to their chastisement. Finally, like the archdeacon, he has the power to excommunicate.[24]

This statement of the archpriest's duties follows the spirit of the chapter *Ut singulae plebes* in the *Decretals*; but whereas the *Partidas* speaks of referring problems to the archdeacon or the bishop, the *Decretals* speaks only of reporting to the bishop, and includes an exhortation to the bishop on the need for archpriests.[25]

We have read earlier[26] of the canonists' agreement that the rural archpriest had ordinary jurisdiction over minor matters; that is, he could hold court as a judge. The sort of case that the archpriest normally was expected to hear is strikingly illustrated by a letter of Innocent III to the archpriest of Hita ordering him to proceed against persons holding the goods of the abbey of Covarrubias.[27]

Hostiensis gives arguments for and against the position that archpriests can hear matrimonial cases. He concludes that this type of court action belongs to the bishop, but he admits the possibility that authorities inferior to the bishop could have such jurisdiction through custom or special privilege.[28] But there was a strong feeling in the curia of Innocent IV that archpriests should not hear marriage cases, because they lacked the necessary training in canon law. This position was given the force of law in the diocese of Salamanca in April of 1245, in the constitutions drawn up by Cardinal Gil Torres and approved by Innocent. The pertinent passage comes in an article on the need to reprimand and curb the insolence of archpriests, "de qua gravis et multiplex pestilentia in perniciem animarum exoritur." First, they illicitly have clerics ordained by bishops outside the diocese. Second, they hear marriage cases:

> Item causae matrimoniales coram eis tractantur perperam, contra canonicas sanctiones, maxime cum peritiam iuris non habeant quae requiritur in causis matrimonialibus decidendis.

Another abuse allegedly committed by archpriests is that they assign parish churches and portions in them without the bishop's or archdeacon's licence. They also present candidates for ordination to the bishop without consulting their archdeacons, to whom they are subordinate. They exact taxes beyond measure, and fail to correct concubinary clerics:

> Concubinarios clericos in suis sordibus computrescere permittentes et eorum interitum praemio seu gratia dissimulatione damnabili procurantes, dum excessus talium tolerant, nec ipsi cum possunt arguunt, nec episcopo vel archidiacono denuntiant corrigendos.

All actions taken by archpriests in marriage cases, and improper actions concerning the ordination of clerics and assignment of benefices are declared void, notwithstanding any contrary custom, which should rather be called a corruption; unfair taxes are to be returned in double measure; and if any archpriest is convicted of receiving anything simoniacally from any cleric (especially one with a concubine) or from any layman, he is to be expelled from his office of archpriest. Not only the bishop but also the archdeacons in their respective archdeaconries are to be diligent in correcting the excesses of the clergy, especially the *concubinarii*, or suffer the canonical sanctions for negligence decreed by the councils held in each province.[29]

Cardinal Torres's list of abuses, practices, and duties may not have had a very close bearing on reality in the diocese of Salamanca. Torres was native of Burgos, but he was from early on attached to the papal curia (he was made a cardinal in 1216), and was no doubt somewhat out of touch with conditions in Castile. He was canon of the cathedral chapter of Toledo, and his fellow-canons tried to bring him back to the diocese by electing him archbishop in 1247; but Innocent IV refused to confirm the election, because his services were needed for the universal Church.[30]

Torres intervened not only in the government of the diocese of Salamanca, but also in that of the dioceses of Ávila, Burgos, Calahorra, Córdoba, Cuenca, Plasencia, Segovia, and possibly Ciudad Rodrigo. However, all of his investigations were carried out from Italy.[31]

Of Torres's constitutions that have been published, besides those for Salamanca, in those for Calahorra, issued in 1249 and again in 1254, and in those for Burgos, issued in 1250 and 1252,[32] there is no censure of archpriests, and no mention of them at all, except that in the Burgos document it is said that archpriests are to be elected and removed by the bishop jointly with the relevant archdeacon (or in some cases, the abbot who has jurisdiction over the area).[33] But in the constitutions for Ávila, issued in 1250, the concluding portion, beginning with the attack on archpriests, is almost identical to the corresponding part of the Salamanca constitutions. Only the names have been changed, and slightly less prominence is given to the archdeacons.[34] In the prologue of the Salamanca document, however, it is said that various points needing reform in the diocese had been reported to the pope,[35] whereas the constitutions for Ávila are said to have been inspired only by the pope's solicitude.

Torres did not write constitutions for the diocese of Segovia, but in October of 1245 he answered various questions and complaints that had been referred to him; and at the end he added his complaint against archpriests, in the wording that he had used six months previously in his Salamanca constitutions.[36]

In view of these repetitions, we are well advised to be cautious in accepting his blanket condemnation of archpriests. There is evidence that the archpriests of Segovia were of a fairly high order, at least earlier in the thirteenth century. When Gonzalo, Bishop of Segovia in the first decade of the century, at the urging of his metropolitan,

Martín López, Archbishop of Toledo, ordered his clergy to put away their women, the clergy resisted, but the archpriests supported the bishop. In the trial against the bishop brought by the clergy, the archpriests of Coca, Cuéllar, Petraza, and Sepúlveda presented evidence in his favor. One witness, the abbot of San Tomé (a collegiate church?) in Sepúlveda, testified that after the bishop's letter of excommunication had been read in chapter to the clergy of the area (presumably it was read by the archpriest of Sepúlveda), the defiant clergy swore to resist and to appeal to Rome. Several other chapters of the clergy reacted similarly.[37] This activity provides an instructive parallel to that of the *Cántica de los clérigos de Talavera*, which we will take up in the next chapter.

The next bishop of Segovia, Giraldo, steered clear of the subject of concubinage, but he did attempt to impose other reforms on the clergy, especially those sanctioned by the Fourth Lateran Council in November of 1215, which Giraldo attended. In the synod that he held at the end of 1216 or beginning of 1217, he included some regulations dealing with archpriests, but there is no allusion to the sorts of abuses Cardinal Torres mentions, except for those connected with the imposition and collection of taxes.[38]

The clergy resisted Giraldo's reforms, and, as before, the archpriests were ranged on the side of the bishop against the clergy.[39] The panel of arbiters appointed to settle the quarrels between the bishop and his clergy approved for the most part the synodal provisions concerning archpriests, including the stipulation that no archpriest was to have a vicar unless he was a resident of the cathedral, or was with the bishop, or was ill, or was away at school, or was on pilgrimage; in such cases, the vicar was to be installed by the archdeacon, with the bishop's consent.[40]

Also approved was the statute requiring that "henceforth no canon is to be made an archpriest unless in the cathedral church."[41] This could mean, in light of the negative style favored elsewhere in the synodal constitutions, that only cathedral canons can be archpriests. Compare, for instance, the order that "no archpriest is to go on visitation in his archipresbyterate except with two mounts and two conveyances, and then he is not to have hunting dogs or birds."[42] This means, as we can see from the canon of the Third Lateran Council (A.D. 1179) which it echoes,[43] that the two mounts and two conveyances are not a minimum requirement but a maximum limit, which one could laudably reduce in the interests of economy and humility. (Motivation for reducing the archpriests' entourages was provided by the arbiters when they declared that no "procurations" or visitation expenses were due to archpriests.)[44]

More likely, however, the statute in question means that the only canons eligible for the office of archpriest are those who make their residence in the cathedral church of Segovia; absentee canons, therefore, and perhaps canons of cathedrals in other dioceses, would be excluded.

We should note that one of the judgments imposed on Bishop Giraldo and his clergy by the arbiters was that "all archpriests are to become priests." That is, the priesthood was a prerequisite for the office. The arbiters also ordered that when archpriests were absent they were each to appoint an honest priest of the area to take his place until he returned.[45] Since the archpriest was able to appoint his own substitute in these cases, the arbiters must not have been talking about formal (or "permanent") vicars, who would be needed for more prolonged absences, and who (as we saw above) were to be authorized jointly by archdeacon and bishop.

It is an anomaly of the system that the higher ranking archdeacons should have had a title referring to a lower major order than the archpriests. In keeping with their designations, archdeacons were required to be no more than deacons, while archpriests were meant to be priests. This was set forth at the Council of Clermont in 1095 and the First Lateran Council in 1123 and incorporated into Gratian's *Decretum*, and a similar regulation from the Council of Poitiers in 1078 or 1079 appeared in later compilations, including the *Decretals of Gregory IX*.[46] At the Third Lateran Council in 1179 it was stipulated that the cure of souls was not to be given to anyone under the age of twenty-five, and anyone so appointed (except for archdeacons) was to be ordained priest within the time fixed by the canons.[47] There was some debate as to what was meant by this last qualification. Bernard of Parma in the *Ordinary Gloss* to the *Decretals* refers to the laws assigning the Ember days as the time of ordination, so that a cleric appointed to a cure should be ordained priest at the next Ember season, or at least within six months.[48] Bernard does not think that the reference is to the canon *Quicumque* and others following it, according to which one must remain a deacon for five years before becoming a priest (and where the age for the priesthood is repeatedly fixed at thirty),[49] for he does not think that one should wait for so long a time. I do not know what the customary practices were in Spain, but we are told that in England thirty was still the canonical age for the priesthood even in the fourteenth century.[50]

II. *Local Norms and Practices*

So far we have seen little evidence of what were the actual duties and conditions of archpriests in Spain, except in the diocese of Segovia early in the thirteenth century. We can expect a certain amount of uniformity between the dioceses of Segovia and Toledo in the Middle Ages, since they both belonged to the province of Toledo. The archbishop of Toledo was also the metropolitan of the province of Toledo, and he held not only diocesan synods but also provincial councils, which often dealt with the same matters. One such council was held around 1220 at Guadalajara by Archbishop Rodrigo Ximénez de Rada to discuss the disputes that had recently arisen between Bishop Giraldo and his clergy in Segovia.[51] The clergy from the diocese of Toledo present at this council would doubtless have reviewed the various recommendations concerning Segovian archpriests, which we treated above, though we cannot know for certain how relevant they were for the diocese of Toledo itself, without corroborating evidence.

Fortunately, the records of many of the synods and councils of Toledo held during the fourteenth and fifteenth centuries are extant,[52] and they provide us with at least some information about archpriests. For instance, when in the synod of 1323 Archbishop Juan of Aragon takes up the question of the kind of cases that archpriests could hear in their judicial role, we can surmise that some archpriests had been going beyond the bounds that he now establishes, and that Cardinal Torres's fears about other dioceses in the previous century were verifiable at this time in Toledo. The archbishop justifies his position by observing that not only canon law but also the practice of the papal curia seems to classify marriage cases as "major," by committing them to bishops alone; for since such cases are to be judged according to the rigor of the law and admit of no compromise or dispensation, it is not right that they be judged by persons ignorant of the canonical statutes (as has happened in the past), if the blind are not to lead the blind. Therefore he orders that no archpriest and no one else ignorant of canon law participate in these proceedings.[53]

In the synod of 1326, convened by Archbishop Juan's vicar-general, Juan Vicente, archdeacons as well as archpriests are singled out among the minor prelates or their vicars who intervene in major criminal cases, which require judges with great (or undisputed) authority.[54] The archpriests and other clergy present at the synod are said to join with the vicar-general in prohibiting minor prelates from hearing criminal cases, unless the crimes and punishments involved are minor, in accord with the lawful jurisdiction of such prelates, or unless one or other of them has authority to hear other cases by statute, custom, or special privilege. But the synod does not mean to prevent any archdeacon, archpriest, vicar, *praecator* (or proctor), or any other judge from arresting a malefactor and delivering him to the archbishop's prison, if necessary by force.[55]

In 1345, the bishops and their vicars as well as archpriests are named as wrongfully intervening in cases that belong to the secular jurisdiction. In the Cortes held that year at Burgos by Alfonso XI, King of Castile and León, there was aired a complaint that the clergy not only heard matters that should come before the king and his judges, but also passed sentences of excommunication on those who refused to accept their proceedings.[56]

The archpriests of the diocese of Toledo, as elsewhere in Spain,[57] were immediately subject to the archdeacon of the archdeaconry in which their archipresbyterates lay. We have seen that Cardinal Torres in his constitutions for the diocese of Burgos and the *Siete partidas* for Castile and León as a whole stipulated that archipresbyterates were to be conferred by both bishop and archdeacon, as Innocent III said was to be done for temporary archpriests. We have also seen that in the diocese of Segovia the vicars of archpriests were to be appointed in this way. But I know of no evidence that archdeacons ever had any official say in the appointment of the archpriests themselves. In the diocese of Sigüenza, which like Segovia was in the province of Toledo, pressure for archidiaconal participation in such appointments seems to have been felt but firmly rejected. When the cathedral chapter was secularized in 1301 by order of Pope Boniface VIII, the constitutions formulated by the bishop, Simón de Cisneros, in conjunction with the bishops of Cuenca and Calahorra, stipulated in the section on archdeacons that the conferral of archipresbyterates was to be the bishop's business alone, as in the past.[58]

Later in the fourteenth century we find indications that the same sort of traditional policy was maintained in other dioceses. When archipresbyterates are included in the roll of expectative graces for students at the University of Salamanca in the register of Pope Clement VII for 1381, all are said to be in the gift of the bishop.[59] In the same roll, there is mention of an unspecified benefice in the gift of the archdeacon of Calatrava, and the fact that archdeacons in the diocese of Toledo conferred some benefices is established in the archidiaconal fee schedule issued by Archbishop Tenorio in 1379.[60] But there is nothing to indicate that among such benefices were archipresbyterates.

Of the twelve expectative graces for archipresbyterates in the above-mentioned Salamanca roll, six are for the diocese of Burgos, three for Palencia, and one each for Toledo, Osma, and Salamanca. The grants are vaguely stated: "an archipresbyterate at the collation of the bishop of Burgos," or "at the collation of the archbishop of Toledo," and so on; and some of the recipients are already priests, while others are not (one of the latter is Juan Rodríguez de Medina de Pomar, cleric of the diocese of Burgos, student in canon law, expecting an archipresbyterate in Burgos). The document must reflect current practices in the dioceses named, and also practices in the curia of Clement VII at Avignon, for the graces were granted as requested. I will speak below of the scholastic requirements for Spanish archipresbyterates observed in Clement's chancery.[61] But I should mention here that the comparatively large number of archipresbyterates expected in Burgos need not correspond to the actual availability of such benefices. Expectative graces were often given in such numbers as to make them virtually useless.[62]

In the diocese of Toledo, archdeacons were dignitaries of the cathedral chapter, where they ranked after the dean but before the master of the school, the cantor, and the treasurer. The diocese was divided into six archdeaconries, each under the jurisdiction of its specific archdeacon.[63] Five of the archdeaconries, those of Toledo, Talavera, Madrid, Guadalajara, and Calatrava, were in existence in the twelfth century,[64] and the sixth, that of Alcaraz, was added sometime before 1234.[65] All of the archdeaconries except Alcaraz were subdivided into archipresbyterates or permanent vicariates. By comparing the fee schedules published by Archbishop Tenorio at the synod of Alcalá in 1379[66] with the data given by Luisa Guadalupe Beraza on ecclesiastical taxes in the diocese at the end of the fifteenth century,[67] we arrive at the following list. I follow the order of the 1379 constitutions, and put in parentheses all names and information not found there:

I. (Archdeaconry of Toledo)
   A. (City of Toledo)
   B. Archipresbyterates:
      1) La Guardia
      2) Ocaña
      3) Rodillas
      4) Canales
      5) Illescas
      6) (Montalbán)

II. (Archdeaconry of Talavera)
   A. Archipresbyterates:
      1) Talavera
      2) Santa Olalla
      3) Maqueda
      4) Escalona

III. (Archdeaconry of Calatrava)
   A. Vicariate:
      1) La Puebla de Alcocer
   B. Archipresbyterate:
      1) Calatrava

IV. (Archdeaconry of Alcaraz)
   A. Archipresbyterate:
      1) Alcaraz

V. (Archdeaconry of Madrid)
   A. Archipresbyterates:
      1) Madrid
      2) Talamanca
      3) Uceda
      4) Buitrago
   B. (Vicariates:)
      1) (Alcolea de Torote)
      2) (Val de Lozoya)

VI. (Archdeaconry of Guadalajara)
  A. Archipresbyterates:
    1) Alcalá
    2) Guadalajara
    3) Hita
    4) Brihuega (a vicariate?)[68]
    5) Zorita
    6) Almoguera
  B. (Vicariate:)
    1) (Brihuega)

The archipresbyterates were of course ruled and taxed by their respective archpriests and the vicariates by their vicars, each of whom operated a chancery. The city of Toledo in the fourteenth century may have included the fifteenth-century archipresbyterate of Montalbán, since no fee schedule is given for Montalbán in 1379; but since there was an archpriest of Montalbán in the thirteenth century, the omission of the schedule may have been accidental. There may have been an archpriest of Toledo in the twelfth century, though the evidence is ambiguous;[69] no hint of such an office, ambiguous or not, is to be seen in later times.[70]

The activities of the various archipresbyteral and vicarial chanceries seem to have been fairly similar, at least in the intention of Archbishop Tenorio, to judge from the schedules he published. But in the districts encompassed by the archdeaconries of Madrid and Guadalajara (except, strangely, in the archipresbyterate of Guadalajara) there are indicated the additional functions of arresting and "dis-arresting." The fee schedule for Hita is as follows (m. = *morabetinus* or maravedí; d. = *denarius* or dinero):

Taxatio cancellariae Archpresbyteratus de Fita

1) Citatio quae fit sine scriptis, quae vulgariter vocatur "coto o señal": 2 m.
2) Litera citatoria simplex, pro sigillo notario seu scriptore: 2 m.
3) Litera monitoria cum excommunicatione, pro sigillo et scriptura: 3 m. et 2 d.
4) Litera denuntiatoria excommunionis, pro sigillo et scriptura: 3 m. et 2 d.
5) Litera de participantibus, pro sigillo et scriptura: 6 m. et 2 d.

6) Litera cum candelis extinctis, pro sigillo et scriptura: 4 m. et 2 d.

7) Litera brachii saecularis, pro sigillo et scriptura: 4 m. et 7 d.

8) Litera absolutionis excommunionis, pro sigillo et scriptura: 3 m. et 2 d.

9) Pro sententia interlocutoria quando lis tractatur in scriptis per libelli oblationem: 3 m.

10) Si vero tractatur sine scriptis, nihil pro ea exigatur.

11) Pro rebellia seu contumacia, quae est quando iudex pronuntiat aliquem contumacem, nihil levetur ex ea neque per iudicem neque per notarium, etiam si ipsam scribat.

12) Litera receptoriae: nihil.

13) Pro sententia definitiva quando lis tractatur in scriptis per libelli oblationem: 6 m.

14) Si vero sine scriptis tractatur, nihil pro eadem levetur.

15) Litera executionis sententiae definitivae: 4 m.

16) Sigillare processum appellationis, pro ipso iudice: 4 m.

17) Praeceptum quod vulgariter vocatur "mandamiento," quod fit in eius curia: 1 m.

18) Publicatio testamenti, pro sigillo et litera: 4 m.

19) Pro eo redigendo in publicam formam, pro eo quod sunt Testes recipiendi et diligenter examinandi et eorum dicta in publicam formam redigenda: 8 m.

20) Auctoritas decreti cuiuslibet scripturae: 6 m.

21) Arrestare aliquem in speciali: 1 m.

22) Ipsum disarrestare: 1 m.

23) Praesentatio testamenti in probationem: 1 m.[71]

It is important to note that the archipresbyterate of Hita in the fifteenth century (and presumably also in the fourteenth) had a much larger purview than the *tierra de Hita* discussed by Manuel Criado de Val.[72] The archipresbyterate proper, which corresponded roughly to the *tierra*, contained twenty-one curacies, but there were ten more in the two dependent vicariates of Cogolludo and Beleña. A third vicariate of the region, that of Mohernando, was under the jurisdiction (at least concerning tithes) of the Order of Santiago. (These vicariates are to be distinguished from the perpetual vicariates like that of Brihuega, which functioned as independent archipresbyterates). In the town of Hita itself there were six curacies (pastorates with cure of souls). Besides the office of curate (that is, rector), the churches of

Santa María de Hita and San Pedro each had an additional three
beneficia servitoria; the churches of San Juan and San Julián each had
one additional *beneficium servitorium*; the curacy of the church of San
Román was dependent on the clergy of Santa María; the church of
San Miguel (combined with that of the village of Taragudo) had a
medium praestimonium in addition to a curate. One of the *beneficia
servitoria* of Santa María was immediately dependent on the archipresbyterate of Hita, as was the combined curacy of the villages of
Majanar and Maluque.[73]

The *Siete partidas* speaks of the archpriest's obligation to visit all of
the churches under his jurisdiction and to report the abuses that he
is not able to correct himself. The synod of Segovia in 1216–17 limited such visitations to once a year, except when necessary or when
ordered by the bishop or archdeacon.[74] We saw that there was an
attempt at that time to limit the size and expense of such visitations,
in accord with the decrees of the ecumenical councils, but there seems
always to have been a tendency for them to expand. There is an elo-
quent testimonial from the diocese of York in the thirteenth century
on how the archidiaconal visitation, which apparently was combined
with that of the rural dean, and perhaps also with the collection of
tithes, had become much more onerous than in the past. The clergy
of the rural deanery of Holderness in the archdeaconry of the East
Riding complained to Archbishop Wickwane (1279–85) that, whereas only the "official" (permanent deputy) of the archdeacon, with the
rural dean and his clerk (or at times with just one of them), used to
come to their churches to hold chapters, with only three or four conveyances, nowadays the official would bring a companion, the dean
would come with clerk, and the archbishop's sequestrator would also
be along, as well as an apparitor recently appointed for their district
by the archbishop's official, and they would have eight or nine conveyances among them.[75]

The Spanish sources that we have been using do not explicitly state
the need for holding meetings or chapters of the clergy of the archipresbyterates, whether in connection with visitations or for other purposes. The chapters that were held in the diocese of Segovia to resist
the bishop were presumably not official gatherings summoned by the
archpriests loyal to the bishop (though it is possible that some archpriests were sympathetic to the clergy), but they may have resembled
such official meetings. Ruridecanal chapters in some areas of Europe

were called Kalendae, perhaps because they were meant to be held at the beginning of the month. In Soissons in the ninth century, their purpose was to provide the opportunity for pious conversation and professional discussion, for the communication of parochial matters, and for the arrangement of prayers for the king, the rulers of the church, and so on. A sixteenth-century statute from the same diocese says that the rural dean is to preside over the Kalendae and to communicate the mandates of the bishop to the clergy.[76] Such meetings were also called Kalendae at Augsburg in the tenth century, at Ferrara in 1278, at Pont-Audemer in 1279, at Rouen in 1335, and at Constance in 1375.[77] Perhaps then it is in keeping with this tradition that the archpriest communicates the mandate of the archbishop to the clergy of the Talavera chapter on the Kalends of April, according to the *Cántica de los clérigos de Talavera*. In twelfth-century León, in the diocese of Orense, there were meetings of the rural clergy called *letaniae*, held mainly, it seems, for the purpose of extracting Lenten offerings. But the unit involved was not the archipresbyterate but rather the archdeaconry.[78]

In England, a record is preserved from the year 1300 of deanery proceedings in the diocese of Worcester that may help to throw light on the differences between chapters of the deanery and those of the archdeaconry.[79] The first two chapter sessions are limited to court cases in which charges are made against persons living within the deanery of Wych (most of the charges deal with fornication and adultery, but one man was accused of mistreating his wife).[80] The third meeting, however, consisted of the rectors and vicars of the whole archdeaconry, who were summoned by the rural dean of Wych, doubtless acting for the archdeacon; the meeting seems to have been presided over by the archdeacon, and it dealt with two vacated benefices.[81] It is not clear who presided over the first two gatherings, which were clearly deanery chapters. It could have been the archdeacon or the archdeacon's official, if he had one. But it could also have been the dean of Wych himself, whether acting as the archdeacon's *ad hoc* deputy or in virtue of his own ordinary jurisdiction. According to the canonist John Acton, who was writing around 1335, rural deans by custom acted in the place of archdeacons and had judicial power of correction.[82] William Lyndwood, writing in the next century but commenting on a statute of the Council of Lambeth of 1261, says that even rural deans in some places have jurisdiction and employ their own summoners.[83] There is evidence also that archdeacons and deans often shared cognition of cases in rural chapters.[84] As in Spain and elsewhere, the deans were forbidden to hear matrimonial cases, on order of papal legate as well as local authority,[85] and attempts were made to reduce their power in other matters. But "even the legislation designed to limit their jurisdiction testifies to its existence."[86]

The courts of the archdeacons and deans did, however, have legitimate jurisdiction over many of the same matters as the courts of the bishops, and were in effect run in competition with these courts in detecting and punishing offenders. As Chaucer's Friar puts it,

> Er the bisshop caughte hem with his hook,
> They weren in the archedeknes book.[87]

The bishop normally had two different kinds of court, the consistory, presided over by his official, and the court of audience, presided over by the bishop himself.[88]

One of the functions of the rural dean was to deliver citatory letters.[89] We have seen the dean of Wych performing this duty for an archdeaconry chapter. But when he did it for an episcopal court, he served for all practical purposes as the bishop's apparitor or summoner.[90] Thus, in the fifteenth-century *N. Town Plays*, "Sim the Summoner," who is charged with bringing Mary and Joseph before the "bishop," is identified in the rubrics as a dean ("den").[91]

Another important duty of the rural dean is illustrated in the constitutions of Archbishop Pecham of Canterbury issued in 1279. The deans and their vicegerents are singled out for special responsibility in seeing to the regular reading at their chapters of the legatine constitution of Cardinal Ottobono Fieschi (nephew of Pope Innocent IV) against concubinary priests. Deans who failed in this obligation were to be punished by fasting every Friday on bread and water.[92]

Were similar functions performed by archpriests in fourteenth-century Castile? We cannot safely extrapolate such activities from outside evidence. Even within England customs and practices varied from diocese to diocese. One general difference between Spain and England was that in Spain the office of archpriest always appears to have entailed a beneficed income in its own right, whereas in England the office of rural dean usually did not (though it was profitable for other reasons: namely the fines and other fees or taxes that could be collected).[93] For instance, the deans of the twelve rural deaneries of the diocese of Bath and Wells were elected or appointed for a year at a time.[94] When we hear of the archpriest of Puckington in that diocese, we are not to think of a rural dean, but rather of the rector of a collegiate church.[95] However, in the diocese of Norwich, the rural deanships seem to have been "perpetual benefices" that could be resigned and exchanged for others.[96]

We will look more closely at the canonical status of archpriests in Spain later on. Here let us consider some questions about the archpriests' supplementary income. In Bishop Giraldo's synod of Segovia in 1216–17 and the arbitration that followed there were various attempts to limit the charges that archpriests could levy in virtue of their office or services. We see the same sort of thing happening in fourteenth-century Toledo, but the archpriests' official standard of living is noticeably higher than in thirteenth-century Segovia. Whereas Bishop Giraldo stipulated, with the subsequent approval of the arbiters, that archpriests could charge nothing for their letters and seals,[97] Archbishop Tenorio, as we have seen, was much more generous, though his archpriests may not have thought so. His establishment of fee schedules came about as the result of complaints presented to Archbishop Tenorio during his visitation of the diocese and in the synod itself against the "inordinate licence of ambition" of certain archdeacons, archpriests, and their deputies in charging more than right and custom dictated; for their chancery fees were almost three times the amounts exacted by the archbishop's own chancery.[98]

The schedules of the archipresbyteral chanceries imply various kinds of court actions, without making it clear that the archpriests served as the judges; but in the schedule for notaries there is reference to "las sentencias de los arcedianos et arciprestes o de sus vicarios."[99] The "vicars" of the archpriests are called not only "lieutenants" (*loca tenentes*), as we have seen, but also "officials."[100]

Archbishop Tenorio gives vent to a long complaint against the delaying tactics of lawyers. He says, for instance: "Horum est officium iura confundere, suscitare lites, dilationes quaerere, supprimere veritatem, fovere mendacium, quaestum sequi."[101] Tenorio distinguishes between the actions heard in the episcopal courts "per vicarios et officiales aut alcaldes nostros, quovis nomine nuncupentur, in curia nostra seu vicariorum nostrorum, ac etiam in villis, ruribus, vel aldeolis et locis aliis quibuscumque nostrae iurisdictioni subiectis," and cases heard "per archidiaconos et archipresbyteros et alios quoscumque [qui] in nostra dioecesi ecclesiasticam iurisdictionem habent, et eorum loca tenentes."[102] He orders that cases involving claims of less than one hundred maravedís be heard with dispatch, and uses the customary phrase to indicate summary procedure: "simpliciter et de plano ac sine iudicii strepitu et figura,"[103] adding that the formalities of written briefs and testimonies are also to be omitted: "et sine scriptis." He goes on to set limits for continuances in the various stages of trials, including those entailed by the submission of "exceptions." Where large sums of money are at stake, and paperwork allowed, the limits for delays are greater.[104] It is quite safe to conclude, as we shall see below, that practicing archpriests in Tenorio's time would have been familiar with court procedures.

There was only one chancery for the six archdeacons, it seems, and it was no doubt situated in the city of Toledo. The chanceries of the archpriests must have been located in the *capites* or capitals of the archipresbyterates, that is, the towns after which they were named. There is a reference to these capitals in the synod of 1323, when the method for (collecting and?) distributing tithes in the archdeaconries of Toledo and Talavera is described: the representative (*nuntius*) of each archdeacon is to go from capital to capital ("capite cuiuslibet archipresbyteratus singillatim"), having with him only one man and one "animal." The bishop's man is also to be present at the distribution, unless some other arrangement is made.[105]

As for the question of the excessive taxation of the clergy, when Archbishop Albornoz took up the matter in the synod of 1346, he included, like Archbishop Tenorio after him, archdeacons as well as archpriests in his injunctions: they are not to tax the clergy without his licence; and if any cleric makes an unlicenced payment, he is to pay a fine of four times the amount to the archbishop.[106] As for those who authorize unlawful taxation, it is the archpriests and vicars rather than the archdeacons who are singled out for punishment, perhaps because as members of the synod they participated directly in formulating and approving the statute (though, of course, the archdeacons and other members of the cathedral chapter would have been represented through their proctors). They are to lose for one year the fruits of the benefices they hold within the diocese of Toledo.[107] He goes on to say that if any expenses are incurred by the archpriests and other clergy in attending the synod or in any other undertaking for the common good, the archbishop himself will see to it that they are reimbursed afterwards, and they are not to levy a tax for the purpose.[108]

An example of a legitimate tax to be paid by the clergy to the archpriests is the *cathedraticum*, which up until 1354 consisted of six maravedís a year; it was thenceforth to be doubled, and another tax, the *luctuosa*, was to be dropped. [109] In 1323, archpriests were appointed collectors not of a tax but of special alms for captives, called the *cruzata*. They were to urge donations from the people both in person and through others, in confession, sermons, and the making of wills, and they were allowed to keep one seventh of what they collected.[110]

The obligation of all archpriests to attend the diocesan synods was clearly set forth by Archbishop Ximeno de Luna in the synod of 1336. He stated that there was to be a synod every year at Toledo on the second Sunday after Easter, unless a letter from the archbishop indicated otherwise; every archpriest and vicar of the diocese was to be present, as well as two clerics from each archipresbyterate and vicarate who were well informed on the state of their respective districts and the churches in them. These synodal members were to come without being summoned, and were to bring copies of provincial and synodal constitutions with them.[111]

In 1354, Archbishop Blas Fernández changed the time of the annual synod to May 1, and specified other clerics who were to attend, as well as the archpriests and vicars and two representatives from each district. The latter, he said, were to be empowered by the clergy of their regions to act for them in the synod.[112] Presumably the clergy of each region would hold a meeting at which their delegates would be chosen and given powers of attorney.

Archbishop Albornoz's method of reimbursing the delegates for their expenses seems not to have proved practicable, for Fernández stipulated that the other clergy were required to contribute towards their expenses (this would be another reason for a meeting to be held). He further instructed the archpriests and vicars to bring lists of all the beneficed clergy and all vacant benefices in their districts.[113]

There is little indication in the records of fourteenth-century synods of how the enactments of the synods were to be imparted to the clergy of the diocese. We shall see in the next chapter that Archbishop Albornoz in 1342 simply ordered the constitution against concubines to be published by the archpriests and other clergy in their churches every Sunday, at the hour when the greater part of the people came to attend services.[114] But a provision of the provincial council held at Aranda in 1473 may throw some light on the subject: the constitutions of the council were to be published in the various dioceses within two months, whether in synods or in the cathedrals, and forty days after such publication they were to be binding in the capitals of the archipresbyterates, to which all of the parish priests were to have been summoned ("in capitibus archipresbyteratu[um], vocatis rectoribus").[115]

That this sort of archipresbyteral chapter was held in earlier times is evident from the documents published by Fidel Fita concerning the efforts of Archbishop Gonzalo Díaz Palomeque of Toledo in the year 1310 to comply with Pope Clement V's attack on the Knights Templar. The archbishop ordered his archdeacons to compile inventories of any Templar holdings in their archdeaconries. As an example of the reports that survive from the archdeaconries of Calatrava, Talavera, and Madrid, Fita gives that of the archipresbyterate of Madrid, as recorded by the scribe of the archpriest of Madrid. On Sunday, June 28, the clergy of the area was assembled in chapter ("estando yuntados a Cabildo los clérigos de la villa e del arraval de Madrit e del dicho arciprestadgo") in the church of San Ginés in Madrid. Martín Martínez de Alfaro, canon of Toledo and proctor of the archdeacon of Madrid, presided over the reading of a letter from the archbishop, which contained the translation of a letter from the pope concerning the confiscation of the goods of the Templars. The archdeacon's proctor then asked the archpriest and all the clerics present if they knew of any such goods existing within the archipresbyterate. They all answered with one voice that six months ago and more they had published in their churches on each Sunday and feastday of obligation a letter from the pope on this point, and that they knew of no Templar holdings in the area; and they promised that if they were to discover any such in the future, they would let the proctor know.[116]

The earlier papal letter referred to by the archpriest of Madrid and his clergy was doubtless the bull *Ad omnium fere notitiam*, one of the several letters issued by Clement V on August 12, 1308, and acknowledged at the provincial council of Toledo held at Alcalá on November 8, 1309. The bull required the goods of the Templars to be turned over to the bishops; and the bishops seem to have ordered the letter to be read in all of the churches under their jurisdiction. We know at least that this was the procedure followed in the diocese of Toledo, from the above-cited report of the archipresbyterate of

Madrid. We know also that the same thing was done in the diocese of Jaén, and we know precisely how it was done (or supposed to be done), from a notarial record of May 28, 1310. On that day, which was the feast of the Ascension, Miguel Sánchez, "arcipreste deste logar," came to the church of Santa María in Andújar, when "muchos omes buenos del concejo sobredicho" (that is, presumably, members of the town council of Andújar) were attending the mass. The archpriest presented a letter, which was then read, from the bishop of Jaén, dated November 25, 1309, addressed to the archdeacon of Baeza and to all the archpriests, vicars, priors, clerics, and chaplains of the arch-deaconry. It contained a translation of *Ad omnium fere notitiam*, with a mandate to publish the bull in each church and to send a record of the publication to the bishop.[117] We note that compliance with the order was not nearly so prompt in this case as it was in the archi-presbyterate of Madrid, perhaps because the archpriest preferred to make the rounds himself to the churches under his jurisdiction rather than entrust the publication to the curates; and it could be done only on Sundays and holydays.

The archpriests' custodial jurisdiction over benefices is brought out in a letter of Archbishop Gonzalo de Aguilar in 1351 to all archpriests and vicars or their deputies.[118] He is addressing the question of whether members of the cathedral chapter were required to take up personal residence in the benefices they held elsewhere in the diocese. He states that they were entitled to the income of these livings as long as all curacies were provided with vicars or chaplains and other benefices were properly staffed. The archpriests, he says, are to protect the chapter members' interests in these benefices.[119] He ends with a tribute to the way in which the archpriests have upheld the customs of the land in the time of his predecessors.[120]

There is surprisingly little in the synodal constitutions about the archpriests' obligations to police the life and morals of the clergy. The synod of 1325 directed the archpriests to admonish married clerics (that is, men who had received the tonsure or even minor orders and who continued to enjoy clerical status even though married) about their hair-style, clothes, and occupations.[121] But there is no word here or elsewhere about their enforcing the laws against clerical concubinage (apart from Albornoz's order in 1342 that they promulgate his con-stitution), or their duties to report offenders to the bishop. We recall that Cardinal Gil Torres laid these obligations on both archpriest and

archdeacon in the constitutions he established for the dioceses of
Salamanca and Ávila in the middle of the thirteenth century, a charge
in keeping with the legatine council of Valladolid held in 1228. The
council was called by John Halgrin of Abbeville, Cardinal Bishop of
Sabina, to promulgate the decrees of the Fourth Lateran Council of
1215.[122] In the similar national council held at Valladolid in 1322
by the papal legate William Godin of Bayonne, O.P., who was also
Cardinal Bishop of Sabina, the obligation of enforcing the law was
placed instead on the bishops and upon special investigators chosen
by them ("praelati omnes et singuli in suis dioecesibus per viros pro-
bos et timentes Deum").[123] In the legatine council of Palencia, held
in 1388 by Cardinal Pedro de Luna, the bishops are directed to appoint *testes synodales* for this purpose.[124] We will take up the content
of the various statutes against concubinage in Chapter III.

Other archipresbyteral duties are set forth in Toledan synodal constitutions of the late fifteenth century. Some of them are clearly new,
for instance, the publication of Archbishop Carrillo's annual Lenten
letter to the archpriests, but several of the functions mentioned in the
letter are no doubt of long standing. The archpriests are to forbid
fortune-tellers, fast-breakers, and concubinary laymen from entering
church; they are to order persons married within the prohibited degrees
of kinship to produce their dispensations; and they are to warn their
"parishioners" not to let their children live with Jews or Moors, under
pain of being excommunicated like public usurers.[125] In the synod
of 1480, Archbishop Carrillo includes archpriests among those who
are to execute the penalties imposed on clerics for not wearing the
proper tonsure or hair style; and archpriests are named among the
judges who are to be punished for allowing illegal divorces (that is,
annulments).[126] An *ad hoc* duty is assigned specifically to the archpriests:
they are to secure authentic formulas from Toledo for the administering
of baptism and extreme unction and distribute them to the curates
of their archipresbyterates.[127] In the synod of 1481, at which Vasco
de Rivera, Archdeacon of Talavera,[128] presided in place of Archbishop
Carrillo, archpriests were directed to examine all prospective converts
from Judaism or Islam and to investigate prejudices against converts
in confraternities. They were also directed to send to their clergy the
proper form for administering communion, and to suspend noncon-
formists or report them to the archbishop.[129]

In 1483, during the tenure of the next archbishop, Cardinal Pedro

González de Mendoza, powers over certain reserved sins were conceded to archpriests.[130] The archpriest of Madrid, who was present at the meeting,[131] observed that all archpriests and curates would have to be informed of the provision (which tells us that some archpriests were not present); accordingly, at his suggestion, multiple copies of the mandate were made.[132]

It is not until the synod of 1497, held by Cardinal Ximénez de Cisneros, that we hear of the obligation of the archpriests to secure their share of newly consecrated holy oils and chrism each year from Toledo and to take them to the capitals of their archipresbyterates for distribution to the various churches, and the subject was only brought up at this time because some archpriests were reportedly charging the clergy a fee for the service.[133] But archipresbyteral supervision of sacramental oils and other appurtenances of the liturgy was traditional, and was insisted on in the legatine council of 1228.[134]

III. *The Canonical Status of Archipresbyteral Benefices*

There is no sign in any of the synodal documents that the archpriest was himself the rector of any parishes within his district, or specifically of the principal church in the capital of his archipresbyterate. In fact, in the constitutions of 1480 there is clear evidence that he was not. In the list of *testes synodales* appointed at the synod, there appear several archpriests, those namely of Ocaña, Guadalajara, and Madrid, and they are singled out for special commendation;[135] among the other *testes* are the *cura* of Santa María, principal church of Escalona, and the *cura* of Santa María of Hita.[136] Therefore, the rector of Santa María of Hita was not the archpriest of Hita; pastors of parishes are distinguished from archpriests. When in the same synod there is reference to the parishioners of archpriests,[137] it must simply be a shorthand way of referring to the parishioners of the curacies within the archipresbyterates. More precise language is used in the same context: "Mandamos a los dichos arciprestes e vicarios que in las iglesias de sus arciprestadgos e vicarias e a los curas en sus iglesias perrochiales fagan leer e publicar la dicha carta e constitucion."[138]

When therefore we hear of an eighteenth-century reference to a grant by Archbishop Albornoz "confirmed by the pope of the time," which seems to refer to "the archpriest of Santa María of the town of Hita," we must be cautious.[139] But the question of whether archpriests or archipresbyterates were attached to certain parishes or churches in Spain before the fifteenth century deserves attention.

When J. F. Rivera refers to Sancho, "arcipreste de la villa" of Maqueda in 1098, and speaks of the "parroquia arciprestal de San Pedro" in Maqueda in the twelfth century,[140] he is perhaps being misled by an obsolete notion of what an archpriest was—for instance, the notion reflected in the canon *In capite quadragesimae* in Gratian, where "archpriests of parishes" are spoken of.[141] When the archbishop of Santiago in the year 1324 speaks of the archpriest of the *villa* of Alba de Tormes in the diocese of Salamanca, he probably means only that Alba was the capital of the archipresbyterate.[142]

More puzzling is the reference in a letter of Pope John XXII in 1325 to the *archipresbyteralis ecclesia* of Daroca in the diocese of Saragossa: the pope grants an expectative grace for the church to a cleric of the diocese of Albi, Raymond Amelii de Penna, canon of the cathedral churches of Albi, Lavaur, and Toledo.[143] Perhaps the phrase represents a mistake made by Raymond in his request; it was the custom in some French dioceses to attach churches to the office of archpriest. Or it may be that the archpriest of Daroca was in charge of, or a member of, a secular capitular or collegiate church, perhaps like the "archipresbyteral collegiate church" of Bergamo. The church of Santa María in Daroca, which was governed by a prior, may be a possibility.[144]

When Pope John writes to Raymond again, in 1332, he simply speaks of him as holding the archipresbyterate of Daroca.[145] He speaks similarly elsewhere of two other archipresbyterates in the diocese of Saragossa. The archipresbyterate of Torellas was first reserved for the nephew of the archbishop of Saragossa, on August 14, 1331, and was conferred on him on October 7. But the grant was revoked on October 23, after a hearing in the Roman curia (that is, at Avignon), and the archbishop and his nephew were ordered to perpetual silence in the matter.[146] The archipresbyterate of Belchite was conferred "by the ordinary authority" on Fortunio García de Turribus, Dean of Segorbe, sometime before August 26, 1330, and in assuming the archipresbyterate he gave up his deanship. This was the condition stated in the expectative grace he received in 1326 for a benefice with or without the cure of souls in the city or diocese of Saragossa.[147]

Another instance in which there seems to have been some kind of connection between an archpriest and specific churches can be seen in Sigüenza. The diocese of Sigüenza, as we have seen, was in the province of Toledo, and was mainly in the kingdom of Castile. Here we have a case of an archpriest in charge of at least some portion of the cathedral city itself and the immediately surrounding area. There were three parishes in the city, namely, the chapel of San Pedro (which was in the cathedral) and the two parochial churches of Santiago and San Vicente. In 1207 and again in 1302, 1309, and 1317, we find the clergy of the two churches acting on their own in disputes with the cathedral chapter.[148] But in 1315 it is "the archpriest and the clerics of Santiago and San Vicente" who are named as the opposing party. A less elliptical mode of expression is employed in a similar dispute in 1318, when it is specified that Alfonso Martínez, Archpriest of Sigüenza, and the clerics of the two churches were joined against the chief chaplain of San Pedro.[149]

It is often difficult to sort out the canonical status of beneficed clergy referred to in documents in which the number and nature of their benefices are not the point at issue. It is a different matter in documents that directly address the subject, especially the letters recorded in the papal registers.

It was a rigorously observed and enforced rule that one must mention all substantial benefices currently held when one seeks another benefice; and we can get some notion of the nature and importance of such benefices from the way they are dealt with. Uniform practice in this matter all over Europe dates from the promulgation of the constitution *Execrabilis* by Pope John XXII on November 19, 1317. In it he restricted all clerics to one benefice with the cure of souls and to one without.[150] In practice, the pope continued to allow the accumulation of non-cured benefices, though under supervision; but the limitation of a single cured benefice to everyone (except cardinals and princes) was maintained. It was a restriction that had been imposed earlier, in 1215, in the decree *De multa* of the Fourth Lateran Council (and duly incorporated into the *Decretals of Gregory IX*),[151] but exemptions from it had become a matter of course.

The "cure of souls" specified by the conciliar canon was interpreted by commentators to include both parochial and jurisdictional obligations. Hostiensis, for instance, says that it applies not only to the penitential forum and not only to a parish church, but also to a cathedral, or to a chapel with parishioners committed to it *de jure* or *de facto*; and it applies as well to dignities or offices without a church, as with many archdeacons, deans, and archpriests who do not rule over a special church and yet have jurisdiction over many places.[152]

Pope John defines benefices with the cure of souls similarly in *Execrabilis*: those that have parishes with the cure of souls, and those whose holders have powers of visitation and correction.[153]

After the promulgation of *Execrabilis*, there was a certain amount of confusion over the precise nature of various benefices. For instance, some archpriests of the diocese of Vienne provisionally resigned their posts, for fear of incurring the penalties of the constitution, until it could be clarified whether they were obliged to relinquish them or not. Pope John replied that since the archipresbyterates were recognized as offices customarily given to rectors of parish churches, who are not perpetual archpriests of these churches, the offices do not fall under the requirement of the constitution.[154]

Sometimes the nature of benefices is spelled out in the papal letters of conferral, which normally reflect statements attested to by the petitioners, but the implications are not always clear. For example, in 1327 a rural archipresbyterate in the diocese of Poitiers was conferred upon a prior of a secular church in the diocese of Perigueux, who was also litigating for a parochial church. He was allowed to retain his priorate, which is described as neither personate, dignity, nor office, but a simple benefice; but he was required to give up the parish church.[155] We cannot be sure whether "simple" means "without cure" or "of little income," or whether the parish church was to be dismissed because of incompatible cures or excessive income.

In another instance, the canonist Jesselin de Cassagnes received an expectative grace to the archipresbyterate of Roquefort in the diocese of Narbonne in 1323. But we are told only in later letters, when he receives non-cured benefices in 1327, 1330, and 1333, that it is the cured archipresbyterate of the church of St. Martin (in Roquefort-de-Sault).[156] Jesselin, by the way, may have been the one responsible for compiling the *Extravagants of John XXII*, which included *Execrabilis*, in 1325. His commentary on the collection, written in that year, became the *Ordinary Gloss*. When he comes to the question of benefices with the cure of souls, as specified in *Execrabilis*, he refers us to what Hostiensis says on *De multa*.[157]

When we turn to Spain, and see a letter reserving a portion in the church of Santo Domingo de la Calzada, for Diego Martínez de Bitoria, notwithstanding the fact that he holds the archipresbyterate of Armentia *cum cura*, in the diocese of Calahorra (province of Burgos) – as well as a half-portion *sine cura* in the town of Bitoria (i.e. Vitoria) in the same diocese[158] – it is only what we should expect to find. However, when we see García Fernández de Biota being granted an expectative grace for a benefice with cure worth seventy pounds, or without cure worth forty pounds, at the collation of the archbishop of Saragossa, with the obligation of dismissing the cured church of Palera in the diocese of Gerona as well as the archipresbyterate of Sarravillo in the diocese of Huesca in Aragon,[159] we must conclude that this particular archipresbyterate was considered to be uncured, because it was compatible with another benefice that was cured. It may have been a temporary rural archipresbyterate or a collegiate office, or had some other peculiar property. But I do not know of any evidence to suggest that rural archipresbyterates in the diocese or province of Toledo were at any time considered to be uncured.

For whatever reason, Spanish archipresbyterates do not seem to have been often brought to the attention of the papal curia. Of the more than 50,000 common letters of Pope John XXII (1316–34),[160] and the 9,000 or so similar letters of Benedict XII (1334–42),[161] there is only one, it seems, that mentions an archpriest of the diocese of Toledo: in 1326, Alfonso Fernández was provided with a canonry and expectation of a prebend in the secular church of Valladolid, notwithstanding his tenure as canon of Zamora and archpriest of Buitrago, and holder of several simple benefices.[162]

But not all papal mandates were registered; and curial clerics, or those with multiple benefices, who predominate in the registers,[163] did not often hold archipresbyterates in Spain, at least through the middle of the fourteenth century (it is hard to be certain on this point, since the registers after the time of Benedict XII have not yet been calendared or published). An exception is Pedro Martínez de Sos, a member of Cardinal Albornoz's retinue, who was appointed to a canonry in the cathedral chapter of Cuenca in 1351, notwithstanding his continued possession of other benefices, including the rural archipresbyterate of Zorita in the diocese of Toledo.[164] Another case, involving a *famulus* and kinsman of the cardinal, Fernando Álvarez de Albornoz, occurs in 1352–53, when a three-way trade of benefices was arranged. One of the benefices was the archipresbyterate of San Pedro del Campo in the diocese of Burgos, which was resigned by an Alfonso Fernández and taken over by Juan Martínez de Salinas, who in turn resigned a portion in the cathedral of Córdoba, which was assumed by Fernando Álvarez de Albornoz.[165]

Another Alfonso Fernández is the first archpriest to appear in the documents gathered by Vicente Beltrán de Heredia. He was archpriest of Carrión in the diocese of Palencia when in 1366 a canonry was sought and procured for him. He is said to be advanced in the study of canon law and well instructed in the ecclesiastical office.[166] In the first generation of students at the Spanish College at Bologna, founded by Cardinal Albornoz, there was an archpriest, Tellio García, who is listed in 1372 as archpriest of Gomara (in the diocese of Osma).[167] In the constitutions of the college as revised in 1375–77, Archpriest Tellio is allowed an extra year beyond the statutory eight.[168] In February of 1380, he is still at the college, as appears from the roll of petitions for benefices sought from Pope Clement VII for students at the college. For Tellio, said to be advanced in the study of canon law, a canonry and prebend in the cathedral chapter of Toledo is requested, along with supplementary incomes, amounting to a worth of forty pounds in all, to be held in addition to his archipresbyterate and other simple benefices (which together do not exceed forty pounds' worth).[169]

We saw earlier that there were a dozen archipresbyterates included in the Salamanca roll presented to Clement VII and approved in 1381.[170] In February of 1379 the rules of the pope's chancery, as set forth by the deputy chancellor Giles Bellemère, show that rural deanships or archipresbyterates with the cure of souls were normally given to university graduates, as were dignities or offices in non-cathedral collegiate churches, while nongraduates were to receive canonries and prebends in such churches.[171] But Bellemère received permission, when dealing with university rolls seeking benefices for students, to grant dignities and other high offices even in cathedral chapters to nongraduates in areas like Spain where there was not an abundance of graduates.[172] In April of 1380 the pope decided that nongraduates were eligible for deanships and archipresbyterates that did not have the rank of *dignitas* or *personatus*.[173] (For all practical purposes, these were synonymous terms.)[174] We will see in the next chapter that the rural archipresbyterates in the kingdom of Castile were considered to be cured dignities, at least by the year 1421.

To sum up. All the evidence indicates that rural archipresbyterates in the province of Toledo, which were a well established institution by the beginning of the thirteenth century, always had the status of perpetual benefices with the jurisdictional cure of souls; the holders of these benefices seem normally to have been unattached to particular churches within the archipresbyteral districts, though there may have been exceptions (perhaps exemplified by the archpriests of Sigüenza).

Archpriests would no doubt get the bulk of their income from sharing in the tithes and other taxes and fees collected from their jurisdictions. In the synod of Segovia held in 1216–17, archdeacons and archpriests were instructed to take nothing from the thirds until they had been divided, and archpriests were to prohibit their *parentes* from doing any of the collecting.[175] Archpriests, therefore, were entitled to part of the proceeds. In the census of ecclesiastical rents in the diocese of Sigüenza taken in 1353, at the wish of King Pedro of Castile, a figure is given for each archipresbyterate as a whole, which seems to be the archpriest's income.[176] Moreover, archpriests of Toledo in the fourteenth century were entitled to additional revenues that were restricted or forbidden in thirteenth-century Segovia: a share in the *cathedraticum*, for instance, the right to charge fees for letters and seals, and the right to collect procurations or visitation taxes.[177] On the latter point, the standard was set by Pope Benedict XII in 1336 in his constitution *Vas electionis Paulus* for the various regions of Europe. For instance, archpriests, who are identified as rural deans, can only charge ten pounds Tournois in England, eight in France, and five in Castile, Aragon, and Portugal, while in still poorer regions like Italy no rate for archpriests is given.[178]

It is possible that archpriests were also entitled to some of the simple benefices in their districts. According to a ruling of the synod of Toledo in 1356, where there is only one *beneficium servitorium* in a given church, it is to be considered *curatum*. Where there are several such benefices, one must be designated a curacy, if it has not already been done by custom or statute.[179] In the late fifteenth century, as we have seen, the church of Santa María at Hita possessed four benefices, one *curatum* and the others *servitoria*, and one of the latter was directly dependent on the archipresbyterate, as was an outlying curacy.[180]

But it is also possible that before 1356 a church of the diocese of Toledo that had no designated curate could be considered to be under the direct administration of the archpriest; or the clergy of the church may have found it necessary or advisable to call upon the archpriest to act as their head, whether temporarily or permanently. Something of the sort seems to have been in effect in Sigüenza, in the cases where the clergy of the parochial churches of Santiago and San Vicente were led by the archpriest of Sigüenza. In 1353, there was no *beneficiatus curatus* at either of these churches, only *beneficiati servitorii*.[181] In some such way, perhaps, the archpriest of Hita may have been called the archpriest of Santa María of Hita in the time of Archbishop Albornoz.

A cured benefice, like a parochial church, a rural archipresbyterate, an archidiaconate, or a cathedral or collegiate deanship (and usually the other dignities in cathedral and collegiate churches), was incompatible with any other cured benefice, and therefore there are always a comparatively fewer number of cured benefices (as opposed to uncured) listed in the papal registers;[182] and a "professional" cleric with multiple benefices would naturally prefer to have for his single cured benefice one with a good income, which would not entail paying an expensive vicar to perform his duties *in absentia*. This is no doubt the main reason why Spanish archipresbyterates were not popular with such clerics in the earlier fourteenth century. They were no doubt given mainly to priests who stayed within their dioceses, and were conferred by the bishops without papal provisions. It was not necessary for benefices to be transferred through the intervention of the pope, except in the case of benefices reserved to the Holy See, though papal provision became increasingly the rule for ordinary benefices as time went on.[183] But it is of fundamental importance to remember that whether a cured benefice (or an important uncured benefice) was conferred by the local ordinary or by the pope, or by the ordinary at the provision of the pope, it had to be mentioned in any subsequent negotiations for benefices.

IV. *Alleged Archpriests of Hita*

We are now in a position to discuss various identifications that have been made of holders of the archipresbyterate of Hita in the fourteenth century.

Let us deal first of all with the claim elaborated by Manuel Criado de Val from a statement by Emilio Sáez and José Trenchs, that Cardinal Albornoz himself was archpriest of Hita from 1353 until his death in 1367.[184] We can say definitely from the evidence provided subsequently by Sáez and Trenchs and their collaborators in the first published volume of the *Diplomatario del Cardenal Albornoz*, which extends from the beginning of 1351 to the end of 1353, that Albornoz was definitely not archpriest of Hita in 1353. Subsequent volumes of the *Diplomatario* will give us the answer for later years, but the answer will almost surely remain negative.

Cardinals and princes were excepted in the constitution *Execrabilis* from the prohibition against accumulating cured benefices.[185] Cardinal Albornoz took advantage of this concession, but in the records of the benefices that he acquired during his first three years as cardinal, though there are nine archidiaconates, three parish churches, two deanships, and two priorates, there are no archipresbyterates.[186] I might add, too, that there are no archipresbyterates in the list of forty-one benefices vacated by the death of Gutierre Gómez, Cardinal of Spain, in 1391.[187]

Criado does not pretend to have encountered documentary evidence that Cardinal Albornoz became archpriest of Hita in 1353, but rather, as I mentioned above, he relies on the authority of Sáez and Trenchs, in an article in which they claim also to have identified earlier archpriests of Hita.[188] But their claims are without justification, and rest on the false assumption that benefices in the gift of the bishop do not have to be named in papal letters.[189]

Sáez and Trenchs say that the archipresbyterate of Hita was possessed by Cardinal Albornoz's nephew, Pedro Álvarez de Albornoz, and when the nephew died (some time before March 3, 1353), the office passed to the cardinal himself.[190] But just as their *Diplomatario* disproves the cardinal's acquisition of the office, it disproves the nephew's possession of it.

When Pope Clement VI addresses the twelve- or thirteen-year-old Pedro on March 7, 1352, he grants him, in spite of his youth, the treasurership of Cuenca, an *officium sive personatus sine cura*, as well as a canonry and prebend in the same church, even though he is already a canon and prebendary of the churches of Toledo and Palencia and has other portions and prestimonies in the dioceses of Toledo and Cuenca.[191] But we hear later, on July 14, 1352, that Pedro gave up two of these portions on becoming canon, prebendary, and treasurer of Cuenca.[192] Pedro died before coming into possession of prestimonies and prestimonial portions in the city and diocese of Cuenca, as we read in a letter of Cardinal Albornoz dated March 3, 1353.[193] In other letters we are informed of the disposal of other benefices vacated by Pedro's death; the archipresbyterate of Hita is not among them.[194]

Criado de Val asserts on the alleged authority of Sáez and Trenchs's article that Pedro de Albornoz's predecessor as archpriest of Hita, from 1343 to 1351, was Pedro Fernández, the administrator of Cardinal Albornoz's goods in Spain and his proctor for the monastery of Villaviciosa. What Sáez and Trenchs actually say is that the archpriest of Hita should not be confused with the administrator of Albornoz's goods in Spain, and specifically in Hita, an office filled by Pedro Fernández, according to a document of Albornoz's preserved at Osma.[195] The authors offer no documentation in their article, but presumably they are referring to a letter written by the newly elevated cardinal on January 7, 1351, which has long been taken to identify Pedro Fernández as the archpriest of Hita. But though Albornoz identifies Fernández as an archpriest, and also speaks of him as his majordomo in the archipresbyterate of Hita, he does not say that he is archpriest of Hita.[196] In an earlier letter, written on June 16, 1350, when still archbishop of Toledo, Albornoz ordered the archpriest of Hita or his deputy to transfer possession of prestimonial portions in Trijueque and Moduex to the sacrist of the Augustinian monastery of San Blas at Villaviciosa in order to alleviate the sacrist's *onera*.[197]

We come now to Juan Rodríguez de Cisneros, whom Sáez and Trenchs identify not only as the archpriest of Hita, but also as the author of the *Libro de buen amor*. Let me point out, first of all, that they have confused Juan Rodríguez de Cisneros with other Juan Rodríguezes, and have also confused the geography of the benefices involved. They say, for example, that Juan Rodríguez de Cisneros was archdeacon of Medina del Campo; but Medina del Campo is in the diocese of Salamanca, and Juan Rodríguez de Cisneros was archdeacon of Medina, that is, Medinaceli, in the diocese of Sigüenza, and he was later archdeacon of Sigüenza itself, while the archidiaconate of Campos in the diocese of Palencia was held successively by two other Juan Rodríguezes: they may have been related to each other as uncle and nephew, with the nephew in effect inheriting the post from his uncle.[198] There may in fact have been two persons named Juan Rodríguez de Cisneros, perhaps similarly related and following a similar career.

The Juan Rodríguez de Cisneros who was the illegitimate son of Arias de Cisneros is dispensed for his illegitimacy every time he appears with a new benefice in the registers of Pope John XXII. The last entry shows him, in 1329, receiving a canonry and expectation of a prebend in the chapter of Toledo, and expectation also of a dignity with or without the cure of souls. He possessed at that time the cured major archidiaconate of Sigüenza and canonries and prebends at Sigüenza, Palencia, and Burgos, and also a quarter portion at Valladolid and simple benefices in Sigüenza.[199] If he had actually received a dignity in Toledo, he would perhaps have been required to relinquish one or more of his other benefices, and if it had been a cured dignity, it would have been mandatory to resign the incompatible archidiaconate of Sigüenza. But in fact he was still archdeacon of Sigüenza as late as 1334.[200] His brother Simón, who remained dean of Sigüenza until at least the middle of 1335,[201] eventually left that post to become archdeacon of Sigüenza, no doubt as soon as the archidiaconate was vacated by Juan. Simón was definitely archdeacon of Sigüenza before March 13, 1343,[202] and probably before the end of 1341.[203]

Sáez and Trenchs refer to a letter (addressed to Pope Clement VI) by Albornoz at the beginning of 1343 in favor of his commensal Juan Ruiz (that is, Juan Rodríguez de Cisneros), who is also a papal chaplain, requesting for him a canonry with expectation of a prebend in Calahorra, notwithstanding other benefices that he holds in the abbey of Santa Leocadia, in Toledo, and in other dioceses. Later in the same year, they say, Juan Ruiz put in the same request for himself.[204] Whether or not this is the same Juan Rodríguez de Cisneros as the one who appears earlier in the registers of John XXII, and the same as the one who appears in 1353 in the registers of Innocent VI, will perhaps become clear once Sáez and Trenchs have identified and published the documents of 1343, so that we can see precisely what benefices were held at that time. (See Addenda, pp. 119–20.)

If the Juan Rodríguez de Cisneros of 1353 is the same as that of the 1320s, we can say the following about his career after 1329: he received the expected prebend in the chapter of Toledo, but not a dignity. Rather, he received a cured dignity at the secular abbey of Santa Leocadia in the city of Toledo, namely, the abbacy, and he accordingly relinquished the cured dignity that he already possessed in the chapter of Sigüenza, namely, the archidiaconate of Sigüenza. He was still canon and prebendary of Sigüenza, Palencia, and Burgos, and no longer worried about his illegitimacy, when, on July 21, 1353, he informed the pope through the good offices of Cardinal Albornoz that he would be willing to give up the posts in Burgos, as well as his quarter portion in Valladolid, in exchange for the canonry and prebend at Calahorra recently vacated by Gonzalo Fernández, Archdeacon of Vizcaya, who died at the Holy See (whereupon all of his benefices were automatically reserved to the pope). The pope agreed to the arrangement on the same day.[205]

In the same letter in which he proposed this exchange for Juan Rodríguez de Cisneros, Cardinal Albornoz also asked the pope to reserve the canonry and prebend of Burgos—which were to be relinquished by Juan Rodríguez de Cisneros in the above-stated way, or relinquished in any other way except by his death ("praeterquam per ipsius obitum")—for his commensal Juan Martínez de la Sierra, doctor of decrees, canon and prebendary of Salamanca, canon, prebendary, and subdean of Santa María in Talavera, cantor of Burgos (under litigation), and holder of portions in Toledo and Ciudad Rodrigo; in return he was willing to give up the above-named holdings in Talavera and Ciudad Rodrigo. The pope agreed to this arrangement.[206]

A similar arrangement was made in the following month, on August 18, for the quarter-portion at Valladolid that was to be relinquished by Juan Rodríguez de Cisneros (again, in any way except by his death). Cardinal Albornoz requested it for another Juan Rodríguez, son of Fernando Rodríguez de Vayllo, who was already possessed of a half-portion in the collegiate church of Fusiellos (which, like Valladolid, is in the diocese of Palencia); and the request was granted.[207] Yet a third Juan Rodríguez in the cardinal's retinue appears in Albornoz's letter of August 18, namely his chaplain, Juan Rodríguez de Espejo, who was giving up a portion in the parochial church of Santiago in Albarracín, in light of an expectative grace in the church of Valencia.[208]

Sáez and Trenchs are clearly mistaken in assuming that Juan Rodríguez de Cisneros was close to death in 1353 because of the expected release of his benefice in Valladolid, and they have no grounds for assuming that he was ever archpriest of Hita. If it is the same Juan Rodríguez de Cisneros who was archdeacon of Sigüenza in the 1320s and 1330s and abbot of Santa Leocadia in 1353, then he could only have assumed the archipresbyterate of Hita, and then given it up again, in the period between circa 1335 and 1343, or in the period between 1343 and 1353; for we are assured by Sáez and Trenchs's report of the letters of 1343 that he could not have been archpriest of Hita at that time. But it is hardly likely that he would have given up the major archidiaconate of the diocese of Sigüenza for an obscure archipresbyterate in the diocese of Toledo, as he would have had to do because of the incompatibility of the two cured benefices.[209]

Juan Rodríguez de Cisneros did in fact give up the archidiaconate of Sigüenza some time between 1335 and 1341 or so. We must conclude either that he vacated it by his death (whereupon it was taken over by his brother Simón, and his other benefices assumed by another relative, also named Juan Rodríguez de Cisneros), or that he vacated it upon assuming the abbacy of Santa Leocadia or some comparable cured dignity, which one will find named in the letters of 1343.

The upshot of all this is that no holder of the archipresbyterate of Hita has yet been identified.

Earlier in this chapter we looked at some of the duties that archpriests in the diocese of Toledo in the fourteenth century would have been expected to perform. The narrator and autoprotagonist of the *Libro de buen amor* does not portray himself as connected with any of these functions. He does not, therefore, manifest himself as the sort of abusive archpriest denounced by the ecclesiastical and secular authorities, who through ambition for power and riches went beyond the limits of his charge as judge, levier and collector of taxes, overseer of benefices, and selector of ordinands; he is no simoniacal conniver with, and concealer of, corrupt or negligent priests. Rather he is himself negligent of whatever ecclesiastical discipline and duties were expected of him. For this reason at least, critics of the *Libro* are justified in considering him only from the viewpoint of the literary "bad archpriest," a figure usually wholly detached from any ecclesiastical function or dereliction of function.

It is, of course, not always clear that the "I" of the story is meant to be Juan Ruiz, Archpriest of Hita, and on one occasion it is clearly not: namely, when the speaker is identified as Don Melón. Don Melón is characterized by Trotaconventos as a lawyer:

> Mas éste vos defendrá de toda esta contienda:
> Sabe de muchos pleitos e sabe de leyenda,
> Ayuda e defiende a quien se le encomienda;
> Si él non vos defiende, non sé quién vos defienda.   (755)

Moreover, he is capable of marriage. He is therefore not a priest, and archpriests were supposed to be priests, as we have seen.[210] However, we will see in the next chapter that one could be dispensed from this obligation, at least for a time.[211] But the holder of this or any kind of benefice would have had to be at least a cleric in minor orders (though perhaps dispensations were possible even from this regulation).

If Juan Ruiz does not show himself to be a functioning archpriest as narrator-character, he comes closer to doing so as narrator-author. Archpriests were required to serve as judges in ecclesiastical courts, and therefore a certain knowledge of canon law would be needed; but they seem to have had a reputation for being untrained in the intricacies of the field, especially the regulations governing marriage, and they were prohibited from hearing cases concerning marriage or cases of great moment. In keeping with this reputation, perhaps, Juan Ruiz speaks modestly of the elementary level of his canonistic knowledge. But we have seen enough to suspect that he may have been a cut above the normal level of archpriest as far as his familiarity with the law was concerned. If he really was an archpriest, he may have received special training in canon law and the law of the land; or his knowledge may be a reflection of actual judicial experience in both areas, experience that local custom or his own ambition as well as his canonical office required of him. We can get some notion of the extent of his judicial knowledge from the episode of Don Ximio, which I will examine below. But first let us deal with the one instance in the *Libro de buen amor* in which an archpriest is seen to be exercising his archipresbyteral functions, namely, the *Cántica de los clérigos de Talavera*.

Chapter Three

The Archpriest at Talavera

I. *Archpriest, Archdeacon, and Subdean*

In order to place the *Cántica de los clérigos de Talavera* into canonical perspective, it will be necessary to discuss the ecclesiastical status of Talavera in the fifteenth century. Let us begin with the celebrated "Archpriest of Talavera." Alfonso Martínez de Toledo has many points of resemblance with the author of the *Libro de buen amor*, as the latter is manifested in his work. With Martínez de Toledo we are fortunate in being able to go beyond the data of his book to solid biographical information, especially as recently expanded and clarified by Vicente Beltrán de Heredia.[1]

There is no doubt about the archipresbyteral status of Alfonso Martínez de Toledo: he was already archpriest of Talavera around 1424, before he had advanced to the priesthood, and he remained archpriest until his death in 1468. He gave his office great prominence when he named his book *Arcipreste de Talavera* in 1438; but the work does not reflect his exercise of the office any more than the *Libro de buen amor* shows Juan Ruiz to be a functioning archpriest—except in the matter of exposing and correcting sin. Juan Ruiz's method of performing this duty is quite different from that employed by Martínez de Toledo, and his sincerity has often been questioned by modern readers. But it is not questioned by Martínez de Toledo, who cites him in the spirit set forth in the Introduction to the *Libro de buen amor*. Like Juan Ruiz, Martínez de Toledo does not claim to be a doctor or master of canon law, but he does claim to hold a bachelor's degree in the

subject (Beltrán thinks it likely that he received such a degree from
the University of Salamanca).² Like Juan Ruiz, he cites Gratian's
Decretum, the *Decretals of Gregory IX*, the *Clementines*, and Cardinal
Hostiensis. Most of his references are specific and can be identified
without trouble. One passage that has proved puzzling is the following:

> Dize el proemio de las *Clementinas* sobre aquella palabra *sylençio*,
> dize:
>> El fablante sea discreto en fablar.
> Dize más Ovidio:
>> Non ay menor trabajo que callar,
>> E mayor pena que mucho fablar,
>> Porque trae consygo el mucho errar.
> Dize Catón que la primera virtud créese refrenar la lengua. Dize
> Sócrates:
>> Dezir me pesó; callar nunca.
> Dize el Arcipreste:
>> Sabieza tenprado callar;
>> Locura desmayado fablar.³

What Martínez de Toledo has done is to quote John Andreae's comment on the word *silentio* from the *Prooemium* to the *Clementines* as
if it were actually a part of the *Clementines*. He is using Andreae's *Apparatus* or *Glossa ordinaria*, which I suggested above may have been
the source for Juan Ruiz's attribution to Gratian of the sentiment that
"la memoria del omne deslesnadera es." In Martínez de Toledo's quotation or adaptation, "Socrates" has been substituted for "Seneca." Andreae says:

> Sit rector discretus in silentio, 43 dist., *Sit rector* [= Gratian,
> *Decretum* 1. 43. 1], in principio: contra illos qui dicunt tacenda.
> Ovidius, *Sine titulo*:
>> Quis minor est unquam quam tacuisse labor?
> Et Cato:
>> Virtutem primam esse puta compescere linguam.
> Et Seneca ait:
>> Dixisse me quandoque poenituit, tacuisse nunquam.⁴

As for the reference to the Archpriest, it has been suggested that Martínez de Toledo was "misquoting from memory" stanza 568 of the
Libro de buen amor, where Juan Ruiz urges the keeping of secrets and

supports the admonition by citing "Cato."[5]

There is no evidence that Martínez de Toledo ever presided personally over his archipresbyteral duties at Talavera. From about 1427 to 1431 he seems to have been legitimately absent in Catalonia on the king's business.[6] But there is indication also that he had not arrived at Talavera before 1427, for on July 3 of that year, a speculator named Francisco Fernández, a priest of Toledo, put in a crudely drafted petition for the post of archpriest of Talavera on the grounds that Martínez de Toledo had forfeited it by marrying. In order to possess a benefice, one normally had to be in minor orders; one was still free to marry at this stage, but in doing so, one would forfeit all benefices. Perhaps a rumor that Martínez de Toledo had married was circulating in the diocese.

However, as Beltrán de Heredia explains, marriage was simply one of the standard reasons set forth in such petitions, and it was usually coupled with the alternative reason that the office-holder had entered a religious order. Shortly afterwards, Fernández submitted a slightly improved petition, in which he added the possible reason that Martínez de Toledo had not been promoted to major orders within the statutory time limit. But nothing came of his efforts.[7]

Also in 1427 we hear of the canons of the collegiate church of Talavera joining with Martín López de Henestrosa, Archdeacon of Talavera, in a petition for indulgences to be granted to persons assisting in rebuilding the church. It was granted at Rome on September 10.[8] Martínez de Toledo was, of course, a dignitary of the chapter, but he had not yet obtained the canonry that usually accompanied the dignity.[9]

The career of Martín López de Henestrosa throws interesting light on ecclesiastical preferments in his time. The cured dignity of the archidiaconate of Talavera was bestowed on Henestrosa in 1410 by Pope Benedict XIII (Pedro de Luna), who declared it vacated by its previous holder, Amadeo de Salucis, on grounds that he had taken the side of the recently elected Pisan pope, Alexander V. Henestrosa received a dispensation because of his youth (he was in his seventeenth year), and as a condition for receiving the archidiaconate he had to give up the scholastries of Toledo and Orense.[10]

In 1418, in a letter addressed to Martin V after the effective deposition of Benedict XIII, Henestrosa is spoken of not as archdeacon of Talavera but rather as secular abbot of Santander: he had been litigating

in the curia of Pedro de Luna over some prestimonies claimed as well
by Juan Rodríguez, doctor of laws and dean of Ávila.[11] Perhaps
Henestrosa had not yet come into possession of the archidiaconate.
But in 1420, within two days of each other, two speculators submitted claims for benefices held by him, including the archidiaconate of
Talavera, and both pointed out that it was unlawful for him to hold
both the archidiaconate and the abbacy of Santander at the same time
without a dispensation.[12] This, of course, was true—if it was true that
he actually held both benefices at once. When John XXII issued his
constitution *Execrabilis* in 1317, Munio Pérez, chancellor of King Alfonso and Queen María of Castile and León, who was abbot of Santander and archdeacon of Campos, surrendered the archidiaconate.[13]
We saw that Juan Rodríguez de Cisneros would have been obliged
to resign the archidiaconate of Sigüenza on becoming abbot of Santa
Leocadia. But perhaps Henestrosa was in the process of dismissing
the abbacy while retaining the archidiaconate, or he may actually have
had a dispensation, whether permanent or temporary. Such dispensations had become fairly common in all three papal obediences, and
were continued under Martin V.[14] We will see below that Alfonso
Martínez de Toledo in 1432 was allowed to hold two cures at once
for a year.

The second of the two petitioners mentioned above wrongly described the archidiaconate of Talavera as the principal dignity of the
collegiate church of Talavera; it was in fact a nonprincipal dignity of
the cathedral church of Toledo. Henestrosa belonged to the Toledo
chapter not only in virtue of his being archdeacon of Talavera but
also by his possession of a canonry and prebend in the same cathedral;
these benefices were usually but not always granted with the dignities.
Some time after 1424, we hear that Henestrosa vacated these posi-
tions by reason of having contracted marriage.[15] His marriage must
have occurred, or have been discovered, only in 1427 or later, for
in that year, as we have seen, he was still named as archdeacon of
Talavera. He would then have been about thirty-four years of age,
and still not advanced to major orders.

Let us turn from the archdeacon of Talavera to the archpriest. According to a petition of the year 1421, rural archipresbyterates in the
kingdom of Castile were considered "dignitates curatae, extra tamen
ecclesias cathedrales."[16] That is, they were non-cathedral dignities that
carried with them the cure of souls. At one point, in 1432, Alfonso

Martínez de Toledo minimized the reality of this pastoral responsibility, as far as his own archipresbyterate of Talavera was concerned ("licet sit curatus, non tamen illi imminet cura animarum"), perhaps because of the large clerical staff of the collegiate church. But it was also in his interests to play down the duties of the post, for he was seeking a dispensation (which was granted) to hold another curacy at the same time for the period of one year—even, his patron Cardinal Casanova says, another rural archipresbyterate which is deemed to be a dignity or a personate.[17] No doubt even ordinary archipresbyterates like that of Hita, which were not attached to a collegiate church, were characterized as dignities by this time.

Beltrán thinks that Martínez de Toledo's assessment of the nature of the archipresbyterate of Talavera is probably correct, and that his successor, Nicolás Fernández, found it advisable to exaggerate the responsibilities of the post.[18] Fernández says flatly of the office, "Cura imminet animarum." But in the papal response granting Fernández's petition, the benefice is described more carefully: the archipresbyterate is rural, and considered by some to be a dignity; and the cure of souls that goes with it is jurisdictional in nature.[19] Beltrán argues that the position was basically *sine cura* because Martínez could be absent without incurring charges of failing to maintain residence. But, as we have seen in the last chapter, it had long been possible to have a permanent vicar appointed to fulfill archipresbyteral duties if the archpriest himself were legitimately excused. Beltrán maintains that the income of the archipresbyterate of Talavera was less than that of a rural pastorate. The point needs discussion. According to a document of March 16, 1433, Martínez de Toledo's proctors had recently accepted such a pastorate for him, only to resign it within a few days, since it conflicted with his archipresbyterate.[20] Was the archipresbyterate preferable only because of its greater prestige, or did it have a greater income? We note that at this time Martínez de Toledo did not yet have a canonry and prebend at Talavera. He was granted these additional benefices only on January 7, 1433, on the death of a canon named Juan González, who was parish priest of Nombela (a town in the archipresbyterate of Escalona, just to the north of that of Talavera).[21] But Martínez de Toledo's right to the posts was under litigation in 1436.[22] In 1433, Martínez de Toledo estimated the income from the canonry and prebend as coming to thirty pounds,[23] and that from the archipresbyterate to be thirty-five pounds.[24] His successor in 1468 valued the archipresbyterate at fifty pounds,[25] which was also the first estimate of Francisco Fernández in 1427.[26] But Fernando García, who claimed the post in 1424, put its value at seventy pounds, and said that the collegiate canonry and prebend which he meant to keep with the archipresbyterate, together with his other benefices in the diocese, would add another thirty pounds.[27]

According to García, who in 1424 was already a canon of Talavera, the archipresbyterate had been conferred on him by the ordinary authority (either the archbishop of Toledo or the collegiate chapter, or both together, or perhaps the archdeacon of Talavera would also have a say),[28] but Martínez de Toledo put in a claim for it before the archdeacon of "Medino," who was papal subexecutor in Spain, and García himself took the matter to the papal court in Rome.[29]

We may conclude from all of this that it would be a mistake to liken the position of the collegiate archpriest of Talavera exactly to that of the archpriest of Hita. But it would also be a mistake to assume an identity of circumstances for Talavera in the fourteenth and fifteenth centuries.

By the fourteenth century, Talavera was one of the principal population centers in the diocese of Toledo, and its collegiate chapter ranked first after that of the cathedral.[30] But dramatic changes took place in the constitution of the Talavera chapter between the time of Archbishop Albornoz and that of Archpriest Martínez de Toledo. As originally instituted, the chapter normally consisted of twelve canons, of whom four were dignitaries, namely the dean, the subdean, the cantor, and the treasurer. But by Martínez de Toledo's time, the subdeanship had been suppressed and replaced by the dignity of archpriest. Beltrán, speaking in the context of the fifteenth century, characterizes this change as "recent," but he unfortunately offers no further precisions, nor does he say what the area of Talavera and its surroundings was called before the time of the change, if it was not an *arciprestazgo*. We have seen that in the fourteenth and fifteenth centuries the areas that were not *arciprestazgos* were called *vicarias*, or, in the case of Toledo, *ciudad*.[31] The earliest archpriest that Beltrán refers to in his discussion of Talavera in this connection is Gonzalo Fernández, who is mentioned in a document of 1417.[32] The subdean still existed after the reign of Archbishop Albornoz. Reference is made in 1354 to the perpetual subdeanship of the secular collegiate church of Santa María of Talavera, and the post is described as a personate, and is said to have been vacated by Juan Martínez de la Sierra upon his appointment as cantor of Salamanca.[33] However, as we saw in the last chapter, the pope in the previous year had required Martínez de la Sierra to relinquish the subdeanship along with his canonry and prebend at Talavera without singling out the subdeanship as a personate.[34]

The new subdean, Juan Fernández, gave up the cured benefice of the church of San Martín in Talavera, and it is likely that the subdeanship was a *personatus curatus*. This surmise is confirmed by letters of Pope John XXII in 1328 and 1330: when Bernardo de Fonte becomes subdean, the post is said to be *cum cura*, as it is when he exchanges it for a parish church held by Jaime de Pertusa. The latter is expecting a dignity *cum cura* or *sine cura* in Valencia, and if he gets one *cum cura* he must relinquish the subdeanship of Talavera.[35]

In the book of constitutions that Archbishop Blas Fernández compiled in 1356, a section from his earlier synod at Alcalá in 1354 is repeated, listing the clergy who are to attend the annual synods. Proctors are to represent the dean and the chapter of the cathedral,[36] and the collegiate churches of Talavera and Santa Leocadia outside the walls of the city of Toledo (of which Juan Rodríguez de Cisneros was abbot in 1353) were to send their subdeans.[37] Perhaps we are justified in concluding, then, that the subdean still existed at Talavera in 1356. Others required to be present at the synod were the priors of the houses of the Order of Santiago in Villahermosa, all archpriests and vicars of the diocese, and two clerics from each archipresbyterate or vicariate.[38] Presumably, then, both the subdean of Talavera and the archpriest (or vicar) of Talavera, if there was one, would be expected to come, the latter to represent the district.

Beltrán speaks of measures taken to reform the religious discipline of Talavera before the time of Archbishop Tenorio, and he refers specifically to a visitation ordered by Archbishop Albornoz; but once again he provides no documentation.[39] Is he simply relying on the usual interpretation of the *Cántica de los clérigos de Talavera* at the end of the *Libro de buen amor*, or is he drawing on some solid data unknown to the biographers of Albornoz?

As for Archbishop Tenorio himself, he attempted to transform the chapter from its secular status to a religious rule. As a result of his own appointments to the chapter (Beltrán says), he was able to tell Pope Clement VII at Avignon that "a certain number of the canons" desired to adopt the religious habit; and on October 25, 1389, the pope gave him authorization to form at Talavera a religious chapter following the Augustinian rule and headed by a prior; the members were to be taken from the present *personae* of the church, provided that they approved of the change and provided that the parochial status of the church was preserved.[40] We find the church still being referred to as secular in 1393;[41] but Beltrán quotes a history published in the year 1600 as saying that Tenorio did succeed in setting up twelve canons, headed by another (called here a dean), in a cloister he built specifically for the purpose, but that after four or five years they gave it up, and the cloister was taken over by the Order of St. Jerome in 1398.[42] Perhaps the archpriest replaced the subdean as a capitular dignitary after the chapter reverted to secular status. But there is reference in Beltrán's *Bulario* to an archpriest of Talavera, one Diego Martínez, in 1369, during the tenure of Gome Manrique as archbishop of Toledo, and the district is called an archipresbyterate in 1379, near the beginning of Tenorio's reign.[43] If indeed there was still a subdean of Talavera at this time, then the office of archpriest may not have been connected to the collegiate church at all.

That is to say, if an archpriest of Talavera can be shown to have existed at the same time as a subdean of Talavera, then the subdean doubtless had no archipresbyteral duties, and the archpriest would have been like the archpriest of Hita, and other rural archpriests of the diocese: he would have had a chancery in Talavera, but belonged to no church. If there was no archpriest at Talavera when there was a subdean, then the subdean perhaps acted as archpriest in the district that came to be called the archipresbyterate of Talavera, whether or not it was so designated at that time.[44]

II. *Decrees Against Concubinage*

Let us now consider the question of what an archpriest is doing at Talavera, in the episode recounted in the appendix to the *Libro de buen amor*. It has usually or perhaps always been assumed that the archpriest who delivers the mandate from Archbishop Gil and the pope is an emissary with no connection with the clergy of Talavera, though the long-held supposition that he is the narrator himself, that is, the

Archpriest of Hita, has recently been contested; for the narrator dissociates himself from this archpriest, and speaks of him in the third person.[45]

It is, of course, entirely possible that a pope or bishop might commission an archpriest to perform a mission outside his archipresbyterate. A case in point is Diego Martínez, who as we saw was archpriest of Talavera in 1369. He was papal subcollector for Toledo, and his district seems to have included not only the city of Toledo itself but also all of the archipresbyterates and vicariates of the diocese.[46] There is a further case in 1395, in which another Alfonso Martínez, Archpriest of Illescas, is one of the negotiators of an accord between the Toledo cathedral chapter and the Franciscan convent of San Clemente in Toledo. But in this instance the archpriest was a member of the committee because he was also one of the canons of the cathedral chapter.[47]

It seems more reasonable, however, that the first possibility we should think of when considering the identity of the archpriest in the *Cántica de los clérigos de Talavera* is that he was the archpriest of Talavera, whose duty it was to attend diocesan synods and to enforce the synodal constitutions and other mandates issued by the archbishop. Whether or not the archpriest of the *Cántica* received his mandate personally at Toledo, he could be said to "deliver" it by announcing it to the meeting of the collegiate chapter, which he is said to have called.

It is not clear whether the archpriest of the *Cántica* is present for the discussion that follows his delivery of the mandate. It is only the *legos* or laymen who are said to adjourn with a view to meeting another day. In strict usage, the word *lego* was meant to be contrasted with *clérigo*, and to designate anyone who had not received the tonsure. No doubt it could also be applied in the strict sense to a tonsured cleric who had lost his clerical immunity (for instance, by plying the trade of a butcher, and not desisting after having been warned by the archpriest, as called for in the synodal constitutions of 1323 and 1325).[48] Perhaps the author of the *Cántica* is referring to the lay servants of the chapter, for as we shall see he understands the mandate of Archbishop Gil to apply to married men with concubines as well as to clerics. Or perhaps he is using the term *legos* loosely to refer to the married clerics of the parish of Santa María. According to Archbishop Juan in 1323, married clerics were obliged to sing the Office on feastdays. The archbishop himself at this point may be inadvertently thinking of them as laymen, for he does not say that they are to sing the Office with the "other clerics," but with the "clerics": "Adiicientes ut in diebus festivis cantent cum clericis, ac in processionibus clericaliter pr[o]cedant induti."⁴⁹

In any case, the author of the *Cántica* says that the archbishop's mandate was for "toda Talavera," and the archpriest would be obliged to announce it to the other clergy of his district. In the late fifteenth century, the archipresbyterate of Talavera contained thirty-two curacies over and above that of the collegiate church of Santa María, as well as other dependencies.⁵⁰

The similarity of the *Cántica* to earlier Latin poems on the same theme has been noticed.⁵¹ Especially interesting is the *Consultatio sacerdotum*, in which the *clerus et presbyteri* of a collegiate chapter gather to discuss the order of their *praesul* to do away with their *ancillulae*. The speakers are the *decanus collegii*; the *capituli doctor et praelatus*, who is said to be well trained in canon law; the *gradu senior*; the *cantor*; the *cellarius*; the *scholasticus*; the *structuarius*; the *ultimus canonicus*; the *primus* of the *presbyteri*, who at one time was *curialis in urbe* and is *tritus et vocalis in iure canonum*; then twenty *presbyteri*, the second of whom is a *vicarius*, the fourteenth a *capellanus*, and the seventeenth *doctus in philosophia*; and finally a *monachus*, who acts as a *praedicator*. The poem ends with a ranking of the members: the lowest are the *clerici*; next are the *monachi* and *canonici*; and third are the *decani* and *praelati*.⁵² It is doubtful that all of these titles or conditions could have been found in any single chapter of whatever kind in the Middle Ages; the appearance of monks in what otherwise looks like a grouping of secular clergy is especially peculiar. Perhaps the author was satirizing a tendency to multiply titles and dignities in the Church.

It is noteworthy that in the *Cántica* there are only three speakers, apart from the archpriest, namely, the dean, the cantor, and the treasurer.⁵³ The four of them together represent the four dignitaries that existed in the collegiate church of Talavera in the fifteenth century; and there is no mention of the subdean, who according to what we have seen (spelling out the implications of Beltrán's assertion) must have been replaced by the archpriest some time after 1354.

If the *Cántica* implies that the archpriest was a member of the collegiate church of Talavera during the time of Archbishop Albornoz, then it must have been written either by a contemporary who was ignorant of the make-up of the chapter, or it was written at a later time when the archpriest was indeed a chapter member, by someone who falsely assumed the same to have been true in the past.

The latter possibility becomes more attractive when we consider that the *Cántica* is found only in the fifteenth-century Salamanca manuscript, and comes only after the author of the *Libro* has announced the completion of his work and dated it. Furthermore, the Salamanca text ends with a note which mistakenly names Albornoz as simultaneously archbishop of Toledo and cardinal, and which gives the otherwise undocumented information that the Archpriest of Hita who composed the book was imprisoned by the cardinal archbishop.

The author of the *Cántica* does not show the same expert knowledge of the laws against concubinage that Juan Ruiz manifests in the *Libro de buen amor*, for he says that clerics as well as married men who have concubines (whether the concubines themselves are married or single) are to be excommunicated:

> Cartas eran venidas, dizen d'esta manera
> Que casado nin clérigo de toda Talavera
> Que non toviés' mançeba, casada nin soltera:
> Qualquier que la toviese descomulgado era. (1694)

But the excommunication of concubinary clerics was abrogated by the decree *Quia clericorum* of William Godin, O.P., Cardinal Bishop of Sabina, in the national council of Valladolid in 1322.[54] He was referring specifically to the penalties of suspension and excommunication set forth by his predecessor Cardinal Halgrin in the council of 1228.[55] Cardinal Halgrin spoke only of excommunication for the concubines of clerics,[56] but in a letter written in 1233 by Pope Gregory IX to the bishop of Astorga, which Raymond of Peñafort included in the *Decretals of Gregory IX*, it is specified that clerics are included in the "major excommunications" levied against their concubines.[57] Cardinal Godin referred to the fact that Pope Alexander IV had subsequently ordered certain Spanish bishops to commute the penalties ordered by Cardinal Halgrin, but the bishops of the province of Toledo may not have been included in this concession. At any rate, the provincial council held at Peñafiel in 1302 remained in accord with the council of 1228, for it ordered suspension and perpetual deprivation for concubinary clerics.[58]

These penalties, then, were revoked by Cardinal Godin in his legatine council of 1322; but at the same time he instituted other severe sanctions in the matter of concubinage. All laymen who forced clerics to

take on concubines were to be excommunicated.[59] All clerics who
had infidel concubines were to be deprived of their benefices and imprisoned.[60] By another statute, *Lex continentiae*, any married man with
a concubine was to be excommunicated, and anyone, whether married or unmarried, who had an infidel concubine was also to be excommunicated. The text deserves to be quoted in full:

> Lex continentiae, et tori coniugalis fidelitas, quandoque per con-
> cubinarium abusum, quandoque per secundas nuptias (quas pleri-
> que de facto, cum de iure non possint, contrahunt contra legis
> divinae praecepta) indebite violatur. Ideoque statuimus ut quicum-
> que coniugatus concubinam publice detinere praesumpserit, vel
> coniugatus aut non coniugatus concubinam infidelem praesump-
> serit detinere, tam ipsi quam ipso [*lege* ipsae] eo ipso sententiam
> excommunicationis incurrant. Praelati vero sententiam huiusmodi
> in ecclesiis faciant saepius publicari.[61]

It is quite clear that this is the legatine constitution that Juan Ruiz
has the Fox's lawyer cite against the Wolf:

> Otrosí le apongo que es descomulgado
> De mayor descomunión por costituçión de legado,
> Porque tiene barragana pública, e es casado
> Con su muger doña Loba, que mora en Vilforado. (337)

A potential objection to this identification is the date that Wolf gives
for the alleged theft and for the trial itself: "Era de mill e tresientos
enl ano primero" (stanza 326). If interpreted as 1301 E.S. (= A.D. 1267),
or even as A.D. 1301, it would antedate the Council of Valladolid.
But it may be that the line is garbled, and a later date intended.[62]
Or it may even be that Juan Ruiz was confused in his dates.

We must consider the possibility that Juan Ruiz knew of Cardinal
Godin's *Lex continentiae* in its renewed form, as set forth by Pedro de
Luna in the legatine council of Palencia, the constitutions of which were
issued on October 4, 1388. The cardinal legate introduced the statute
by drawing on Psalm 31:9. This verse was quoted by Juan Ruiz in
the Introduction to the *Libro de buen amor*: "Nolite fieri sicut equus
et mulus, in quibus non est intellectus" (lines 71–72), and of course
it follows immediately upon Juan Ruiz's principal sermon-text, "In-

tellectum tibi dabo," and so on (Psalm 31:8). The cardinal also extended the statute to exclude offenders from ecclesiastical burial.[63]

Such a late source for the *Libro de buen amor* would take it beyond the Salamanca manuscript date of 1381, even Incarnationally interpreted, but it would still fall short of the *terminus extremus* of the Gayoso manuscript, which was probably completed on Thursday July 22 or Friday July 23 of the year 1389.

Pedro de Luna also renewed Cardinal Godin's *Quia clericorum* against concubinary clerics; he slightly reduced the schedule of punishments,[64] but extended the prohibition of ecclesiastical burial to the clerics as well as to their concubines.[65] He complained that William's constitution remained unobserved up to the present time.[66] This seems to be a fair conclusion, as far as the diocese of Toledo is concerned. There is no reference to the constitution of 1322 or to the problem of clerical concubinage in any of the extant synodal constitutions of the fourteenth century—with one exception. Only Archbishop Albornoz addressed the subject, in a constitution dated April 16, 1342. Since this was two days after the second Sunday of Easter, the date set by Archbishop Ximeno de Luna in 1336 for the annual synod,[67] the constitution was probably introduced and ratified at the synod for that year.

It has been suggested that Albornoz was stimulated to enact his statute by the letter addressed to the archbishops and bishops of Spain by Pope Benedict XII on January 21, 1342, on the need to draw the clergy from the vice of incontinence.[68] The pope says he has heard that some of the clergy in Spain, including even bishops, have not hesitated to indulge in public incontinence. He urges the archbishops to try to effect voluntary reform. But the public *concubinarii* and *alii in talibus delinquentes* are to be punished according to law. The archbishops are to report clearly disobedient bishops to the pope, who will see to suitable remedies.[69]

If Albornoz's constitution is a reply to this letter, it is a very indirect one. He takes action not against the offending clerics but rather against their concubines. He does not refer to the pope's letter but only to Godin's constitution, which he says many have been negligent in enforcing. Furthermore, he alludes only to its final clause, which prohibits ecclesiastical burial to clerical concubines, and he thereby gives the impression that the constitution calls for no other measures against concubinage.

The text of Albornoz's constitution is as follows:

Aegidius miseratione divina archiepiscopus toletanus, Hispaniarum primas, et regni Castellae cancellarius, dilectis in Christo archidiaconis, archipresbyteris, vicariis, clericis, et capellanis civitatis et dioecesis toletanae, salutem in Domino.

Quamvis in constitutione recolendae memoriae domini fratris Guillielmi, quondam episcopi sabinensis, in his partibus apostolicae sedis legati, quae incipit *Qu[i]a clericorum*, caveatur expresse quod concubinae publicae clericorum careant ecclesiastica sepultura, quia tamen in eiusdem constitutionis observatione se multi exhibent negligentes,

Nos, ut periculosa illorum negligentia huiusmodi nostrae constitutionis executione suppleatur, volentes detestabili et horrendo libidinis morbo, prout nobis est possibile, viam praecludere, statuimus ut quicumque publicam clerici concubinam in ecclesia vel coemeterio ecclesiastico sepeliverit, vel sepulturae interfuerit, si clericus unum vel plura beneficia ecclesiastica vel capellaniam perpetuam obtinens fuerit, ut suum poena auctorem teneat, nulla etiam monitione praemissa, illo beneficio seu beneficiis seu capellania praesentis constitutionis auctoritate sit privatus. Si vero fuerit temporalis capellanus aut alius clericus qui nondum ecclesiasticum beneficium obtinuerit, capellania praedicta dimissa, eo ipso usque ad unum annum reddatur inhabilis ad ecclesiasticum beneficium obtinendum. Laici quoque, qui huiusmodi ecclesiasticae sepulturae interfuerint, excommunicationis incurrant sententiam ipso facto.

Insuper, ut lubricis luxuriandi materia amplius adimatur et ipsae concubinae ab invio, poenitudine ductae, resiliant, statuimus ut, si qua aut si quae clericorum vel laicorum publicae concubinae nostram toletanam aut aliquam aliam ecclesiam, dum divina officia in ea celebrantur, intraverint, portari[us] et clericuli [chori] ecclesiae nostrae, et eorum quilibet, ipsam nostram ecclesiam, sacristae vero et clericuli aliarum ecclesiarum, ipsas ecclesias intrantes, vestes quas ea[e]dem concubinae induerint exuant, et huiusmodi vestes ipsis portario et clericulis seu sacristis cedant. Si quis autem ipsas concubinas ecclesias, ut praemittitur, intrantes ne denudentur defendere praesumpserint, eo ipso excommunicationis sententiae se noverit subiacere, a qua, quo[u]sque poenam unius sacrilegii exsolverit, minime absolvatur;

Districte omnibus et singulis archipresbyteris et clericis praeci-

pientes ut hanc constitutionem singulis diebus dominicis in suis
ecclesiis, dum maior populi multitudo convenerit ad divina, publi-
cent seu faciant publicari.[70]

It is quite clear that Albornoz was unwilling to attack the practice
of clerical concubinage head-on. Though archpriests are singled out
for special responsibility in communicating the constitution to the
churches of their area (which was in accord with their office), it is
not the sort of message we see the archpriest delivering to the chapter
of Talavera in the *Cántica de los clérigos de Talavera*. The only clerics
marked out by Albornoz for punishment are those who provide ecclesiastical burial to clerical concubines,[71] and excommunication is
threatened only against laymen who participate in the prohibited obse-
quies, and also against anyone who tries to prevent the bizarre procedure of denuding concubines who enter a church during services
(at this point, Albornoz is speaking about the concubines of the laity
as well as those of the clergy). It seems, therefore, that the archbishop
has despaired of trying to reform the clergy who have taken women,
and is attempting to combat the practice only by frightening and sham-
ing the women into desisting.

Let us suppose that Alfonsus Peratinensis or Paratinensis, who
mistakenly reported Albornoz to have been a cardinal before his time,
was also the author of the *Cántica*, which seems erroneously to place
an archpriest in the chapter of Talavera before one existed, and which
inaccurately depicts the sanctions in force against concubinage in the
fourteenth century. If Peratinensis did not invent the date of 1381,
which appears in stanza 1634 of his text, but found it in the received
text and interpreted it as A.D. 1343, he would have had sufficient reason
to situate the Archpriest of Hita in the time of Archbishop Albornoz.
He could have invented the story of his imprisonment from the
reference to "esta mala presión" in the first stanza of the *Libro*; or,
more likely perhaps, he may have composed the beginning stanzas
himself and placed them before the authentic prose Introduction, along
with the explanatory rubric: "Ésta es oración quel açipreste fizo a Dios
quando começó este libro suyo." Peratinensis has usually been taken
to be the author of the numerous rubrics peculiar to the Salamanca
text, which vastly increase the role of the archpriest in the poem.

When, according to our *ad hoc* hypothesis, Peratinensis decided to
modernize the *Consultatio sacerdotum* or some such work and attribute

it to the composition of the Archpriest of Hita, he may have had some vague knowledge of the constitution of the synod of 1342, in which Archbishop Albornoz reemphasized earlier strictures against public concubines. But he may also have known of the documents sent out to various dioceses in the previous century by Cardinal Gil Torres, in some of which archpriests were denounced for conniving at concubinage within their jurisdictions. He may even have mistaken Cardinal Torres for Cardinal Albornoz, since the texts of the constitutions do not identify him by surname: "Egidius divina patientia sanctorum Cosme et Damiani Diaconus Cardinalis."[72] He may not have realized that Albornoz was not cardinal deacon of Sts. Cosmas and Damian, but rather cardinal priest of St. Clement and later cardinal bishop of Sabina. For even modern historians have mistaken Albornoz's title.[73] The fact that these constitutions were forwarded with covering letters from the pope might have inspired Peratinensis to characterize the order delivered by the archpriest of Talavera not only as "las cartas del arçobispo don Gil" and "el mandado," but also as a constitution sent by the pope: "El papa nos enbía esta constituçión."

Peratinensis may have singled out Talavera for attention not only because it had a collegiate chapter with dignitaries who could be designated as speakers in his satire, but also because he knew something of Archbishop Tenorio's unsuccessful attempt to impose religious discipline on the church.

If it was a late author like Peratinensis who wrote the *Cántica* and formulated the colophon of the Salamanca manuscript, he may also, as I hinted above, have invented the date of 1381 in order to tie the work (for reasons of his own) to the reign of Archbishop Albornoz. For if the date in his received text was 1368, as in the Toledo manuscript, he would have found it too late if interpreted according to the Christian era, and too early if read according to the Spanish Era (that is, A.D. 1330).

We cannot be certain of what lies behind the composition of the *Cántica de los clérigos de Talavera*. We can only say that there is good reason for thinking it was composed near the time that Alfonso Martínez de Toledo became archpriest of Talavera. We can also say that there is good reason for doubting all of the hitherto accepted connections of the original *Libro de buen amor* with the time and person of Archbishop Gil de Albornoz.

Chapter Four

Procedure in the Court of Don Ximio

1. *Charge, Countercharge, and Conclusion*

Let us turn our gaze back from the suspect outskirts of the *Libro de buen amor* to an episode that is solidly present in all of the manuscripts, namely, the trial of the Fox upon a capital accusation brought by the Wolf.

The relevance of the episode to its context is not made clear by the rubrics of Alfonsus Peratenensis in the Salamanca manuscript. The passage comes at the end of a series in which the author accuses Love of associating with various vices, and some of these vices are illustrated by beast fables. The rubric before stanza 317, *Aquí dize del pecado de la açidia*, gives the impression that the last vice treated is *acedia*, and that the trial episode that follows must somehow be illustrative of it. But in fact the last vice to be treated is hypocrisy:

> Otrosí con açidia traes ipocresía,
> Andas con grand sinpleza pensando pletisía,
> Pensando estás triste, tu ojo non se erzía,
> Do vees la fermosa, oteas con raposía. (Stanza 319)

Ostensibly, the story of the trial is to show how Love, like Wolf, accuses others of doing what he himself does:

> De quanto bien pedricas, non fazes d'ello cosa,
> Engañas todo el mundo con palabra fermosa;
> Quieres lo que el lobo quiere de la raposa. (320)

This purpose is confirmed after the tale:

> Tal eres como el lobo, retraes lo que fazes,
> Estrañas a los otros el lodo en que yazes,
> Eres mal enemigo a todos quantos plazes,
> Fablas con grand sinpleza porque muchos enlazes.
>
> (372)

However, Juan Ruiz clearly becomes carried away with the sheer joy of putting the dry regulations of judicial procedure into verse. But he has stated another purpose in telling the story, which to some extent justifies the lengths to which he goes; he tells it for the instruction of lawyers:

> Abogado de fuero, oy' fabla provechosa!   (320d)

It is often supposed that Juan Ruiz is mocking the judicial procedures he elaborates. In my opinion, this is barking up the wrong tree. Though he clearly treats everything with high good humor, his main intent seems to be to set ignorant lawyers straight on court formalities then in force.

In creating a judge as authoritative as Don Ximio, Juan Ruiz invites the conjecture that he himself had judicial experience, whether as an archpriest or in some other capacity. If he were a functioning archpriest, he would have served as judge of an ecclesiastical court, and if he were good at his job he would have been well acquainted with the peculiarities of secular court procedure as well.

There was a certain overlapping between the ecclesiastical and secular courts. The sorts of cases tried in both tribunals were often the same, and there were sometimes jurisdictional disputes over which court had the right of cognizance in particular instances. We have seen that a complaint was made at the Cortes of 1345 that ecclesiastical judges, including archpriests, were claiming authority over cases the secular judges believed to be reserved to themselves.[1]

In Spain, ecclesiastical and secular law as well as court procedures were both based directly on Roman civil law. Such was not the case in England, where the secular courts were ruled primarily by the native tradition of common law. It was an accepted principle on the Continent that cases could be supported in the civil forum by citing canon law; and, conversely, Roman law was recognized as binding in the ecclesiastical courts, in all matters where there was no conflict between the two traditions.[2]

Furthermore, certain procedures, like those dealing with excommunication, were imposed by canon law upon the secular courts. This was true for England as well as for Spain. There were, of course, differences between the secular and ecclesiastical courts; for instance, mutilation and death could be imposed by the former and not by the latter. But these differences and peculiarities were often expounded upon by the sort of canonistic authorities that Juan Ruiz cites in his discussion of confession.

Most commentators upon the Don Ximio episode have made the mistake of thinking that Spanish secular law in the Middle Ages was a law to itself.[3] This is precisely the error reproved by Don Ximio in his rhetorical address to the *abogado de romance* (stanza 353); a lawyer must take note of current procedure, for which a knowledge of Latin is required.

In the following pages, I would like to set out some of the canonistic material that has a bearing on the trial presided over by Don Ximio, with a view to encouraging further research.

The form of trial involved in Wolf's charge against Mrs. Fox is a cumbersome procedure known as *accusatio*, which was inherited both by canon law and Spanish secular law. By the fourteenth century, the *accusatio* had been largely replaced in the ecclesiastical courts by a new kind of trial called the *inquisitio*, in which, when initiated *ex officio*, it was not necessary for a specific individual to bring a formal charge against a defendant.[4] Cardinal Albornoz in fact introduced inquisitorial procedures into secular law courts, in the constitutions that he arranged to be drawn up for the March of Ancona, which he promulgated in 1357.[5] The *accusatio*, however, continued to be given full treatment by the canonists, especially in commentaries on the first title of the fifth book of the *Decretals of Gregory IX*: *De accusationibus, inquisitionibus, et denuntiationibus*, and in works on court procedure like William Durantis's *Speculum iudiciale*.

To initiate an accusation, the accuser must submit to the judge a *libellus accusationis*. Durantis describes the required contents:

Est ergo notandum quod libellus accusationis haec continere debet, scilicet:
Nomen iudicis cui porrigitur, et accusatoris, et accusati;

Item, crimen, et eius qualitatem seu magnitudinem;

Item, cum qua persona, et in quo loco commissum est, et etiam locum loci: puta in tali angulo domus, vel pomarii, vel vineae . . . [he gives an example from the case of Susanna and the Elders in the Book of Daniel];

Item, annum et mensem commissi criminis; diem vero et horam ponere non tenetur;

Item, annum et mensem et diem dati libelli;

Item, nomen imperatoris, et papae in patrimonio beati Petri—vel etiam ubique, si velit; vel regis in regno. Non consulis, quia hodie non sunt.[6]

The *libellus* is to conclude with the accuser formally binding himself to the *poena talionis*, by an *inscriptio*. The model form that Durantis gives for the *inscriptio* includes the date of the *libellus* as well as the promise to prove the accusation or else suffer the penalty for bringing a false charge or for failing to prove it:

Ego Lucius profiteor me hunc libellum dedisse anno Domini 1270 mensis Maii intrantis die 9, et praefatam accusationem me legitime prosecuturum et probaturum promitto; profiteor etiam, et ad hoc me specialiter obligo, poenam calumniae seu talionis me subiturum, si hanc accusationem calumniose instituero, vel si in probatione defecero praedictorum.[7]

Durantis then refers to entries in Gratian's *Decretum* and Roman civil law where these procedures are established. [8] The term *talio* appears only in Gratian.

The prescribed form of accusation in the *Siete partidas* is simpler:

En la carta de la acusacion deve ser puesto el nome del acusador, e el de aquel a quien acusa, e el del juez ante quien la faze, e el yerro que fizo el acusado, e el lugar do fue fecho el yerro de que lo acusa, e el mes e el año e la era en que lo fizo.

The judge himself is to note the date of the accusation and to make the accuser affirm on oath that he believes the charge to be true:

E el judgador deve recebir la acusacion, e escrevir el dia en que gela dieron, rescibiendo luego·del acusador la jura que non se mueve maliciosamente a acusar, mas que cree que aquel a quien acusa que es en culpa, a que fizo aquel yerro de quel faze la acusacion.[9]

In the *Libro de buen amor*, Wolf follows the fuller form to the extent of naming the reigning monarch, but neither he nor Don Ximio takes special note of the date on which the charge is submitted. We do know, however, that it is in the same year as the alleged crime, which Wolf says occurred during the past February: "en el mes que pasó de febrero" (stanza 326).[10] It must be fairly late in the year, since Don Ximio later sets the term for sentencing to after the Epiphany (January 6); and an interval of longer than a month or two would be unreasonable, even given the occurrence of the Christmas holidays (of which the Epiphany was one), when the courts could not convene.

The Wolf binds himself to the *talio*, in accord with the norms described by Durantis, and also specifies what the penalty at issue is, namely, death, in keeping with the rule that the gravity of the crime must be indicated:

Pido que la condenedes, por sentençia e por ál non,
Que sea enforcada e muerta como ladrón;
Esto me ofresco provar so pena de talión.   (Stanza 328)

It is noteworthy that the *Partidas* does not specify such a commitment on the part of the accuser, and Gregorio López seems to hold that the requirement had fallen into disuse at the time when the code was compiled. He cites Durantis as testifying that the *inscriptio ad talionem* was no longer practiced in many regions, and he takes John Andreae's discussion of the point in the *Additions to the Speculum* as praising this development.[11]

There are, however, two laws in the *Partidas* declaring that an accuser who fails to prove his charge is to have the same penalty that the accused would have had if proof were forthcoming.[12] It may be, therefore, that even if there was to be no explicit inscription, it was taken as understood: the accuser would know what his punishment would be.

There is another law in the *Partidas* noting that the *inscriptio ad talionem* is not to be used in certain cases where a husband accuses his wife of adultery and requests a decree of separation:

Obligar non se deve a pena de talión el que acusare su muger por razon de adulterio, quanto a departimiento del lecho.

The reason, of course, is that there should be no separation if adultery cannot be proved. But when the accusing spouse demands a punishment prescribed by law, the *inscriptio* is required:

Mas si la accusa a pena, segund manda el fuero de los legos, estonce se deve obligar a pena de talión.[13]

Since, therefore, the *inscriptio* is to be used in these cases, perhaps it is still to be used in other criminal accusations as well.

The purpose of the above-cited rule was to bring Spanish law into conformity with a decretal of Innocent III, which Raymond of Peñafort included in the *Decretals of Gregory IX*. Innocent says that when a man accuses his wife of adultery before a secular judge with a view to inflicting the penalty set by law, which would make it a case where the *inscriptio ad talionem* is required, the husband must make the *inscriptio* in person and not through a proctor. But when he makes an accusation of adultery before an ecclesiastical judge and requests a separation, the *talio* is not applicable.[14]

The law in the *Partidas* is taken from the *Summa de matrimonio* of Raymond of Peñafort, which he added to his *Summa de casibus* after completing the *Decretals*.[15] The same law in the *Partidas* notes that husbands who are delinquent are to be punished in the same way as wives, in keeping with the law of the Church, but that women do not have the same rights before a secular judge (which is in keeping with Roman civil law).[16] Earlier, the *Partidas* noted that a wife as well as a husband could bring a charge of adultery and petition for separation to the ecclesiastical court of the bishop or his official, and that the husband could do the same before a secular judge.[17] (But some other man could charge a husband with adultery, thus acting in effect for the wife.)

We see in these texts not only an awareness of the differences between the secular and ecclesiastical courts, but also a confirmation of the ecclesiastical policy of reserving marriage cases to the bishop (and prohibiting them from being heard by archdeacons and archpriests).[18]

We are to take it that Mrs. Fox has been served a formal summons to hear the charge laid against her. Don Ximio refuses her request that he appoint a lawyer for her. She is to find her own lawyer and answer the charge in just twenty days:

> Pero yo te dó de plazo que fasta días veinte
> Ayas tu abogado; luego al plazo vente. (Stanza 330)

According to the *Justinian Novels*, or *Authenticae*, a deliberative delay of twenty days is to be given to a defendant.[19] The stipulation is repeated by Gratian,[20] but the *Ordinary Gloss* notes that it applies to civil rather than to criminal cases.[21] However, Azzo of Bologna in his *Summa* on the *Justinian Code* suggests that the same interval be given in criminal accusations as well.[22] The *Siete partidas* makes it definite; the judge is to give the accused twenty days to reply:

> E despues desto, deve emplazar al acusado, e darle traslado de la demanda, señalandole plazo de veynte dias, a que venga responder a ella.[23]

Gregorio López assumes that the *Partidas* is drawing on Azzo,[24] but it is possible that the procedure had already become common.

On the appointed day, Mrs. Fox's lawyer, Sheepdog, immediately enters two exceptions against Wolf, one of crime (specifically, that Wolf is a notorious and proven thief himself) and the other of excommunication (namely, that Wolf has been automatically excommunicated for having both a wife and a concubine).[25] These points are among the exceptions that can be made against an accuser, as listed by Durantis.[26]

In this case, the decisive exception will be found to be that of crime. The ineligibility of a criminal to be an accuser is clearly explained by the *Ordinary Gloss* to the first chapter of the title *De accusationibus* of the *Decretals of Gregory IX*.[27]

Don Ximio will later classify the first of Sheepdog's exceptions as peremptory and the second as dilatory. Exceptions are treated more fully by canonists than by civilians, but not always very clearly. The basic difference between the two principal classes of exceptions is set forth by Azzo of Bologna. Some exceptions are perpetual and peremptory, others are temporary and dilatory. Peremptory exceptions repel plaintiffs permanently, and destroy the point at issue. The defendant can raise peremptory exceptions any time before sentencing.[28] That is, he can raise them before the case is contested, which is the normal time for submitting dilatory exceptions, and afterwards as well (at which time he is usually bound to submit all such motions before a date set by the judge).

When exceptions are made, the judge first rules on their admissibility, and then normally sets a term for the defendant to prove his charges, first of all by having the plaintiff or accuser interrogated under oath.[29] In our case, two terms would be in order, the mandated short term of nine days for the exception of excommunication (which need not be explicitly set by the judge) and a longer term for the exception of crime. But it seems that this process is short-circuited by Sheepdog and Wolf, who, realizing or at least believing that the charges can be readily proved, fearfully and reluctantly confess all (stanza 339). That is, they apparently admit the truth of both exceptions.

A confession is sufficient proof in itself for the exception of crime, as Don Ximio will point out, but not, perhaps, for the exception of excommunication.

Mrs. Fox then enters a *reconventio* or countercharge against Wolf, and, it seems, against Greyhound, Wolf's lawyer, and demands that they be given the death penalty without further trial:

> Señor, sean tenidos
> En reconvençión; pido que mueran, e non oídos.
>   (Stanza 339)

The countercharge of course could not be directed at matters already decided in court (*res iudicatae*) but only at hitherto unprosecuted crimes.

The further activity of both sides is then summed up in a single line, followed by a call to the judge to set a day for sentencing, which he does:

> Ençerraron razones de toda su porfía;
> Pidieron al alcalde que asinase día
> En que diese sentençia qual él por bien tenía.
> Él asinóles plazo después de Pifanía. (Stanza 340)

It does not seem that the reference to the "whole case" should be taken to mean that the trial proceeds to the principal matter (Wolf's accusation) and concludes with a definitive sentence. What is called for at this point is an interlocutory sentence on the exceptions and a ruling on the admissibility of Mrs. Fox's countercharge (more on this later). It was a general principle that subsidiary questions which, if established, would prevent the case from continuing had to be adjudicated before the principal matter.[30]

If the judge were to find that neither of the exceptions were proved, the case would have to be "contested," that is, Mrs. Fox would have to enter a plea to Wolf's charge. If her plea were "Not guilty," Wolf would have to "found" his charge with proofs, which Mrs. Fox would attempt to assail. If, however, one of the exceptions were found to be proved, the case would be halted; and if the proved exception were classified as peremptory, perpetual silence would be imposed on the accuser.[31]

We find the latter turn of events in our case. Don Ximio's sentence deals mainly with the exceptions submitted by Sheepdog. He finds the exception of crime to be proved by Wolf's admission, and he imposes silence on Wolf: "Por ende pongo silençio al Lobo esta saçón" (stanza 362). The last two words are not to be taken to mean that Wolf can ever qualify to raise the issue again. The accusation simply cannot be received:

> Pronunçio que la demanda que él fizo e propuso
> Non le sea resçebida.   (Stanza 363)

Furthermore, it *has* not been received, for the case did not arrive at the point of contestation: "Nin fue el pleito contestado" (stanza 367). When sentence is given on exceptions that have been heard after the contestation of the case, this fact must be mentioned.[32] Finally, a definitive sentence is usually named as such explicitly.[33]

In his sentence, Don Ximio runs through the case as consisting of Wolf's original charge (stanza 348), Mrs. Fox's exceptions and Wolf's reply and replications:

> E vistas las excusas e las defensiones
> Que puso la Gulharra en sus exepçiones,
> E vista la respuesta e las replicaçiones
> Que propuso el Lobo en todas sus razones.
>   (Stanza 349)

The next phase of the trial was Mrs. Fox's *reconventio*, and finally there was the demand for sentence on both sides:

> E visto lo que pide en su reconvençión
> La comadre contra el Lobo çerca la conclusión;
> Visto todo el proçeso, quantas razones son,
> E las partes que piden sentençia, e ál non. (Stanza 350)

It seems, then, that the puzzling line in stanza 340, "Ençerraron razones
de toda su porfía," refers only to a discussion of the exceptions and
the basis for Mrs. Fox's countercharge; and in fact Don Ximio recalls
one of Wolf's reasons for invalidating his confession of guilt, namely,
that it was made out of fear:

> Non le preste lo que dixo, que con miedo e quexura
> Fizo la confesión, cogido en angostura.   (Stanza 365)

The term "reasons" must no doubt be taken to mean *allegationes iuris*,
the arguments of law entered by the advocates after the facts have
been set forth.[34] The term "replications" technically refers to counterexceptions made by a plaintiff, which, if they are ruled admissible,
are to be proved after the defendant has submitted proofs for his
exceptions.[35] Since no such activity is in evidence in the previous nar-
ration, we must conclude either that Don Ximio is using the alternative nontechnical sense of replication noted by Durantis, to indicate
a simple response,[36] or that, if Wolf did enter counterexceptions, they
were not admitted by Don Ximio.

   This outline of the case does not leave me altogether satisfied,
however, because of the final objection made by the lawyers against
Don Ximio's procedures:

> Dixiéronle otrosí una derecha razón:
> Que, fecha la conclusión en criminal acusaçión,
> Non podía dar liçençia para aver conpusiçión:
> Menester la sentençia çerca la conclusión.[37] (Stanza 370)

One might think that a case could hardly be taken as concluded if
it had never been contested; and it would seem more reasonable to
forbid an accord after a term had been set for a definitive sentence
than during the interval before an interlocutory sentence.

   I can find no statement of any restriction on transacting an accord between the conclusion of a case and the delivery of the sentence. The *Siete partidas* says simply that in cases involving the death penalty or amputation of a member, such transactions can occur before the sentence:

> Tenemos por bien que, si la avenencia fuere fecha ante que la sentencia sea dada sobre tal yerro como este, que vala.[38]

Hostiensis says that the *transactio* can occur after the case is contested or before ("lite pendente vel futura"), but not after sentence is given ("contra sententiam latam").[39] He notes that according to canon law no true *transactio* can take place in criminal cases, because crimes are not punished by blood (that is, in ecclesiastical courts); but he says that some authorities allow a free agreement ("gratuita pactio").[40] Furthermore, if a *transactio* occurs in cases of injury or theft, the judge can accept it.[41] Here at least we have some notice of a judge's discretionary powers, of the sort claimed by Don Ximio when he says that his royal commission authorizes him to accept a *transactio* between conclusion and sentence (stanza 371). But perhaps the point at issue in the *Libro de buen amor* does not hinge upon a *transactio* in particular, but upon any action or motion brought forth after the concluding term has been reached, even if the term is only for an interlocutory sentence.

Durantis points out, as we shall see later, that the exception of excommunication is unusual in being admissible even after conclusion.[42] It is a general rule that after the parties in a case "renounce and conclude," no exception, allegation of fact, witness, or instrument is to be admitted, unless some clear reason convinces the judge otherwise, or unless the judge *ex officio* seeks further information.[43]

There is some dispute over whether a renunciation of the right to make further allegations constitutes in itself a conclusion of all motions.[44] John Andreae in his *Additions to the Speculum* says that there is less doubt involved when the renunciation is made on some "emergent" question (an example would be Mrs. Fox's exceptions), and in any event the words used and the particular customs of the individual court are to be taken into consideration.[45]

In our case, however, there has been no formal renunciation but instead a petition for the judge to set a day for sentencing. Durantis holds that in these circumstances the agreed-upon date for the delivery

of the sentence is itself to be considered the term for the conclusion.[46]
This is clearly not the local custom in Don Ximio's court, for he agrees
with the advocates that the conclusion has already occurred by the
time the day of sentencing has arrived.

The solution to the doubt I raised above on the conclusion of the
case of Wolf versus Fox would seem to lie in the fact that an interlocutory sentence upholding a peremptory exception, even though
it might not technically be considered definitive,[47] nevertheless has
definitive force, for it has the effect of closing the matter for good.[48]
Furthermore, any interlocutory sentence is like a definitive sentence
in that it converts to a *res iudicata* within ten days if not appealed.[49]
Durantis states that all of what he says about the ways in which advocates should ask for sentences and in which judges should seek the
counsel of learned men holds for interlocutory as well as for definitive
sentences.[50]

II. *The Instructions of Archbishop Tenorio*

It may be enlightening to consider here the rules for procedure set
forth by Archbishop Tenorio in the synod of 1379.[51] Tenorio is speaking of civil actions rather than criminal cases, but the fundamental
stages of all trials were similar. We must also remember that Tenorio
is at pains to cut down on unnecessary delays, and therefore is thinking primarily of unjustifiable objections, and does not enter into the
procedures called for when exceptions are proved.

In cases involving claims of more than 100 maravedís, the plaintiff
must submit a *libellus*, which corresponds to Wolf's *demanda* or *libellus accusationis*. But whereas Mrs.Fox is given twenty days to respond
(which is also the usual term in monetary cases), Tenorio sets a limit
of nine days for the plaintiff to contest the case. In actions involving
lesser sums, where an oral petition is made, only five days are allot-
ted.[52] However, if the plaintiff enters an exception refusing the judge,
or submits other exceptions against the plaintiff, such as *spoliatio*[53] or
excommunication, or cites a previous court ruling (*res iudicata, transacta, vel finita*), he is permitted to prove his objections; if he fails to
prove them, he is to be held a confessed calumniator, unless he can

show cause why he is to be excused from the taint of calumny; in which case, after the judge's pronouncement, the plaintiff will be ordered to contest the case in another nine days. But if any such exception (apart from *res iudicatae*, it seems) is entered after the case is contested, it is to be heard before all else, in accord with the canonical traditions.[54]

After the case is contested, the defendant is given ten days in minor cases or twenty days in major ones to submit all peremptory exceptions, and no exception is to be entered after this term expires, unless the defendant can affirm on oath that it deals with something newly come to light.[55] When the defendant enters a simple denial of the suit (that is, pleads "Not guilty" and submits no peremptory exceptions immediately), all further allegations are to be set aside and the plaintiff assigned a reasonable time to prove his case. If, however, during this time the defendant submits a peremptory exception, the judge is to set him a term to prove it; but if the plaintiff should see fit to replicate against it before such a term is set, the same moderate term is to be set for both parties, the one to prove the exception and the other the replication.[56] But if the defendant submits a peremptory exception at the contesting of the case, the same term is to be assigned to both parties: the plaintiff to prove his suit, and the defendant to prove his exception. If the plaintiff thinks a replication is required, even after such a term for proof is set, he can have ten days to act, but no more, unless he can swear that some new cause for replication has emerged; if the judge agrees to admit it, he will set a further moderate term and then rule on its truth.[57]

The experienced judge is to use his discretion in diligently avoiding all further replications, whether they are called triplications or some additional name. (This is a matter that even Durantis became confused over.[58] Tenorio remarks that these motions should rather be considered "implications," the sort of thing that the cunning of lawyers often finds to prorogue cases and confound the truth.) The judge is to admit them, if an urgent case requires it (which rarely happens), or to repel them, in the interests of justice (which is more expedient).[59]

The judge is to bear in mind that if he conducts himself badly, whether through malice or negligence, through ignorance or favor or baseness, in the foresaid matters, that is, by unwarrantably admitting frustratory and superfluous complications and cavillings, he will not escape the condign retribution of the archbishop's displeasure, in addition to being held accountable for the expenses and losses of the complaining party.[60]

If one or both of the parties should submit articled points on the principal matter or on the exceptions or replications, the other party is to respond to them under oath, without his lawyer's intervention, and they must do so whenever such articles are submitted. But if one of the parties should contumaciously refuse to reply, the judge is to consider him to have confessed concerning the exception or article, and to proceed accordingly, having received the proofs of the case and published them in due time, and enacted whatever other matters he considers the quality of the case to require.[61]

The judge is then to assign a term for renunciation and conclusion; and if one of the parties contumaciously avoids complying with it, with no legitimate impediment standing in the way, the judge is to declare the case closed in spite of his contumacy. He is then to hand down a definitive sentence after twenty days in cases involving claims of over 200 maravedís, or, where lesser sums are at stake, within fifteen days.[62]

If any judge fails to obey this salubrious mandate, he will not only be liable for the losses that a party will have suffered because of it, but will also be automatically fined 100 maravedís.[63]

This, then, is the streamlined procedure that Archbishop Tenorio expected all of his judges, including archpriests and their deputies, to follow in ordinary civil suits. But the traditional longer procedures were to be observed in more important cases, such as those dealing with benefices and marriages (and, we might add, serious criminal complaints), where there is greater danger and where greater caution and expertness are required.[64]

III. *Summary Justice*

We can see that in comparison with the normal course of a trial Don Ximio handles the case of Wolf versus Fox with great dispatch, and only allows himself a certain expansiveness when it comes to delivering his sentence. He has been scrupulous in observing the cautions not to reveal his opinions on the case beforehand,[65] and he is unaffected by the attempted bribes of the parties.

Since both parties, when offered a last-minute opportunity to trans-act an accord, declare themselves to be intransigent, Don Ximio pro-ceeds to the sentencing, after first having seated himself. The canonists as well as the civilians accepted a rule deduced from Roman civil law that a sentence is void unless it is delivered while the judge is seated.[66]

Don Ximio begins his sentence "en el nombre de Dios" (stanza 348), in accord with some of the models given by Durantis.[67] There is no set form for sentences, but the judge should state the plaintiff's peti-tion and the defendant's response and exceptions, and in general sum-marize whatever has been petitioned or alleged on both sides.[68]

Using fairly standard terms,[69] Don Ximio states that he has con-sulted with learned men and is impartial:

> Avido me consejo, que me fizo provecho,
> Con omnes sabidores en fuero e en derecho,
> Dios ante los mis ojos e non ruego nin pecho.
>
> (Stanza 351)

After reviewing the case, he pronounces Wolf's *libellus* well formed, and then enters into a discourse on Mrs. Fox's exceptions.

He makes the point later that the peremptory exception of crime is sufficiently proved by Wolf's confession. But the exception of ex-communication, which in these circumstances must be classified as dilatory, cannot be established by a confession, it seems (unless we are to take it that Wolf confessed only to the exception of crime), but needs documentation, testimonial or otherwise, which must be presented within nine days; furthermore, the constitution that was cited must be specified by name (stanzas 354–55).

In making these observations, Don Ximio is following one of Inno-cent IV's *novellae constitutiones*, namely, *Pia consideratione*, which Boni-face VIII incorporated into the *Liber sextus* at the end of the thirteenth century. Pope Innocent complains that the exception of excommuni-cation is frequently entered out of malice in ecclesiastical cases, with the result that the cases are deferred and the parties are worn out with unnecessary work and expense. He therefore decrees that whoever enters such an exception must state the species of excommunication (which Sheepdog did: it was the major excommunication) and also the name of the excommunicator, and must be able to prove it in open court within eight days, not counting the day on which the exception is alleged, by means of unambiguous documents.[70] Don Ximio follows the inclusive method of counting used by Archbishop Tenorio: the term is nine days, counting the day on which the motion is made.[71]

We note that Pope Innocent was limiting his attention to ecclesiastical courts, but his immediate successor Alexander IV ordered secular judges as well to repel excommunicates (under pain of being themselves excommunicated), in a decretal that was also put into the *Sext*.[72]

In the fourteenth century, Clement V decreed that the dilatory exception of excommunication could be entered at any time during a trial, even after the peremptory term set by the judge for receiving exceptions. But he noted that the decretal *Pia consideratione* was to be observed.[73] Presumably the pope was referring not only to the necessary documentation but also to the time-restriction for submitting proof.

According to Don Ximio, the time limit of nine days is also observed in the secular courts for dilatory exceptions of excommunication, but a longer period is to be given when the exception is peremptory:

> Quando la descomunión por dilatoria se pone,
> Nueve días a de plazo para el que se apone;
> Por perentoria, más.[74] Esto guarda, non te encone,
> Que a muchos abogados se olvida e se pospone. (Stanza 356)

When a specific term is mandated by law, it begins to run whether the judge assigns it or not. But if our case had proceeded to this point, and if there had been only the exception of excommunication at issue, it does not seem that Mrs. Fox and Sheepdog would have been entirely on their own in knowing about the term, at least if *Pia consideratione* was in full force, since Don Ximio would have been required to specify the expenses that Mrs. Fox would have to pay to Wolf if the exception were not proved within the time-limit.[75]

For most other exceptions, it was up to the plaintiff himself to ask for expenses in case of failure to prove. Durantis warns each side to remember to petition for expenses when asking for a sentence.[76] In a criminal action, the judge can "supply" a request for expenses that a party incurred after the contestation of the case but failed to ask for, but not for unpetitioned expenses incurred before the contestation.[77] We see from this the meaning of stanza 367:

Non apellaron las partes, del juizio son pagados,
Porque non pagaron costas nin fueron condenados:
Esto fue porque non fueron de las partes demandados,
Nin fue el pleito contestado, porque fueron escusados.

Wolf and Mrs. Fox are thereby exempted from paying the other's costs. But, of course, they must still pay their own costs, specifically the fees of their lawyers. Durantis notes that it is permissible for advocates to receive pay, and also to stipulate that a greater fee be paid in case of victory; and the fees have to be agreed upon before the contestation of the case.[78]

What about fees owing to Don Ximio himself? According to Durantis, no fee is to be exacted if a judge holds judgment in his own town (which Don Ximio does not); and expenses are not to be paid if he receives a public salary. In general, he says, local custom is to be followed, but he objects against the practice of some ecclesiastical judges of exacting fees before the contestation of the case. Fees should however be exacted before the final sentence is handed down, because both parties to the case are more willing to pay at that point.[79] He is obviously not talking of the sort of delicacies that Wolf and Mrs. Fox offer to Don Ximio while he deliberates over his interlocutory sentence.

We saw above that there was no need to set or observe terms for proving the exceptions because of Wolf's confession. Since the confession of crime would be decisive, it would not be necessary to prove the excommunication, if Wolf's confession on this point did not constitute valid proof. It may be, then, that Don Ximio's discourse on the exception of excommunication is purely academic, as far as the means of proof are concerned. The exception would be "a little erroneous" only because her lawyer failed to specify the papal legate and his constitution, and not because he failed to submit proper proof in time. The stanzas would therefore be punctuated as follows:

La exepçión primera muy bien fue alegada,
Mas la descomunión fue un poco errada:
Que la costituçión deviera ser nonbrada.
E fasta nueve días deviera ser probada:

Por cartas e testigos o por buen instrumente

De público notario devié sin fallimente
Esta tal dilatoria provarse claramente.
Si se pon perentoria, esto es otramente. (Stanzas 354–55)

If the last-cited line refers to ordinary peremptory exceptions, like the exception of crime, it is perhaps being contrasted with the dilatory exception of excommunication not only in the length of time given for proof, but also in the methods of proof allowed (for instance, confession may not be sufficient).[80] But if the line looks ahead to the following stanzas and refers to excommunication objected with peremptory force, the indicated contrast must be of time limits only, for excommunication would have to be proved in the above-stated way, no matter what effect the proof would have on the course of a trial.

Presumably the reason why excommunication is thought to be fundamentally dilatory and not peremptory in nature is that excommunication need be only temporary: one can be absolved from it. The exception is admitted to be anomalous in that it can be entered at any time. It can be dilatory by turning aside the trial (*declinatoria iudicii*), as well as by delaying the outcome (*dilatoria solutionis*). But it can also have peremptory effect. Durantis gives only one specific example of the exception of excommunication being truly peremptory, namely, when it is entered against a canonical election.[81] Don Ximio gives two other instances: when it is objected against a judge or against a witness.

Don Ximio is saying in effect that even if Mrs. Fox's charge of excommunication had been leveled against Wolf after the case was contested, it would still be dilatory in nature, if proved. The decretal *Pia consideratione* specifies that a plaintiff in such circumstances is simply to be excluded from the proceedings until such time as he is absolved from the excommunication, but the proceedings up to the time of exclusion remain valid.[82] Furthermore, the decretal says that when such an exception is proved against the plaintiff after sentence has been given, it does not invalidate the sentence but only impedes its execution.

Let us look at Don Ximio's examples of when excommunication would have peremptory force, as given in the first three lines of stanza 357. In the Gayoso manuscript the text reads:

Es toda perentoria la descomonion atal
Si pone contra testigos en [e]l pleyto principal
E contra jues publico, ca su proçeso non val.

The Salamanca version goes thus:

> Es toda perentoria la escomunion atal
> Quando se pon contra testigos en pleito criminal;
> Contra juez publicado, que su proçesso non val.

The Gayoso reading of *principal* is doubtless to be preferred to *criminal*, since the same procedure applies in civil as well as in criminal cases and, furthermore, the exception takes on its peremptory character when it is proposed during the trial of the principal question, after the contestation of the case, when witnesses for the plaintiff are regularly admitted. (It is true, of course, as Don Ximio indicates, that the defendant can use witnesses to prove exceptions before the contestation takes place, and the same is true of plaintiffs who submit replications, and peremptory objections can be made against these witnesses.) In the third line, the Gayoso reading of "e contra" is to be preferred to "contra," for the exception against the judge is a second example, not an elaboration of the exception against witnesses. As for the variants *publico* and *publicado*, neither is quite satisfactory; perhaps we should read *publicada*. At any rate, the meaning is quite clear: it refers to a publicly excommunicated judge – *iudex publice excommunicatus* – all of whose actions are completely null.[83]

The clearest discussion I have found of such exceptions occurs in Bernard of Parma's *Ordinary Gloss* to the *Decretals of Gregory IX*. The exception of excommunication is partly dilatory, partly peremptory. It can be proposed at any time, both before the contestation and even after the sentencing, whether or not the sentence is appealed, for sometimes it nullifies the judgment retroactively; but even here it is dilatory in a sense, if the case can be reheard.[84]

Durantis says much the same thing, though he stresses the lack of time-restrictions on when the exception of excommunication can be proposed, and does not explicitly note its peremptory aspect in cases of nullification.[85] But it is quite clear that when a trial is retroactively invalidated, it is destroyed and not simply delayed, even though a new trial can be had.

Durantis also points out that the exception of excommunication can be lodged at any time against a witness, and also, in a case of criminal accusation, against the accuser; and it can also be submitted after the conclusion of the case, and even after the sentence, against the execution of the sentence, as stipulated by Innocent IV in *Pia considera-tione*.[86] He does not indicate which of the instances listed here have peremptory force. We have seen that exceptions against plaintiffs (into which category an accuser would fall) and against the execution of the sentence are only dilatory. As for witnesses, Don Ximio's assertion has the ring of truth: when excommunication is proved against a witness testifying on the principal matter in a trial, his testimony is to be thrown out of court.

Further confirmation of Don Ximio's presentation comes from John Andreae in his *Novella* on the *Liber sextus*. He cites with approval Archdeacon Guido of Baysio's comment that the mandated short term of eight days does not apply to exceptions of excommunication lodged against the judge or a witness, for then a suitable term in keeping with the gravity of the circumstances is to be assigned. Andreae also gives approval to the opinion of Abbas Antiquus that the exception of excommunication cannot be entered with peremptory force whenever one wishes.[87]

Ordinary peremptory exceptions against witnesses, specifically exceptions of hitherto uncharged crimes, are to be submitted before sentence is handed down in the case, according to the decretal *Denique* of Celestine III. The *Ordinary Gloss* notes that when it is not the person of the witness but the truth of his testimony that is being impugned, the objection can be made for twenty years after the case is terminated (or with no time limitation in marriage cases); but if the objection is made before the sentence is delivered and is not proved, it cannot be raised again after the sentence, unless the case is appealed.[88]

Don Ximio's ruling on Mrs. Fox's *reconventio* or counter-accusation follows naturally from his discussion of exceptions. He disqualifies the accusation on two grounds, first because of the equal seriousness of charge and countercharge, and second because Wolf's crime was proved by the process of exception, and is therefore not punishable:

> Fallo, más, que la Gulpeja pide más que non deve pedir,
> Que de egual en criminal non puede reconvenir.
> Por exepçión non puedo yo condenar nin punir,
> Nin deve el abogado tal petiçión comedir.[89] (Stanza 358)

The canonical tradition differed somewhat from the civilian on the subject of *reconventio*. Alexander III, in the decretal *Ex literis*, states simply that a judge is to have the plaintiff answer the defendant's countercharge, and then hear both charges together and hand down a single sentence at the end.[90] However, the *Ordinary Gloss* notes that no *reconventio* is allowed in criminal cases, citing Gratian and the *Justinian Code*.[91] John Andreae cites the same authorities, but wonders whether *reconventio* is in fact not possible in such cases, since according to the Roman law *Neganda* the accused is meant to turn the accuser's *inscriptio ad talionem* against him, even during the trial, and he is also allowed to enter a countercharge of a greater crime.[92]

The *Siete partidas* repeats the provisions of *Neganda*; specifically:

Non podria acusar a otro por razon de yerro que fuesse menor o ygual de aquel de que lo acusasse, fasta que fuesse acabado el pleyto de su acusacion.[93]

In the law of the *Partidas* corresponding to Alexander III's *Ex literis* (according to which *conventio* and *reconventio* are to be heard together), it is explained that in criminal cases a lesser charge is not heard until the greater is disposed of.[94] The gravity of a crime, we should note, is determined by the gravity of the punishment prescribed for it.[95]

Durantis interprets the traditions on *reconventio* to mean that a defendant in a criminal accusation cannot make a countercharge once he is truly a defendant, that is, after the case is contested. But before the contestation, he can enter a countercharge of a greater crime, which moreover involves an *inscriptio* (that is, he must agree to the *poena talionis*).[96]

However, when it is a question of accusing an accuser of a crime by way of exception, in order to repel him from the accusation, it is sufficient to allege any kind of crime, whether greater, equal, or less.[97] The decretal *Denique* notes that when witnesses are convicted of or confess to crimes objected solely by way of exception, they cannot be penalized by the ordinary punishment, since the accusation has not followed the ordinary course of the law. It is sufficient that such witnesses be repelled from testifying.[98] The same would hold for crimes excepted against a party to an action (in our case, accuser Wolf), as Don Ximio points out:

Maguer contra la parte o contra el mal testigo

Sea exepçión provada, no l' farán otro castigo;
Desecharán su demanda, su dicho non val un figo;
La pena ordinaria non avrá, yo vos lo digo. (Stanza 359)

Don Ximio goes on to note that if he does have the power to torture
a false or vacillating witness in criminal proceedings, it is not because
of charges made through exceptions, but rather *ex officio*:

Si non fuer' testigo falso o si lo vieren variar,
Ca entonçe el alcalde puédelo atormentar,
Non per exepçión, mas porque lo puede far:
En los pleitos criminales su ofiçio ha grand lugar. (Stanza 360)

The *Ordinary Gloss* to Gratian's *Decretum* lists the persons who may
be tortured by judges. A witness may be tortured in both civil and
criminal cases, if he is a slave or a "vile" person, or even if he is a
free man who is a criminal or infamous or of obscure or unknown
origin. A free man may also be tortured, even though not of vile estate,
if he vacillates in giving witness: "Torquetur etiam libera persona, licet
non sit vilis, dum tamen vacillet in testimonio." This statement is justified by a law in the *Justinian Digest*, where, however, the point is put
negatively: "Ex libero homine pro testimonio non vacillante quaestionem haberi non oportet."[99]

The *Siete partidas* gives "ordinary" judges (like Don Ximio) power
to torture vacillating witnesses if they are of vile condition, in order
to discover the truth; and when the witnesses are found to have given
false testimony, the judge can punish them *ex officio*.[100] This law, therefore, might seem to grant both more and less than what Don Ximio
claims for himself. It is true that Don Ximio, in accord with the
canonistic authorities, places no restriction of status on the witnesses
he is allowed to torture (though he does seem to restrict the right
to criminal proceedings). But when he says he cannot punish a witness, he is not speaking of witnesses found to be perjured, but of witnesses found guilty of other crimes by the process of exception.[101]

Don Ximio is, of course, speaking of the use of torture in the secular
courts, but there was no clear canonical prohibition of torture in ordinary ecclesiastical courts. The *Decretals of Gregory IX*, issued in 1234,
contains a rule that simply stipulates that torture is not to be used
at the beginning of a trial.[102] In practice, however, it seems not to

have been used at all in church courts until after it was authorized for papal inquisitors against suspected heretics later in the thirteenth century.[103] At the beginning of the fourteenth century, Clement V prohibited the inquisitors from using torture except in the presence of the local bishop or his official.[104] But as for church courts in general, John Andreae in his *Novella* simply follows the rule formulated by Huguccio of Pisa at the end of the twelfth century: that only moderate forms of torture should be used. Therefore, the church courts should not use the rack, or claws and cords, which are sometimes employed by the secular courts, but rather rods or switches, or leather whips of the sort that the Italians call *scorezate* (or *correggiate*).[105] Ecclesiastics were also thought to be restricted in their use of torture by the general prohibition against the spilling of blood by clerics in major orders, and by the law forbidding the church courts to inflict punishments involving bloodshed.[106] Whipping was a normal penalty prescribed by ecclesiastical judges,[107] and so was enforced fasting,[108] and one can see how such punishments might be thought appropriate for other purposes.[109] I do not know what the local practice was in the diocese of Toledo in the fourteenth century. Cardinal Albornoz authorized the use of torture in the secular courts of the Papal State of Ancona in 1357, but only with the express permission of the rector, or governor, of the State. [110]

Don Ximio sums up his remarks on the limited role of exceptions in court by saying that they can only void an accusation and repel or challenge witnesses, but cannot result in a formal condemnation or execution:

> Por exepçión se puede la demanda desechar,
> E puédense los testigos desechar e aún tachar.[111]
> Por exepçión non puedo yo condenar nin matar:
> Non puede más el alcalde que el derecho mandar. (Stanza 361)

I have not been able to answer all of the questions that are raised by the fate of Wolf's accusation against Mrs. Fox in Don Ximio's court. For instance, I do not know if Don Ximio is within his rights to speak to Mrs. Fox as if the charge of theft has somehow been proved against her:

> Dó liçençia a la Raposa: váyase a salvagina,

> Pero que non la asuelvo del furto tan aína,
> Mas mando que non furte el gallo a su vezina. (Stanza 366)

I may have overlooked some problems or misconstrued others. But I have seen enough to conclude that we must think twice before assuming any procedural error in Don Ximio's handling of the case. His confident and dogmatic tone seems to be abundantly justified. His knowledge of proper judicial formalities is of the sort that could only have come from solid experience in the courtroom. And, of course, the same must hold true for Juan Ruiz. Even though his experience may have been in the ecclesiastical courtroom, the canonical authorities with which he must have been familiar would have given him detailed knowledge of secular court procedures.

Chapter Five

Conclusion

The main part of the *Libro de buen amor*, including everything in the Toledo manuscript and everything in the Gayoso and Salamanca manuscripts except for the appendixes (and excluding the front matter of the Salamanca text), was written by a man sufficiently familiar with canon law to make easy and accurate reference to it, sufficiently current in the discipline to name the works of outstanding canonists, aware of the contents of conciliar and synodal constitutions, and thoroughly informed about court procedure. The fact that he cites the *Novella* of John Andreae shows that he must have been writing after A.D. 1338. He must have finished before A.D. 1389, the scribal date of the Gayoso text. The prose Introduction of the Salamanca manuscript, which also cites canon law and draws on jurisprudential maxims, is probably by the same author.

If this author, "Juan Ruiz," really was a rural archpriest, as he claimed, he may have acquired his knowledge of the law through the exercise of his office. Rural archpriests in Spain, like the rural deans of other lands, were generally accorded the right to examine and conclude minor matters of church discipline, and they sometimes overreached their charge to adjudicate more serious cases or to encroach upon the secular jurisdiction.

If the Toledo manuscript date of 1368 is authentic, it cannot be interpreted as A.D. 1330, but must mean A.D. 1368. In this case, we can more easily think of Juan Ruiz as the author not only of the main part of the *Libro de buen amor* but also of the *Cántica de los clérigos de Talavera*, since there was an archpriest of Talavera by A.D. 1369 (though he may not yet have been a member of the chapter of the collegiate church of Santa María). This possibility would appear even greater if he finished the bulk of the work in A.D. 1381: if, that is, the Salamanca reading of 1381 is the authentic one and signifies the Dominical year. (The Toledo date of 1368 would in this case have to be ascribed to a scribal alteration.) But the *Cántica* does not show the same expert knowledge of conciliar law that Juan Ruiz manifests in the undisputed portion of his work.

If, on the other hand, the date of 1381 is not only authentic but signifies the Caesarian year, corresponding to A.D. 1343, the *Cántica* is probably by another author, since the satire seems to date from a time when the archpriest of Talavera had replaced the subdean in the collegiate chapter. The change must have occurred after 1354, for the subdeanship still existed in that year. The author of the *Cántica* must have been writing fairly long after the change, at a time when the archpriest was well established and could be thought of as existing from time immemorial, or at least as far back as the reign of Archbishop Albornoz (1338–50). Perhaps the author was Alfonsus Peratinensis, the scribe of the Salamanca manuscript, who mistakenly characterizes Albornoz as a cardinal while he was in charge of the see of Toledo. If Alfonsus Peratinensis is the Alfonso de Paradinas who was born in 1395, the Salamanca manuscript must be placed well within the fifteenth century. But since this identification is not certain, we must allow for the possibility that the manuscript dates from the final years of the fourteenth century. Peratinensis may have found the date 1381 in his received text and interpreted it, rightly or wrongly, as A.D. 1343, which may have provided him the inspiration to concoct the romance of Juan Ruiz's imprisonment at the order of Cardinal Albornoz. Or, if his received text contained the date of 1368, Peratinensis may himself have substituted the date of 1381 and invented the story of Juan Ruiz's association with Albornoz out of whole cloth.

Since life must go on, for medievalists as well as for the normal run of mankind, I suspect that even those of my readers who admit the cogency of my arguments will formulate a dominant working hypothesis for the *Libro de Buen amor*, rather than leaving all of the possibilities suspended in an emulsion of uncertainty. One such hypothesis could be that the bulk of the *Libro de buen amor* was written by Juan Ruiz, archpriest of Hita, in the time of Archbishop Albornoz, and finished in the year 1343; and that the *Cántica de los clérigos de Talavera* was added by Alfonso de Paradinas in the next century, while he was a student at the University of Salamanca. Nothing that I have said can disprove such a hypothesis. But I do not encourage it, for it is too comfortable: it fits in too well with traditional ways of thinking about the *Libro de buen amor*. I myself lean towards a hypothesis that would put the work at the forefront of the great burst of poetic activity that occurred in Spain in the 1380s.

As an outsider to the world of medieval Spanish literature, perhaps I may be allowed to point out what I find to be the prevailing fault of scholars in the field. It is to take too much for granted in the way of received opinion, and to show too little interest in areas that should be of vital concern. Many essential questions have been unasked and unanswered. There has been, for instance, almost no cross-referencing between literary studies and ecclesiastical history. There have been sporadic attempts to look for allusions to archpriests of Hita in the 1330s and 1340s, but no effort to look for other archpriests in fourteenth-century Spain, or to ask what kind of a position the office of archpriest was: what were its duties, what sort of person was normally entrusted with it, what was its income, how many and what sort of other benefices could be held with it, what were the actual mechanisms by which one was appointed to it, and how were its duties perceived and performed by the incumbents. In the thirteenth and early fourteenth centuries, archpriests had a reputation for being ignorant of the niceties of canon law. By the end of the fourteenth century and during the fifteenth century we hear of better-trained archpriests, who, however, exercised their functions through deputies. Alfonso Martínez de Toledo, for example, was an absentee archpriest with a bachelor's degree in canon law. Perhaps Juan Ruiz represents a short-lived breed of archpriest who not only knew canon law but practiced it. The archives and libraries of Spain and the Vatican are waiting to be explored by scholars with such questions in mind. For instance, the as yet uncalendared registers of Popes Clement VI (1342–52), Innocent VI (1352–62), Urban V (1362–70), Gregory XI (1370–78), and Clement VII (1378–94) are bound to yield important results. I hope that my essay will provide something of the necessary stimulus for such research.

Appendix

Persons named Juan Rodríguez

appearing in papal registers, 1305–42[1]

1) Juan Rodríguez de Cisneros, illegitimate son of Arias de Cisneros, nephew of Simón, Bishop of Sigüenza. In 1312, in his sixteenth year, he is in minor orders and is canon and prebendary of Sigüenza, having been dispensed locally for defects of age and birth; the pope grants similar dispensations, confirms his present benefices, allows him to receive others, and to proceed to major orders (C 9775). In 1318, he is archdeacon of *Metinen.*, that is, Medinaceli, in the diocese of Sigüenza,[2] and still canon of Sigüenza, and dispensed again for illegitimacy and defect of age (he is still said to be in his sixteenth year) (J 7470). In 1319, he becomes a canon of Palencia, even though he has an archidiaconate with the cure of souls, and a canonry and prebend, in the diocese of Sigüenza, and a portion in Palencia and a quarter portion in Valladolid (J 10598). He is probably no longer archdeacon of Medinaceli by this time but rather archdeacon of Sigüenza, as he is in 1320;[3] and he is so addressed by the pope in 1321, when he is dispensed for illegitimacy for the fourth time, on this occasion at the intercession of the king and queen of Castile and León, and he is given permission to become bishop after attaining his thirtieth year (J 13692).[4] He is dispensed again for his illegitimacy in 1326, when he adds a canonry at Burgos,

with the expectation of a prebend, to his previous benefices (J 24699, cf. 24697–98). In the next year he is named a papal chaplain (J 28047), and at the same time given a three-year permission for nonresidency, while studying at a university or residing in a church where he is or will be beneficed (J 28036, cf. 28035). In 1329, he is named canon of Toledo, with expectation of a prebend, and expectation also of a dignity, personate, or office with or without the cure of souls, with prestimonies and prestimonial portions, in spite of his holding the major archidiaconate of Sigüenza, with cure of souls, and the other benefices previously mentioned; and he is dispensed once again for illegitimacy (J 45657).

2) Juan Rodríguez de Rojas, in 1318 archdeacon of Calahorra (J 8029). While still only a deacon he is named bishop of Mondoñedo in 1327, and is dead two years later (E 343; cf. J 27203, 27205, 28376).

3) Juan Rodríguez, cleric of Queen María of Castile-León, in 1320 receives a canonry in Córdoba (J 12611). In 1325, when he is described as a familiar of King Alfonso, he is made canon of Palencia (J 22043: for "Gerunden." read "Corduben.").

4) Juan Rodríguez, sacrist, canon, and prebendary of the secular church of Valladolid, in 1321 becomes archdeacon of Campos in Palencia and canon of Palencia, and has to give up the sacristy at Valladolid, but not the canonry and prebend (J 13143–44, 13147). In 1326, when he is called a cleric of the king of Castile, he adds a canonry and prebend of the secular church of Oviedo (J 26266), and in 1328 he is given an additional canonry and prebend, this time in Burgos, while remaining canon and prebendary of Palencia, Oviedo, and Valladolid, and archdeacon of Campos (J 41823). In 1327, he receives an executory letter along with Juan Rodríguez no. 8 (J 28425), to whom he is perhaps related (as uncle to nephew?).

5) Juan Rodríguez, canon of Seville in 1323 (J 18647); perhaps the same as Juan Rodríguez de Cornuciello, who is canon of Seville in 1325 (J 23033–34), and the Juan Rodríguez who is canon of Seville in 1329 and 1332, and no longer in 1333 (J 43990, 57901, 62142).

6) Juan Rodríguez of Ripa Acuta in the diocese of Calahorra, pastor of Saxo Albo in the diocese of Orense, in 1324 becomes canon of Zamora (J 20194); in 1329, when he is designated as cleric and nuncio of Queen Eleanor of Aragon, he is given an expectative grace to a dignity in Zamora, with the obligation of relinquishing his pastorate (J 48269).

7) Juan Rodríguez, Bishop of Cartagena, in 1326 is appointed bishop of Calahorra-Calzada by John XXII (E 156; cf. J 26388–89, 26878, 58506, 58510). But when he was elevated from being dean of Cartagena to bishop of Cartagena by Clement V in 1311, he was identified as Juan Muñoz (E 168). He lived until 1346.

8) Juan Rodríguez, canon of Valladolid, in 1327 becomes canon of Salamanca (J 28424). At the same time, he and the archdeacon of Campos (Juan Rodríguez no. 4) receive an executory letter from the pope (J 28425). He later receives the uncured sacristy of Valladolid (which we saw was given up by Juan Rodríguez no. 4 in 1321 on becoming archdeacon of Campos), and gives it up around 1339 on becoming archdeacon of Campos (B 7689; cf. 6774–75).⁵

9) Juan Rodríguez, holder of a prestimonial benefice at Villa María in the diocese of Burgos, in 1327 receives a canonry at the church of Valpuesta in the same diocese, with expectation of a prebend and prestimonies pertaining to it, which are at the disposition of the archdeacon of the same church (J 27527). (We note that the archdeacon of Valpuesta is here called archdeacon of the church of Valpuesta, rather than archdeacon of Valpuesta in the church of Burgos.)

10) Juan Rodríguez, scholar, in 1328 is to be granted a canonry at Calahorra (J 42805); perhaps he is the canon of the same name who is heard of in 1339 and 1341 (B 6776, 8619).

11) Juan Rodríguez de Sasamón has a son, Francisco, who in 1328 receives a canonry at Burgos, at the intercession of King Alfonso of Castile (J 41820). Cf. no. 15 below.

12) Juan Rodríguez, canon of Jaén, in 1329 receives the canonry of Mondoñedo vacated by Álvaro, successor of Bishop Juan Rodríguez de Rojas (no. 2 above), at the intercession of Cardinal Pedro Gómez (J 47029).

13) Juan Rodríguez in 1329 becomes canon of Palencia by favor of the bishop, while retaining portions in Palencia and in *Sussellen.* in the diocese of Palencia (J 47714).

14) Juan Rodríguez in 1333 is chancellor of King Alfonso of Castile-León (J 60508-9).

15) Juan Rodríguez de Sasamón, cleric and familiar of King Alfonso of Castile-León, portioner and chaplain of the church of Sts. Cosmas and Damian at Covarrubias in the diocese of Burgos, in 1338 re-

ceives a canonry in the church of Santa María Major, Valladolid
(B 5654). Cf. no. 11 above.

16) Juan Rodríguez of Fonteboronia, who died before 11 November
1339, was treasurer of Seville (B 6786).

Addendum: *The Registers of 1343*

I have been able to consult the pertinent *Registra supplicationum* for the year
1343 in the Vatican Archives (I used the microfilm copies in the library of
the Pontifical Institute of Mediaeval Studies in Toronto, by the kind favor
of Father Leonard Boyle, O. P.), and can now throw light on the matters
discussed on pp. 69–71 above.

On March 8, 1343, Pope Clement VI approved Archbishop Albornoz's
request of benefices for seven of his commensals. The first of them, the *nobilis*
Juan Rodríguez de Cisneros, chaplain of the Apostolic See, is provided with
a canonry in the cathedral of Calahorra, with expectation of a prebend, in
spite of the fact that he already possesses the abbacy of Santa Leocadia, a
canonry in Toledo as well as a prebend (but he is litigating over the latter),
and canonries and prebends in the cathedrals of Burgos, Palencia, and Sigüenza, and a half portion in Valladolid (*Reg. sup.* 3, fol. 87). But after word
of the pope's approval was received, a further supplication was sent to repair
deficiencies in the petitions for two of the commensals, namely, Juan
Rodríguez de Cisneros and Martín Muñoz, Archdeacon of Albarracín. In
the case of the latter, it was neglected *per oblivionem* to mention in the list
of benefices already possessed that he was canon-prebendary of Segorbe-
Albarracín. In the case of the noble Cisneros, it was neglected *per errorem*
to mention his defect of birth; the pope is now asked to grant him a dispensation to hold the benefices in Calahorra and to confirm the dispensations
already granted for taking holy orders and for assuming and transferring his
other benefices. The pope approved these requests around August 8, 1343,
but directed that they be made effective retroactively to the original date
of March 8 (*Reg. sup.* 4, fol. 149). These documents clearly refer to Juan
Rodríguez de Cisneros, Archdeacon of Sigüenza, who was made canon of
Toledo in 1329 (see no. 1 above). The expected dignity in Toledo came
about in the form of the abbacy of Santa Leocadia, but the expected prebend still eluded him, fourteen years later (in 1343). However, he had increased his interest in Valladolid from a quarter portion to a half portion.

I do not think it likely that he is the same person as the Juan Rodríguez
de Cisneros who turns up ten years later, in 1353, as a commensal of Cardinal Albornoz. Even though he too is a papal chaplain, abbot of Santa

Leocadia, and canon and prebendary of Toledo, Sigüenza, Palencia, and Burgos, he has only a quarter portion at Valladolid, is not yet canon of Calahorra, and is not illegitimate. It is not probable that the elder Cisneros would have reduced his holding in Valladolid without noticeable gain (unless he gave up a quarter portion when finally taking possession of the Toledo prebend). It is also unlikely that Albornoz and the elder Cisneros would have made the same mistake in 1353 that they made in 1343, by failing to mention the impediment of illegitimacy. The second supplication of 1343 makes it very clear that they believed a new dispensation to be necessary every time an additional benefice was obtained; they understood that every failure to mention all of the pertinent details made them run the risk of having the grant declared "surreptitious" and invalid. When asking Innocent VI for a vacant canonry and prebend in Calahorra in 1353, they would hardly have neglected to say that Clement VI had already granted Cisneros a canonry and expectation of a prebend in that church, and had moreover given him the necessary dispensation for his illegitimacy.

In the register containing that despensation, there also appears a request for a canonry in León by Juan Rodríguez de Sasamón (no. 15 above), who is designated as a lawyer (*iurisperitus*). His petition was granted on July 19, 1343 (*Reg. sup.* 4, fol. 81v). A bit later, there is registered the supplication of the Infante Fernando (son of Alfonso IV of Aragon), Marquess of Tortosa and Duke of Albarracín, asking that the *generosus vir* Juan Rodríguez de Espejo, student in (Roman) civil law, be named canon of Gerona; the pope complied around August 13, 1343 (*Reg. sup.* 4, fol. 153). When Espejo appears as a commensal of Cardinal Albornoz in 1352–53, he is called *nobilis* and said to be a bachelor in laws (I mention him on p. 70 above; I should note here that the dates I give on pp. 68–70 for Cardinal Albornoz's petitions to the pope do not indicate the times of writing but rather the days on which the pope approved them).

I have explained above (p. 71) why it is unlikely that the elder Cisneros would have become archpriest of Hita before becoming abbot of Santa Leocadia. It is also unlikely that the younger Cisneros would have acquired such a benefice in the course of duplicating the career of his elder namesake. Unlike the elder and younger Cisneros, both Espejo and Sasamón are identified as having had formal legal training. Espejo could technically have become archpriest of Hita before acquiring the parish church in the diocese of Valencia which he possessed in 1352. But his interests are largely limited to Aragon, especially Valencia, and his native tongue may have been Catalan. More promising is the jurist Juan Rodríguez from Sasamón in the diocese of Burgos; but if he were given an archipresbyterate after 1343, it is more likely that it would have been in the diocese of Burgos than in the diocese of Toledo.

Notes
and
Indices

Notes to Chapter One

Canons, Canonists, and Dates in the Libro de Buen Amor

1. I use the edition by Emil Friedberg, *Corpus iuris canonici*, 2 vols. (Leipzig, 1879–81, repr. Graz, 1959). Vol. 1 has Gratian's *Decretum*; vol. 2 contains the *Decretals of Gregory IX*, the *Sext* (of Boniface VIII), the *Clementine Constitutions* (of Clement V), the *Extravagants of John XXII*, and the *Common Extravagants*. The *Glossae ordinariae* to all of these compilations can be found in the Roman edition of 1582 or one of its reprints; I use that of Lyons, 1606.

2. Unless otherwise noted, I follow the edition of the *Libro de buen amor* by Jacques Joset, 2 vols. (Madrid, 1974), in the series Clásicos castellanos, nos. 14 and 17 (replacing the 1913 edition by Julio Cejador). I will sometimes refer also to the editions of Giorgio Chiarini (Milan, 1964) and Joan Corominas (Madrid, 1967). For manuscript readings, I use the parallel-text paleographic edition by Manuel Criado de Val and Eric W. Naylor, Clásicos hispánicos 2.9 (Madrid, 1965) and the same editors' facsimile edition of the Toledo MS, 3 vols. (Madrid, 1977); the facsimile edition of the Gayoso MS by the Real Academia Española (Madrid, 1974); and the facsimile edition of the Salamanca MS edited by César Real de la Riva, 2 vols. (Madrid, 1975).

3. Joset finds an example of "maestro nin doctor" elsewhere and concludes that it is a stereotypical formula.

4. Félix Lecoy, *Recherches sur le Libro de buen amor de Juan Ruiz, Archiprêtre de Hita* (Paris, 1938), reissued with Prologue, Supplementary Bibliography, and Index by A. D. Deyermond (Farnborough, Hants., 1973), pp. 196–97.

5. Gratian, *Decretum* 2. 33. 3: *Tractatus de poenitentia* (Friedberg, 1:1159–1247). Lecoy, followed by others who rely on him, mistakenly names Case 23 instead of Case 33, and uses the obsolete edition reprinted in Migne's *Patrologia latina* (PL).

6. Gratian, *De poenitentia* 1, dictum ante can. 1 et dictum post can. 60 (Friedberg, 1:1159, 1175).

7. Gratian, *De poenitentia* 1. 1: *Petrus doluit* (Friedberg, 1:1159); see Lecoy, p. 197, for the texts.

8. Gratian, *De poenitentia* 1. 88: *Quem poenitet* (Friedberg, 1:1187–89), Chaps. 10–11 of *De vera et falsa poenitentia*, PL 40:1122–23; see Lecoy, p. 196. Clelianna Fantini, "Il trattato ps.-agostiniano *De vera et falsa paenitentia*," *Ricerche di storia religiosa* 1 (Rome, 1954): pp. 200–9, has collected scholarly opinions on the treatise.

9. *Lib. b. amor* 1145; Gratian, *De poenitentia* 6. 1: *Qui vult confiteri* (Friedberg, 1:1242); Lecoy, p. 198.

10. Gratian, *Decretum* 2. 20. 3. 2: *Proclivis* (Friedberg, 1:849).

11. Gratian, *Decretum* 2. 12. 1. 1: *Omnis aetas* (1:676): "Omnis aetas ab adolescentia in malum prona est." The *impuberes* or *adolescentes* among the clergy are to be under an older member, "ut lubricae aetatis annos non in luxuria sed in disciplinis ecclesiasticis agant." A somewhat similar sentiment can be found in the *Justinian Novels* 5. 2: *Hinc autem*, par. 2: *Si vero is quidem*: "Humana enim natura quodammodo labitur ad delicta." See *Corpus iuris civilis*, ed. Paulus Krueger et al., 3 vols., 3 (repr. Berlin, 1959), 32.

12. José Sánchez Herrero, *Concilios provinciales y sínodos toledanos de los siglos XIV y XV: La religiosidad cristiana del clero y pueblo*, Estudios de historia, vol. 2 (La Laguna, 1976), p. 181. The synod was held by Archbishop Juan, Infante of Aragon (see below, n. 64, and Chap. 2 at n. 53). The point that he is making here is that no priest is to say mass without having the text of the canon of the mass at hand with a light to read it by. Juan's constitution was included in the *Libro de constituciones sinodales* published at the synod of 1356 by Archbishop Blas Fernández (Sánchez Herrero, pp. 223–42, esp. 235–36). As we shall see below, the *Libro de buen amor* may have been composed well after 1356. Archpriests were expected to have copies of provincial and synodal constitutions in their possession and to bring them to meetings of the synod (see below, Chap. 2 at n. 111). Cf. the document recording the reorganization of the cathedral chapter of Sigüenza in 1301: it was drawn up "propter labilitatem humanae memoriae et hominum inconstantiam." See Toribio Minguella y Arnedo, *Historia de la diócesis de Sigüenza y sus obispos*, 3 vols. (Madrid, 1910–13), 2:361–62. Cf. also the judgment given by Rodrigo Ximénez de Rada, Archbishop of Toledo, in the dispute between the clergy of Atienza and the clergy of the *aldeae termini sui*: that is, between the clergy of the *villa* of Atienza (diocese of Sigüenza) and the clergy who live outside the town within the bounds of the archipresbyterate of Atienza. The archbishop begins by saying: "Quia ea quae fiunt in tempore simul labuntur cum tempore nisi aut a scripti memoria aut a voce testium recipiant firmamentum," etc. See Minguella, 1:534–35 no. 171, document of 29 June 1219.

13. John Andreae, *Ordinary Gloss* to *Clementines* 5. 11. 2: *Saepe contingit*, ad v. *clarior* (col. 338, ed. cit. n. 1 above), and see Gratian, *Decretum* 1. 23. 12: *Praeterea sciscitaris* (Friedberg, 1:83). Andreae goes on to cite something similar from civil law, namely, *Justinian Code* 6. 22. 8: *Hac consultissima lege*, par. lb, which reads: "At cum humana fragilitas, mortis praecipue cogitatione turbata, minus memoria possit res plures consequi, patebit eis licentia voluntatem suam, sive in testamenti sive in codicilli tenore compositam, cui velint scribendam credere" (*Corpus iuris civilis*, 2:253). I cite other comments of Andreae on the same constitution (*Saepe*) below, Chap. 4, nn. 54, 66. The idea of *memoria* as *labilis* was clearly proverbial. In addition to the examples given in the previous note, we see Thomas Aquinas saying that in formal criminal cases the accusation has to be in writing, because "ea quae verbotenus dicuntur facile labuntur a memoria" (*Summa theologiae* 2-2. 68. 2). Two centuries later, in the trial nullifying Joan of Arc's condemnation, the notaries say they put the acts in writing so that, even *labente memoria hominum*, the record would remain: *Procès en nullité de la condemnation de Jeanne d'Arc*, ed. Pierre Duparc, 2 vols. (Paris, 1977–79), 1:1. John Gerson uses the expression in 1423 in his *De laude scriptorum, Oeuvres complètes*, ed. Palémon Glorieux, 9 (Paris, 1973), 425: "Legentibus autem atque dictantibus, si defuerint auxilia scriptorum, cum memoria sit labilis, obrepet protinus obliteratio dictatis aut de lectis oblivio." Dante, *Paradiso* 20. 11–12, speaks of songs fleeting and falling from his memory ("canti Da mia memoria labili et caduci"). Closer to home, the canonist Juan Alfonso de Madrid, who was a bachelor in laws and arts in 1393 and later held the chief chair in law at the University of Salamanca, justified his writing of compendia as follows: "Memoriae labilitas, negotiorum multiplicitas, scientiarum prolixitas, vitae brevitas, librorum gravitas ad compendiorum suffragium modo nos astanter compellunt et quae naturali docte [*lege* dote] non valemus, velut artificiali memoria contingamus." As he continues, he gives a good example of the "humility *topos*": he is a doctor of both laws, though unworthy of the degree: "Quam ob rem ego Ioannes Alfonsi de Maiorito, utriusque iuris doctor, licet indignus, nativus de Ispania, de diocesi Tolletana, et domini papae prothonotarius, per alphabetum sequentes tabulas ordinavi." See Antonio García y García, "La canonística ibérica medieval posterior al *Decreto* de Graciano," part 3, in *Repertorio de historia de las ciencias eclesiásticas en España*, 5 (Salamanca, 1976): 351–402, esp. 374–77. Juan Alfonso had his J.U.D. in 1407, but García is mistaken in saying that he resigned a canonry in Talavera in that year. Rather he resigned a benefice *sine cura* in the church of Robillo in the diocese of Toledo, which was given to a canon of Talavera, namely, Diego González Cornejo, who later became archpriest of Talavera, the predecessor

of Alfonso Martínez de Toledo. García is also mistaken in saying that Juan Alfonso became archdeacon of Briviesca in 1407: he was granted this post in 1409 by Benedict XIII, and was dispensed to hold the incompatible cured deanship of Santiago at the same time. See Vicente Beltrán de Heredia, *Bulario de la Universidad de Salamanca (1219–1549)*, 3 vols., Acta Salmanticensia: Historia de la Universidad, vols. 12–14 (Salamanca, 1966–67), 1:613–14 no. 398; cf. 621–22 no. 413 (where *ad decanatu* should read *ac decanatu*).

14. The date of 1326 given by Johann Friedrich von Schulte, *Die Geschichte der Quellen und Literatur des canonischen Rechts von Gratian bis auf die Gegenwort*, 3 vols. (Stuttgart, 1875–80, repr. Graz, 1956), 2:217, is mistaken. See Stephan Kuttner, "The *Apostillae* of Johannes Andreae on the *Clementines*," in *Études d'histoire de droit canonique dédiées à Gabriel Le Bras* (Paris, 1965), 1:195–201, esp. 196. Kuttner shows that Andreae composed a supplement (*Apostillae*) to his *Apparatus* sometime between 1324 and 1330.

15. Gratian, *Decretum* 2. 50. 5. 3: *Nostrates* (Friedberg, 1:1105): "Haec sunt, praeter alia quae ad memoriam non occurrunt, pacta coniugiorum solemnia."

16. Gratian, *Decretum* 3. 4. 113: *Si nulla extant* (1:1396–97): "Qui autem possunt meminisse quod ad ecclesiam veniebant cum parentibus, possunt recordari an quod eorum parentibus dabatur acceperint. Sed si hoc etiam ab ipsa memoria alienum est, conferendum eis videtur quod collatum esse nescitur." Cf. 1. 84. 2: *Nuntiatum* (1:295): some bishops are "immemores honoris sui."

17. Gratian, *Decretum* 2. 13. 2. 29: *Fatendum* (Friedberg, 1:730–31): "Fatendum est, nescire quidem mortuos quid hic agatur, sed dum hic agitur; postea vero audire ab eis qui hinc ad eos moriendo pergunt, non quidem omnia, sed quae sinuntur etiam isti meminisse, et quae illos, quibus haec indicant, oportet audire."

18. *Justinian Code* 1. 17. 2, par. 13 (*Corpus iuris civilis*, 2:72). Later (par. 18), he says: "Humani vero iuris conditio semper in infinitum decurrit." Cf. the sentiment from the *Justinian Novels* cited in n. 11 above.

19. William Durantis, *Speculum iudiciale*, Book 2, part 2, rubric *De instrumentorum editione*, paragraph 8 (*Restat*), no. 16; vol. 1, p. 661 of the edition of Venice, 1585 (titled *Speculum iuris*); the similar edition of Basel, 1574 (repr. Aalen, 1975), has a slightly different pagination (in this case, p. 658).

20. Azzo, *Summa* (Venice, 1581), col. 2 no. 3.

21. Ibid., col. 29 no. 4.

22. Hostiensis, *Summa aurea* on *Decretals of Gregory IX* 1. 3 (title *De constitutionibus*), paragraph *Qualiter constitutionibus derogetur*. In the edi-

tion of Lyons, 1537 (repr. Aalen, 1962), fol. 5 no. 12, the text reads: "Et est ratio diversitatis, quia in rescriptis continentur facta quorum habere memoriam et in nullo peccare," etc. The edition of Venice, 1574 (repr. Turin, 1963), col. 24 no. 12, is similar. But the wording as I give it in the text above is that quoted by Geoffrey Barraclough, *Papal Provisions* (Oxford, 1935), p. 175; Barraclough in his bibliography (p. 180) cites the edition of Venice, 1490, and a Munich MS (Cod. lat. Monacen. 24) for the *Summa aurea*. Perhaps the original reading was "quia omnium," and was misread as "quorum."

23. Bernard of Parma, *Ordinary Gloss* to *Decretals* 1. 3. 17: *Cum adeo*, ad v. *moderemur* (col. 49, ed. cit. n. 1 above); and to 2. 30. 6: *Porrecta*, ad v. *non credamus* (col. 987). See Stephan Kuttner and Beryl Smalley, "The *Glossa ordinaria* to the Gregorian *Decretals*," *English Historical Review* 60 (1945): 97–105.

24. Gratian, *Decretum* 2. 12. 1. 10: *Nolo* (Friedberg, 1:680).

25. Bernard, loc. cit.: "Quandoque tamen ipsum fallit oblivio, 23 Dist., *Praeterea*, et 30 q. 4, *Quod autem* [Gratian 2. 30. 4. 6], ubi oblitus fuit Urbanus, cum omnium habere memoriam," etc.

26. Gratian, *De poenitentia* 4. 8: *Si ex bono*, § 1 (Friedberg, 1:1231): "Et tamen antequam factum esset, iam filii Dei erant in memoriali Patris sui inconcussa stabilitate conscripti."

27. Gratian, *Decretum* 2. 30. 1. 6: *De his* (Friedberg, 1:1098): "Domino dicant, 'Delicta ignorantiae nostrae ne memineris.'"

28. Gratian, *De poenitentia* 4, dictum post 19 (Friedberg, 1:1237).

29. Gratian, *De poenitentia* 1. 74: *Ne forsitan* (Friedberg, 1:1179): "Ne forsitan peccati memores tardius revertantur." Cf. *De poenitentia* 1, dictum post 87, § 1 (1:1184–85): men are urged to remember their sins and not to forget them. Cf. also *De poenitentia* 3. 36: *Iudas poenituit* (1:1223): "Magnum est ut quis peccata sua agnoscat, et memoriam eorum perseveranter retineat. Nullum invenitur delictorum tale remedium, sicut eorum continuata memoria."

30. Gratian, *Decretum* 3. 3. 28: *Venerabiles imagines* (Friedberg, 1:1360): "Ad memoriam et recordationem primitivorum venerantur eas et adorant." Gratian's rubric reads: "Imagines sanctorum memoria sunt et recordatio praeteritorum." For other kinds of reminders, see 3. 1. 26: *Placuit* (1:1300–1301): no memory of martyrs is to be accepted as probable without their bodies or certain relics; 3. 2. 37: *Dum hostia* (1:1327): when the host is broken at mass, the Passion of Christ is called to memory; see also 3. 2. 54: *Liquido* (1:1334); 3. 2. 71: *Iteratur* (1:1341); 3. 2. 76: *De hac* (1:1345); 3. 2. 82: *In Christo*, § 4 (1:1348). In 2. 15. 1. 4: *Mulier* (1:747), an animal a woman sinned with is killed to obliterate the memory of the deed. According to 1. 81. 9: *Valet* (1:283), the place where one

has committed sins reminds one of them. In 2. 7. 1. 9: *Denique* (1:570), a thurible in which incense was wrongly offered is to be exhibited as a memorial of the divine indignation.

31. Gratian, *Decretum* 2. 12. 2, dictum ante 64 (Friedberg, 1:707): "Ne vero longinquitate temporis obscuretur conditio originis, tempore suae manumissionis scribant liberti professionem." Cf. 1. 81, dictum ante 1 (1:281), where Gratian adds an epilogue for our memory: "Praecedentibus cohaerentia quaedam sub epilogo ad memoriam subiciamus."

32. Gratian, *Decretum* 1. 80. 4: *Illud sane* (Friedberg, 1:280): "Quod sanctorum Patrum divinitus inspirata vetuerunt decreta."

33. Gratian, *Decretum* 2. 24. 3. 12: *Cum sancti* (Friedberg, 1:994): "Scriptura sacra duobus modis maledictum memorat."

34. Gratian, *Decretum* 1. 23. 17: *Exorcista* (Friedberg, 1:84): "Exorcista cum ordinatur accipiat de manu episcopi libellum in quo scripti sunt exorcismi, dicente sibi episcopo: 'Accipe et commenda memoriae.'"

35. Gratian, *De poenitentia* 2. 5: *Caritas* (Friedberg, 1:1191–92).

36. Gratian, *De poenitentia* 3. 25 (Friedberg, 1:1216–17).

37. I follow the Salamanca MS reading of *las*, since *decretales* is feminine; in Latin, it is short for *litterae decretales*.

38. *Decretales Gregorii IX* 2. 28. 41: *Secundo requiris* (Friedberg, 2:424).

39. G. Mollat, "Les Clémentines," *Dictionnaire de droit canonique* (DDC), ed. R. Naz, 7 vols. (Paris, 1935–65), 4:635–40; Stephan Kuttner, "The Date of the Constitution *Saepe*, the Vatican Manuscripts, and the Roman Edition of the *Clementines*," *Mélanges Eugène Tisserant*, vol. 4, part 1, Studi e testi, vol. 234 (Vatican City, 1964), pp. 427–52, esp. 428–30.

40. *Clementines* 1. 1. 1: *Fidei catholicae* (Friedberg, 2:1133).

41. He is quoting the beginning of verse 15; see the text given by J. N. D. Kelly, *The Athanasian Creed* (London, 1964), pp. 17–20.

42. Sánchez Herrero (n. 12 above), p. 206 (on the date of 1338, see below, Chap. 3 n. 31); *Statutes of Exeter II*, Chap. 20, ed. F. M. Powicke and C. R. Cheney, *Councils and Synods with Other Documents Relating to the English Church*, vol. 2: *A.D. 1205–1313* (Oxford, 1964), p. 1017. See also pp. 304, 423, and 610. Powicke and Cheney say on p. 982 n. 2 that the bishop's family name was spelled Quinel in the thirteenth century, but in later times has been read as Quivel. For councils that refer to the work as a *tractatus*, see Powicke and Cheney, pp. 268, 345, 403. The custom of singing the *Quicumque* daily was introduced in Cluniac circles. But it was more common to sing it only once a week, at Prime on Sundays. See Kelly (n. 41 above), p. 44. Kelly says that the title of *symbolum* began to be generally applied to the piece only in the thirteenth century (pp. 1, 44). Other names given to the work were *fides*, *sermo*, *libellus*, and *hymnus*. See A. E. Burn, *The Athanasian Creed*, Texts

and Studies, ser. 1 no. 4 (Cambridge, 1896), p. 41; J. Tixeront, in *Dictionnaire de théologie catholique*, 1:2178. None of these authorities notice the names of *psalmus* and *tractatus*.

43. No doubt more juristic maxims will be uncovered in time. I suggest as a possibility the counsel of not putting one's sickle to another man's crop. Juan Ruiz brings it up as a rule in the matter of confessional jurisdiction: "Non deve poner omne su foz en miese ajena" (1146c). It was applied to jurisdiction in the external forum when the bishop of Beauvais sought permission from the chapter of Rouen to proceed against Joan of Arc in Rouen; the chapter acknowledged the bishop's good intentions: "non intendens tamen falcem suam in messem nostram absque nostro consensu ponere" (*Procès de condamnation*, 1:17; see below, Chap. 2, n. 90).

44. The alternative reading of the first line (from the Salamanca MS) is not reported by Joset. In the last line, I have substituted the Salamanca reading *Diratorio* for the Gayoso reading *Decretorio* (accepted by Joset) for reasons that will be explained below.

45. See Schulte (n. 14 above), 2:144–56; L. Falletti, "Guillaume Durand," DDC (n. 39 above), 5:1014–75, esp. 1030; Stephan Kuttner, "Duranti, William, the Elder," *New Catholic Encyclopedia* (NCE) 4:1117. The first edition of the *Speculum* was produced between 1271 and 1276, the second ca. 1289. The final version of the *Repertorium*, or *Breviarium*, was completed between the two editions of the *Speculum*. The *Repertorium* sets forth problems in the order of the titles of the *Decretals of Gregory IX*, and the *Confessorium* comes after title 38 (*De poenitentiis et remissionibus*) of Book 5 (see Falletti, col. 1052). I have consulted the Paris, 1513, edition, which is entitled *Breviarium aureum*, in which the *Confessorium* appears on fols. 173v–86. On fols. 184v–85, Durantis lists some three dozen specific sins that are supposedly reserved to the bishop, but concludes by counseling the priest in effect to ignore the list, since it places too great a restriction on his powers: "Verum tot casus ponere nihil aliud est quam sacerdotum potestatem restringere, quae tamen sibi in his est plenarie attributa." He determines that the priest has power over all hidden sins except those explicitly reserved by law, but adds the general principle that cases of particular enormity or difficulty should be referred to one's superior, and he also stresses that local custom should be observed in the matter (fol. 185r–v). He notes, however, that a priest can absolve reserved sins in an emergency: "Fateor etiam quod in necessitatis articulo in praedictis casibus et aliis etiam sibi alias non concessis potest per sacerdotem quilibet absolvi" (fol. 185v). He cites Gratian, *Decretum* 2. 26. 6. 14: *Presbyter* (Friedberg, 1:1041), which reads: "Presbyter inconsulto episcopo non reconciliet poenitentem, nisi absente episcopo ultima

necessitas cogat," and *Decretals of Gregory IX* 3. 28. 14: *Parochiano* (Friedberg, 2:554), which reads: "Parochiano tuo, qui excommunicatus pro manifestis excessibus, videlicet homicidio, incendio, violenta manuum iniectione in personas ecclesiasticas, ecclesiarum violatione, vel incestu, fuit, dum ageret in extremis, per presbyterum suum iuxta formam ecclesiae absolutus, non [debet] coemeterium et alia ecclesiae suffragia denegari." Cf. *Libro de buen amor*, stanza 1156:

> Segund común derecho, aquésta es la verdat;
> Mas en ora de muerte o de grand neçesidat,
> Do el pecador non puede aver de otro sanidat,
> A vuestros e ajenos, oíd, absolved, quitat.

46. For this last point, I am grateful to Dr. Thomas Izbicki, of the University of Notre Dame.

47. Antonio García y García and Ramón Gonzálvez, *Catálogo de los manuscritos jurídicos medievales de la catedral de Toledo*, Cuadernos del Instituto Jurídico Español, vol. 21 (Madrid, 1970), pp. 91–94.

48. See Schulte, 2:123–29; Charles Lefebvre, DDC 5:1211–27; idem, NCE 7:170–71.

49. See J. A. Cantini, "Sinibalde dei Fieschi," DDC 7:1029–39, esp. 1031.

50. K. W. Nörr, "Guido de Baysio," NCE 6:841–42. Guido also commented on the *Sext* (see below, Chap. 4, n. 87).

51. For another possible use of the term *directorium* at the same time, see n. 62 below. Somewhat later, in 1332, a French Dominican, probably Raymond Estienne, wrote the *Directorium ad passagium faciendum*, ed. Charles Kohler, *Recueil des historiens des croisades: Documents arméniens*, vol. 2 (Paris, 1906), pp. 367–517; see Jean Richard, *La papauté et les missions d'Orient au moyen âge (XIIIᵉ–XVᵉ siècles)* (Rome, 1977), p. 170 n. 4. Still later in the century, in 1376, the Catalan Dominican Nicholas Eymeric produced the first version of his *Directorium inquisitorum*. See J. Quétif and J. Échard, *Scriptores ordinis praedicatorum* (Paris, 1719–23, repr. New York, 1959), 1:710; J. Perarnau, "Tres nous tractats de Nicolau Eimeric," *Revista catalana de teología*, 4 (1979): 70–100.

52. Demetrio Mansilla, *Catálogo de los códices de la catedral de Burgos* (Madrid, 1952), pp. 71–72: "Incipit suma que vocatur diritorium iuris in foro conscencie et iudiciali composita a fratre Petro Quesuel de ordine fratrum minorum ex iuribus et doctorum sententis diversorum." The MS contains only the first three of the four parts of the work. Mansilla seems to think that the author is a Spaniard and gives his name as Petrus Consuel.

53. See Josiah Cox Russell, *Dictionary of Writers of Thirteenth-Century England* (London, 1936), pp. 102–3. He cites John Bale's *Index* for the Norwich possession of the book.

54. C. L. Kingsford, *Dictionary of National Biography*, s.v. Quesnel.

55. Schulte, 2:262.

56. This point was noticed by F. M. Powicke, *The Medieval Books of Merton College* (Oxford, 1931), p. 142 n.

57. He does however note that a Peter Quesnel was designated by the Benedictine abbey of Montebourg (in Normandy) to be its representative at Westminster in 1288. Could the author have been confused with Peter Quinel, Bishop of Exeter (see above, n. 42), who died in 1291? Quesnel in the *Directorium* does not follow the tradition noted in Quinel's statutes of referring to the Athanasian Creed as a psalm, but rather calls it a *symbolum*: "et in symbolo Athanasii *quicumque wlt*" (fol. 2rb of the Yale MS; see next note).

58. Yale University, Beinecke Rare Book and Manuscript Library, MS 429 (unless otherwise indicated, I follow the older foliation; a newer foliation increases each number by one). My colleague Richard Rouse has identified the hand as English, ca. 1320.

59. Yale MS, fol. 1va.

60. Oxford University, Merton MS N 3.6, Coxe 223 (fourteenth century). Cf. the title of the Burgos copy (n. 52 above) and that of the Toledo copy (n. 69 below). Like the Burgos copy, the Merton manuscript contains only Books 1–3, with Book 4 omitted. The alphabetical index for Books 1–2 appears on fols. 202v–32. The Introduction, the title of which I have given in the text above, is copied not at the beginning but at the end, after Book 3, starting on fol. 339va. The title is imperfectly transcribed by Powicke and Russell, and Russell also makes a mistake in the incipit of the Introduction, which reads correctly: *Si quis ignorat, ignorabitur.*

61. The title *Directorium iuris* at the beginning of the Merton manuscript is in a different hand from that of the text, but at the end of the third book the text scribe concludes thus: "Explicit tertius liber. Directorii iuris" (fol. 339rb). In the Yale manuscript the list of chapters at the end is titled: "Prologus sive tabula generalis super summam que directoria vocatur" (fol. 423vb). But at the end of each of the two alphabetical tables that follow the neuter singular form is used: "Explicit tabula directorii iuris primo et secundo libro" (new fol. 437ra) and "Explicit tabula directorii iuris libro tercio et quarto" (new fol. 450ra).

62. Yale MS fol. 1rb: "constitutiones extravagantes que ab aliquibus liber septimus nuncupantur." Just above, he cites "extra. de fid' katho' fidei.§.fi .1. vij°.," that is, the chapter *Fidei catholicae* of the title *De summa Trinitate et fide catholica* of the first book of the *Clementines*, the final

paragraph (Friedberg 2:1134). See above at n. 40 for Juan Ruiz's citation of the same decretal. John Andreae objected to the designation of the *Clementines* as *Septimus liber*; see the *Glossa ordinaria* to the *Prooemium* of the *Clementines*, ad v. *in unum volumen* (ed. of Lyons, 1606, col. 4). See Schulte 2:48 n. 9, and Kuttner, "Date" (n. 39 above), p. 437 n. 43. The name however does appear in the manuscript tradition and was used by several commentators, among them Nicholas of Anesiac or Ennezat in his *Tabula super Septimum*, compiled in 1319 (Schulte 2:232); Schulte at one point refers to it as Nicholas's *Directorium* (2:48 n. 10), but he may not mean to imply that this title has manuscript authority.

63. Yale MS fol. 1rb–1va: "Nec aliquem doctorem adhuc viderim qui ista iura noua posuerit integre et perfecte."

64. Kuttner, "Apostillae" (n. 14 above), pp. 197–98. William dedicated his work to the Infante Juan, who later in 1319 was elected to the see of Toledo (see n. 12 above). Another commentary on the *Clementines*, that of Matthew of Rome, may also have been written before Andreae's *Apparatus* (ibid., p. 198).

65. See Quesnel's list of authors, Yale MS fol. 1va; William appears as "G de monte Laudinno." G. Mollat, "Guillaume de Montlauzun," DDC 5:1078–79, dates the *Lectura* ca. 1306–16.

66. Yale MS fol. 2rb: "et Jo. An. extra. .c. Fideli l' vj." See Cyprian M. Rosen, "Johannes Andreae," NCE 7:994–95. The *Novella* on the *Sextus* was finished much later, after 1338, and in the meantime he had composed some *Additiones* to the *Glossa*.

67. Yale MS new fol. 450ra: "Anno domini M° .ccc° .xxij° compilatus est liber iste per suum auctorem." In the second column of this page there appears, in large letters and a later hand (early seventeenth-century English?), the inscription: "Georgius Nicolaus/ Stoll/ Studiosus a° g 1·3·22." Why Stoll would put the date *anno gratiae* 1322 after his name is not clear.

68. See Amédée Teetaert, "Quesvel, Pierre," *Dictionnaire de théologie catholique*, 13:1536–37.

69. Luke Wadding, *Scriptores ordinis minorum* (Rome, 1650), pp. 287–88, after listing the titles of the four books, says: "Quae omnia diu MSS servabantur in Bibliotheca Norvicensi. Extat adhuc MS in Bibliotheca Vaticana, et Minorum Toletana, littera X, num. 81. Titulus libri est: Summa, quae vocatur Directorium iuris, in foro conscientiae et iudiciali, composita a Fratre Petro Quesvel de Ordine Fratrum Minorum, ex iuribus doctorum et summis diversorum." The manuscript is not listed by Atanasio López, *Descripción de los manuscritos franciscanos existentes en la Biblioteca Provincial de Toledo* (Madrid, 1926), or in López and L. M. Núñez, "Descriptio codicum franciscalium bibliothecae ecclesiae primatialis toletanae," *Archivo ibero-americano*, 1 (1914–15), 369–90, 542–63; 3

(1915), 88–103; 7 (1917), 255–81; 11 (1919), 72–91; 12 (1919), 390–409; 13 (1920), 81–96.

70. Yale MS, fols. 24v–37v.

71. Ibid., fols. 29v–33v.

72. Chiarini (n. 1 above) ad loc.

73. Corominas (n. 1 above) ad loc.

74. José Luis Bermejo Cabrero, "El saber jurídico del Arcipreste," in *El Arcipreste de Hita: El libro, el autor, la tierra, la epoca,* ed. Manuel Criado de Val, Actas del I Congreso Internacional sobre el Arcipreste de Hita (Barcilona, 1973), pp. 409–15, esp. 411 and n. 5. Of the latter work, he says: "Fue muy conocida la obra del Cronista Juan Andrés: *Novellae super Decretalibus.*" It is bizarre to refer to Andreae as a "chronicler," and Bermejo himself could hardly have confused him with the literary historian Juan Andrés, S.J. (1740–1817). Is "Chronista" a misprint or editorial mistake for "Canonista"?

75. García and Gonzálvez (n. 47 above) pp. 7, 83; cf. p. 103. On the constitutions of Innocent IV and Gregory X, see Stephan Kuttner, "Decretalistica," *Zeitschrift der Savigny-Stiftung für Rechtsgeschichte, Kanonistische Abteilung* 26 (1937): 436–70, esp. 460–61, 466–69; Martin Bertram, "Zur wissenschaftlichen Bearbeitung der Konstitutionen Gregors X," *Quellen und Forschungen aus italienischen Archiven und Bibliotheken* 53 (1973): 459–67.

76. Benedict XI, *Ex eo* (*Common Extravagants* 5. 3. 1, Friedberg, 2:1290), referring to Boniface VIII, *Per hoc* (*Sext* 5. 2. 17, Friedberg, 2:1076); Benedict XI, *Inter cunctas* (*Common Extravagants* 5. 7. 1, Friedberg, 2:1296–1300), removing the *novitas* introduced by Boniface VIII's *Super cathedram*; Clement V, *Dudum* (*Clementines* 3. 7. 2, Friedberg, 2:1161–64), giving the text and reestablishing the authority of *Super cathedram*; *Registrum Hamonis Hethe, diocesis Roffensis, A.D. 1319–1352,* ed. Charles Johnson, Canterbury and York Society 48–49 (Oxford, 1948), p. 368. For another reference to *Super cathedram,* see below at n. 89; as it touches upon confession, Boniface's constitution allows friars to hear confessions in dioceses with or without the bishop's permission, but limits their powers to those of local parish priests, unless the bishop allows them further authority. Benedict XI does not seem to have wished to change Boniface's instructions on this point when he issued *Inter cunctas*: he says there that friars cannot absolve from sins reserved to the bishop, and he gives a list of such sins.

Another example of the use of the adjective *novella* can be found in Bernard Gui, *Practica inquisitionis haereticae pravitatis,* ed. C. Douais (Paris, 1886), completed around 1323: see Antoine Dondaine, "Le manuel de l'inquisiteur (1230–1330)," *Archivum fratrum praedicatorum* 17 (1947):

85–194, esp. 115–17. At one point Gui gives a formula in which the heresy–inquisitor requests the bishop's participation, "iuxta tenorem novellae constitutionis" (Part 1, no. 34, pp. 28, 29), but later (in a part, however, which was written earlier) he identifies it: "in constitutione novella Clementis papae V, *Multorum querela*" (Part 4, p. 182; cf. p. 187), referring to *Clementines* 5. 3. 1 (Friedberg, 2:1181). For a reference to the *novellae constitutiones* of Bishop Trefnant of Hereford, issued in 1394, see *The Hereford Breviary*, ed. W. H. Frere and L. E. G. Brown, Henry Bradshaw Society 26, 40, 46 (London, 1904–15), 3:xlvi; cf. 1:354, 430.

77. This is the title of the edition of 1581 which was reprinted at Turin in 1963, with an Introduction by Stephan Kuttner. The Introduction was reprinted with additional notes as "Joannes Andreae and His *Novella* on the *Decretals of Gregory IX*," *The Jurist* 24 (1964): 393–408.

78. Kuttner, Introduction, pp. x, xii (*Jurist* 24:401–2, 406); Franz Gillmann, "Zur Frage der Abfassungszeit der Novelle des Johannes Andreä zu den Dekretalen Gregors IX," *Archiv für katholisches Kirchenrecht* 104 (1924): 261–75, esp. 265.

79. Antonio García y García, "La penetración del derecho clásico medieval en España," *Anuario de historia del derecho español* 36 (1966): 575–92, esp. 578–79.

80. Candido Mesini, "Gli Spagnoli a Bologna prima della fondazione del collegio di Egidio d'Albornoz (1364–69)," in *El cardenal Albornoz y el Colegio de España*, ed. Evelio Verdera y Tuells, 6 vols., Studia albornotiana, vols. 11–13, 35–37 (Bologna, 1972–79), 2:41–71, esp. 54–55.

81. These conclusions have been reinforced and substantiated by Father Cyprian Rosen, O. F. M. Cap., of St. Francis High School Seminary, Lafayette, N. J., in a personal communication. He points to five early versions of Andreae's commentaries on specific decretals, which later appear with additions in the *Novella*, contained in MS S. II. 3 of the Biblioteca Malatestina in Cesena; in these texts there is no mention of the *Novella*. He also notes that Andreae refers to one of these early commentaries, that on the decretal *Fraternitatis* (*Decretals of Gregory IX* 2. 20. 17) in his *Apparatus* or *Glossa ordinaria* to the *Clementines* 2. 8. 2: *Testibus*, sub verbo *testibus* (ed. of Lyons, 1606, col. 113), where he calls it simply a *commentum*: "Et quia decretalem illam solemniter commentavi, et ipsius commenti habetur copia, facilius hanc transibo." Andreae is saying that a copy of the *commentum* is available from the Stationarius of the University of Bologna; for all solemn or public disputations were published in this way. See Rosen, "Notes on an Earlier version of the *Quaestiones mercuriales*," *Bulletin of Medieval Canon Law*, n.s. 5 (1975): 103–14, esp. 111. The earlier version of Andreae's *Quaestiones mercuriales* (later revised to become part of the *Novella* on the *Liber sextus*), discussed by Father

Rosen in this article, is also contained in the Cesena manuscript, and here we do find some references to the *Novella*; some of them are cited by Kuttner, Introduction, p. x. Father Rosen points out that most of these references use the future tense, e.g., "quam gl. videre poteris in novella." There is one exception: on fol. 113va, we read: "ut scripssi in novella." But this too could be explained by the classroom context.

82. García and Gonzálvez (n. 47 above), pp. 22–26, MSS 8-7, 8-10, and 8-5 respectively. On matching days of the week to years, see n. 90 below. Andrew makes a more obvious mistake in the year when dating Book IV in MS 8-7: he puts m.iii.lviiii for m.ccc.lviiii.

83. Ibid., p. 23, MS 8-6.

84. Ibid., p. 111, MS 28-7.

85. *Decretales Gregorii IX* 1. 24. 3 (Friedberg, 2:154), and the *Glossa ordinaria* in the edition of Lyons, 1606, col. 320.

86. Bernard of Montmirat (ca. 1225–96), Abbot of Montmajeur, later referred to as Abbas Antiquus, to distinguish him from the fifteenth-century Sicilian abbot, Nicholas Tudeschi (Panormitanus). See Stephan Kuttner, "Wer war der Dekretalist 'Abbas antiquus'?" *Zeit. Savigny* 26 (cit. n. 75 above): 471–89; cf. Pierre Legendre, NCE 2:341.

87. John Andreae, *Novella* on *Decretales* 1. 24. 3. in glossam ultimam, in fine (Turin, 1963, 1:195): "Et hoc videntur Innocentius et Abbas intelligere de graviter peccantibus. . . . Si intellexerunt de casibus episcopo reservatis, id non placet Hostiensi, qui dicit quod sine speciali commissione episcopi archipresbyter in illis non absolvet; quod verum credo. . . . Et sic nota: secundum Hostiensem, quemlibet habere tres qui praesunt animae: papam cum suis vicariis; episcopum cum civitatense archipresbytero, in hoc eius vicario; et curatum."

88. *Decretales Gregorii IX* 1. 24. 4: *Ut singulae plebes*; *Glossa ordinaria* ad v. *cuncta tamen referant* (col. 321); Andreae, *Novella* on *Decretales* 1. 24. 4 in glossam ultimam (fol. 195): "Alias ista litera esset sibi contradictoria, secundum Hostiensem. Unde dicebat Innocentius quod terminabit minora secundum ordinationes episcopi."

89. Andreae, *Ordinary Gloss* on *Sext* 5. 10. 2 (*Si episcopus*), ad v. *suo subdito* and *reservantur* (col. 702); *Novella in Sextum* (Venice, 1499; repr. Graz, 1963), p. 286, on *Si episcopus*.

90. See the Criado-Naylor edition, pp. xv, 577, 648. The "corrector" of the manuscript interpreted the date as "20 de Julio 1389," and Martín Sarmiento read it as "el jueves 23 de Julio, del año de 1382," neither of which can be right. For a ready method of ascertaining days of the week, see C. R. Cheney, *Handbook of Dates for Students of English History*, Royal Historical Society Guides and Handbooks, vol. 4 (London, 1961); on p. 158, we see that Easter Sunday in 1389 fell on April 18, and the

Easter table for that day (pp. 138–39) gives all of the days of the year. For typical mistakes in writing Roman numerals, see above at n. 82.

91. Chiarini, p. ix.

92. Ramón Menéndez Pidal, "Un copista illuste del *Libro de buen amor* y dos redacciones de esta obra," *Poesía árabe y poesía europea, con otros estudios de literatura medieval* (Buenos Aires, 1941), pp. 124–28. Part of this note is taken from his review of Ducamin's edition of the *Libro*, *Romania* 30 (1901): 434–40, where, however, he simply identifies the scribe as an Alfonso who was a native of Paradinas (p. 435). See also Manuel García Blanco, "D. Alonso de Paradinas, Copista del *Libro de buen amor*," *Estudios dedicados a Menéndez Pidal*, vol. 6 (Madrid, 1956), pp. 339–54. Photographs of Paradinas's sepulcher and epitaph and of the last page of the Salamanca text of the *Libro* are given facing pp. 346–47.

93. García Blanco, p. 340.

94. García Blanco, p. 347, cites the epitaph from a secondary source as beginning ALFONSO DE PALADINAS, without noticing that in the picture he provides it clearly reads ALFONSO DE PARADINAS.

95. Vicente Beltrán de Heredia, *Bulario de la Universidad de Salamanca* (above, n. 13), 2:527 no. 1052: "quidem alius, Alfonsus de Paradinas, dicens se ius ad dictam cantoriam." If this is the same person as the future bishop, he must not yet have acquired the dignity of archdeacon, which, as we shall see below, usually ranked higher than that of cantor in Spanish cathedral chapters.

96. Deyermond (above, n. 4), p. xiii.

97. See Criado and Naylor, p. 553.

98. According to R. Dean Ware, "The dating formula of this style is distinctive in that the word *annus* never occurs, only *era*." See his "Medieval Chronology: Theory and Practice," in *Medieval Studies: An Introduction*, ed. James M. Powell (Syracuse, 1976), pp. 213–37, esp. 223. He is speaking of Latin formulas, but of course the same rule normally applies to the vernacular as well. For instance, when the *Fuero real* or *Fuero de las leyes* was authorized by King Alfonso XI on 8 Februrary 1348 A.D., the year was stated thus: "era de mil e trecientos e ochenta e seis annos": *Códigos antiguos de España*, ed. Marcelo Martínez Alcubilla (Madrid, 1885), p. 687. But sometimes *año* was used together with *era*, as in the *Gran crónica de Alfonso XI*, Chapter 207, ed. Diego Catalán, 2 vols., Fuentes cronísticas de la historia de España, vol. 4 (Madrid, 1976), 2:184: "año de la era de mill e trezientos y setenta y quatro años," that is 1374 E.S. = A.D. 1336. The *Gran crónica* was elaborated between A.D. 1376 and 1379 from the earlier *Crónica* of Fernán Sánchez de Valladolid of 1344 (Catalán, 1:162, 242–50).

99. Chiarini, p. xxix.

100. See J. F. Rivera Recio, *Los arzobispos de Toledo en la baja edad media (s. xii–xv)*, Publicaciones del Instituto provincial de investigaciones y estudios toledanos, ser. 2, no. 3 (Toledo, 1969), pp. 53, 85–87. For Cardinal Torres, see below, Chap. 2 at n. 30. Lecoy (n. 4 above), pp. 234–35, suggests that the *Cántica* was inspired by Albornoz's synod held at Toledo on April 16, 1342, but as I will show below, Chap. 3 at n. 70, the archbishop's constitution was directed not against concubinary clerics but rather against their concubines.

101. H. H. Arnold sets forth a solution in his review of Lecoy in *Hispanic Review* 8 (1940): 166–70. He concludes: "The gaps of G (supplied by S) seem then to be omissions either accidental or intentional from an original like S and not additions to a shorter text" (p. 168).

102. Joset, 1:xli–xlii.

103. See José Vives, "Cómputo eclesiástico medieval," in *Manual de cronología española y universal*, ed. Jacinto Augustí y Casanovas, Consejo superior de investigaciones científicas, Escuela de estudios medievales: Estudios, vol. 25 (Madrid, 1952), p. 11: The Council of Tarragona in 1180, with the royal approval, made dating by the Christian Era obligatory in Catalonia. In Aragon, the use of the Spanish Era persisted until 1350, in Valencia until 1358, in Castile until 1383, and in Portugal until 1422.

104. See the *Crónicas de los reyes de Castilla don Pedro, don Enrique II, don Juan I, don Enrique III, por don Pedro López de Ayala*, ed. Eugenio de Llaguno Amírola, 2 vols. (Madrid, 1779–80), 2:626–27. For legal documents to be valid, the king said, they had to be dated thus: "Dada en el año del Nascimiento de nuestro señor Jesu–Christo de 1384 años."

105. Demetrio Mansilla Reoyo, *Catálogo documental del archivo catedral de Burgos (804–1416)*, Monumenta Hispaniae sacra: Subsidia, vol. 2 (Madrid, 1971), p. 406, no. 1617: Protest of the Chapter of Burgos, April 16 "del anno del Señor de mill e trezientos e ochenta e un annos"; no. 1618: the bishop's reply from Valladolid, April 18, "anno del nascimiento de nuestro Señor Jesucristo de mill e trescientos e ochenta e un annos." Cf. the formula *año de era de años* from the *Gran crónica* noted in n. 98 above.

106. Mansilla, *Catálogo*, p. 423 no. 1680: "de março, era de mill e quatrozientos e treinta annos."

107. *Crónicas* (n. 104 above), 2:649. Another example, from 1395, is on p. 662.

108. See, for example, Luciano Serrano, *Fuentes para la historia de Castilla* (Silos, 1907), 200–201, 11 April 1345: "Dada en Burgos, onze dias de Abril, anno Domini millesimo ccc° xl quinto." Other examples are on pp. 230–31 (A.D. 1371) and 281–82 (A.D. 1403). On pp. 268–69, there is a dating for 1395 by the *annus Nativitatis* at the end of a letter in Spanish:

"anno a nativitate Domini millesimo trecentesimo nonagesimo quinto."
Mansilla, *Catálogo*, p. 477 no. 1879, records the Spanish variant *año de año*: "anno del nascimiento. . . de mill e quatrosientos e siete anno."

109. Mansilla, *Catálogo*, p. 414 no. 1647. Cf. p. 469 no. 1847, 7 January 1406: "Jueves a vii dias del mes de enero de mill e cccc e vi annos." Cf. also pp. 484–85 nos. 1907 and 1912: documents made at San Juan de Ortega in 1408 on January 22 and January 23 respectively, dated according to the formula "mes de enero del nascimiento de Nuestro Señor Jesucristo de mill e quatrocientos e ocho annos." But no. 1913, written at the same time and place uses "anno del nascimiento . . ." whereas nos. 1908–11 use the Latin *anno Domini* formula. Cf. the article cited below, Chap. 3 n. 31.

110. *Cancionero de Juan Alfonso de Baena*, ed. José María Azaceta, Clásicos hispánicos, 2. 10 (Madrid, 1966), p. 599 no. 289.

111. Joaquín Gimeno Casalduero, review of Erik von Kraemer's edition of the *Disputa* (Helsinki, 1956) in *Romance Philology* 16 (1962–63): 367–72.

112. See Jerry R. Craddock, "La nota cronológica inserta en el prólogo de las *Siete partidas*: Edición crítica y comentario," *Al-Andalus* 39 (1974): 365–89. Cf. the corrupted text in the edition of Gregorio López, 7 vols. (Salamanca, 1555; repr. 7 vol. in 3, Madrid, 1974), vol. 1, fols. 3v–4. On the date of the *Siete partidas*, see below, Chap. 2, n. 18.

113. *Crónicas*, ed. Llaguno (n. 104 above), 1:586–88.

114. Ibid., 588–90.

115. Ibid., 590–92.

116. Ibid., 558–70. It is possible, of course, that Pedro IV transformed Pedro the Cruel's dates from the Spanish to the Christian Era when recording the letters in his memorial, or that a similar adjustment was made by Pedro Miguel Carbonell, who preserved the memorial in his chronicle.

117. See Marilyn A. Olsen, "Three Observations on the *Zifar*," *Corónica* 8 (1979–80): 146–48 (pointed out to me by Professor Eric W. Naylor). She edits the passages, which appear on fol. 1 of the Paris MS, as follows (except for my suggested emendation of the ungrammatical *vino* to Boniface VIII's numeral):

En el tienpo del honrrado padre Bonifaçio vino [*lege* viii°] en la era de mill e trezientos años, el dia de la naçencia de Nuestro Señor Ihesu Xpisto, començo en el año Jubileo, el qual dizen çentenario porque non viene synon de çiento a çiento años, e cunplese por la fiesta de Ihesu Xpisto de la era de mill e quatro çientos años. . . .

E porque luego non se podia tornar lo que cada uno devia segund dicho es, e lo podiesen pagar, oviesen los perdones mas conplidos, dioles plazo a que lo pagasen fasta la fiesta de resurreçion, que fue fecha en la era de mill e trezientos e treynta e nueve años.

118. Such a long imprisonment would, of course, have been unusual. The papal legate William Godin of Bayonne in the national council of Valladolid in 1322 ordered the loss of benefices (which would presumably include archipresbyterates) for clerics with infidel concubines, and also a minimum of two years in prison; by implication the prison sentence could be extended, especially for the unrepentent. The text of this provision, in the constitution *Quia clericorum*, ed. G. D. Mansi, *Sacra concilia*, 25:702, reads as follows:

Ac tam beneficiati quam non beneficiati qui ea [*lege* eas] sic detinere praesumpserint per suos praelatos per biennium ad minus in carcere detrudantur; quibus etiam per dioecesanos seu alios dictorum clericorum praelatos poenae graves aliae, prout eorum discretioni videbitur, imponantur. Si tamen hi clerici ad cor redeuntes vere poenituerint de peccato et ad vitam honestam continuaverint, concedimus quod ipsorum dioecesani cum eis post quinquennium, numerandum a sua correctione dumtaxat, possint quoad ordines et simplicia beneficia obtinenda misericorditer dispensare.

Lecoy (above, n. 4), p. 234, does not notice that these penalties refer to clerics with infidel concubines. Cf. his remarks on pp. 235–36, referring to the council of 1473, which extended the statute of 1322 to include nuns as well as infidels held by clerics as concubines (Sánchez Herrero [above, n. 12], p. 289). The 1473 text confirms that the Mansi reading of *ea* is a mistake for *eas*; *ea* would refer to the subtracted benefices of the *beneficiati*, whereas the statute is referring to the nonbeneficed clergy as well.

Perpetual imprisonment (and a diet of bread and water) was ordered by the provincial council held in 1302 by Gonzalo Díaz Palomeque, Archbishop of Toledo, for priests who broke the seal of confession: "Mandamus quod si tam nefandi criminis rei inventi fuerint, tanquam deportati et in metallum damnati perpetuo carceri mancipentur, pane et aqua sibi pro vitae sustentatione solummodo reservatis" (Sánchez Herrero, p. 167). Cf. the decree *Omnis utriusque sexus* of the Fourth Lateran Council in 1215 (*Decretals of Gregory IX* 5. 38. 12) requiring everyone to go to confession to his or her own parish priest. The penalty for breaking the seal of confession is perpetual penance in a strict monastery: "ad agendam perpetuam poenitentiam in arctum monasterium detrudendum" (Friedberg, 2:887–88).

Notes to Chapter Two

Archpriests and the Archpriest of Hita

1. Joset, 1:xv n. 13; José María Aguado, *Glosario sobre Juan Ruiz* (Madrid, 1929), p. 184.

2. On the life of St. Raymond, see J. Giménez y Martínez de Caraval, "San Raimundo de Peñafort y las *Partidas* de Alfonso X el Sabio," *Anthologica annua* 3 (1955): 201–338, esp. 302–14.

3. *Decretals of Gregory IX* 1. 24. 1 (Friedberg, 2:153–54); see Gratian, *Decretum* 1. 25. 1: *Perlectis,* § 12: *Archipresbyter* (Freidberg, 1:91). The passage is a later interpolation into the original letter. Isidore's authorship of the letter itself is put into doubt by Roger E. Reynolds, "The 'Isidorian' *Epistula ad Leudefredum*: Its Origins, Early Manuscript Tradition, and Editions," in *Visigothic Spain: New Approaches,* ed. Edward James (Oxford, 1980), pp. 251–72. For the *Archipresbyter* interpolation, see pp. 253–54.

4. *Decretales Gregorii IX* 1. 24. 2–4 (Friedberg, 2:154–55). See A. Amanieu, "Archiprêtre," DDC 1:1004–26, esp. 1015; and A. Hamilton Thompson, "Diocesan Organization in the Middle Ages: Archdeacons and Rural Deans," *Proceedings of the British Academy* 29 (1943): 153–94, esp. p. 194 n. 1. All four chapters appear in Bernard of Pavia's *Breviarium extravagantium* (ca. 1190; later known as *Compilatio prima antiqua*) 1. 16. 1–3, 5, ed. Emil Friedberg, *Quinque compilationes antiquae* (Leipzig, 1882; repr. Graz, 1956), pp. 6–7; and also in the still earlier *Collectio parisiensis secunda* 6. 1–4 and the *Collectio lipsiensis* 33. 6–9, ed. Friedberg, *Die Canones-Sammlungen zwischen Gratian und Bernhard von Pavia* (Leipzig, 1897; repr. Graz, 1958), pp. 33, 123.

5. *Decretales Gregorii IX* 1. 23. 7: *Ad haec* (Friedberg, *Corpus,* 2:151–52), taken from *Compilatio quarta* 1. 11. 1 (compiled after 1215): "Archipresbyteri . . . a pluribus decani nuncupantur"; "Quaesivisti utrum decani rurales, qui pro tempore statuuntur, ad mandatum tuum solum, vel

archidiaconi, vel etiam utriusque institui debeant vel destitui; . . . cum commune eorum decanus officium exerceat, communiter est eligendus vel etiam amovendus."

6. "Ibi adesse debent archipresbyteri parochiarum, id est, presbyteri poenitentium." This is the reading of the pseudo-Theodoran penitential canon in PL 99:940, chap. 11; see John T. McNeill and Helena M. Gamer, *Medieval Handbooks of Penance* (New York, 1938), p. 180.

7. Gratian, *Decretum* 1. 50. 64: *In capite quadragesimae* (Friedberg, 1:201): "Ibi adesse debent decani, id est, archipresbyteri parochiarum, et presbyteri poenitentium." In this reading, Gratian follows Ivo, *Decretum* 15. 45 (PL 161:867). Burchard, *Decreti* 19. 26 (PL 140:984) identifies even the priests of the penitents with the deans: "decani, id est, archipresbyteri parochiarum, id est, presbyteri poenitentium." Regino of Prüm, *De synodalibus causis*, ed. F. G. A. Wasserschleben (Leipzig, 1840; repr. Graz, 1964), p. 136, has a different explanation: "Ubi adesse debent decani, id est, archipresbyteri parochiarum, cum testibus, id est, presbyteris poenitentium." On arch-priests' "parishioners," see below at n. 137.

8. Gratian, *Decretum* 1. 60. 1: *Nullus episcopus* (Friedberg, 1:226), sum-mary of a statute of the Council of Clermont in 1095. Gratian's text reads, "Nullus episcopus in ecclesia sua, nisi diaconus sit, archidiaconum institere, nec archipresbyterum aut decanum, nisi presbyteri sint, ordinare praesumat." But Gratian in his rubric uses the nondisjunctive *vel* rather than the usually disjunctive *aut*: "Archipresbyter, *vel* decanus, aut archi-diaconus nonnisi presbyter aut diaconus ordinetur." The reported text of the council makes it clear that *decanus* is another name for *archipresbyter*: "Ut nullus fiat decanus in ecclesia nisi presbyter; nullus archidiaconus, nisi levita. Ut nullus clericus teneat archidiaconatum, nisi ipsius dignitatis habeat gradum. Ut nullus fit archipresbyter, quo alicubi dicitur decanus, nisi sit sacerdos ordinatus": G. D. Mansi, *Sacra concilia* 20:817.

9. *Glossa ordinaria* to Gratian, *Decretum* 1. 50. 64: *In capite*, ad v. *archi-presbyteri* (Lyons, 1606, col. 266): "Videtur ergo quod alius sit decanus, alius archipresbyter, et sic est contra 60 dist., cap. 1. Sed ibi ponitur haec dictio *aut* subdisiunctive. Vel loquitur hic de rurali decano."

10. *Glossa ordinaria* to *Decretales* 3. 39. 6: *Cum apostolus*, ad v. *decani*; and to 5. 4. 1: *Praeterea*, ad v. *decani* (Lyons, 1606, cols. 1341, 1647). Innocent IV, *In quinque libros Decretalium commentaria* (Venice, 1578), fol. 50 no. 4, on *Decretales* 1. 23. 7: *Ad haec*, where Innocent III speaks of rural deans, refers us to the last chapter of the title *De officio archipresbyteri*.

11. For city deans, see n. 70 below. Hostiensis, *In primum [-quintum] Decretalium librum commentaria*, 6 vols. (Venice, 1581, repr. Turin, 1965), 3:150a and 5:27a, has glosses similar to those of the *Glossa ordinaria* cited above. In commenting on the third chapter on archpriests, *Decretales* 1.

24. 3, which specifies the archpriest *de urbe*, he says that this refers to city archpriests, whereas the next chapter refers to rural archpriests, who also in some places seem to be deans (1:129a); but when he comes to the fourth chapter, he mistakenly says it deals with city archpriests (1:130). Later, commenting on *Decretales* 2. 28. 63: *Dilecto* (2:199a), he says that in the third and fourth chapters on archpriests the archpriest of the city is called rural: "Sic et dicitur archpresbyter de urbe ruralis." Here the text must originally have read: "Sic et dicitur archipresbyter de urbe *et* ruralis," the point being that archpriests are distinguished as either urban or rural. In the *Summa aurea* (Venice, 1574, repr. Turin, 1963), Book 1, rubric *De officio archipresbyteri* (col. 268), Hostiensis says that there are two kinds of archpriests, city and rural; these are also called rural deans or city [deans]: "Quot sunt genera archipresbyterorum? Duo, scilicet civitatensis . . . et ruralis. . . . Hi etiam vel rurales decani sive civitatenses vocantur." Later, in Book 5, rubric *De poenitentiis et remissionibus*, no. 25 (col. 1782), he lists possible sins that archpriests could commit, and says, "Et hoc intelligas de archipresbytero civitatensi." He goes on: "Idem de rurali, qui aliquando vocatur archipresbyter ruralis [referring to *Decretales* 1. 24. 4: *Ut singulae*], qui et aliquando decanus vocatur [1. 23. 7: *Ad haec*], aliquando plebanus [1. 31. 3: *Cum ab ecclesiarum*], quandoque abbas, licet improprie [1. 9. 3: *Ex transmissa*]." In this last passage, he seems to be speaking only of the rural archpriest. But earlier in the *Summa*, when discussing the functions of the urban archpriest, he does clearly speak of city deans: "Haec quae supra diximus videntur pertinere ad officium archipresbyteri sive decani de urbe vel civitatensis" (col. 272).

12. Hostiensis, *Commentaria* to *Decretales* 1. 6. 18: *Cum inter universas*, ad v. *ad decanum* (1:46): "Nota quod absente decano (qui honorabilior est in capitulo . . . , unde etiam et interdicit . . .) potest fieri electio, secundum Ioannem; sed contra . . . , quod dic." The *Glossa ordinaria* is similar, except that unlike Hostiensis it upholds the right of the chapter to have an election without the dean: "Nota quod absente decano potest electio fieri, licet sit honorabilior pars capituli." In the *Summa*, Book 5, *De poenitentiis*, no. 23 (cols. 1781–82), Hostiensis has a special section on deans of chapters and their possible sins.

13. Thompson (n. 4 above), p. 171; see also Kathleen Edwards, *The English Secular Cathedrals in the Middle Ages: A Constitutional Study with Special Reference to the Fourteenth Century*, ed. 2 (Manchester, 1967), p. 137 n. 2.

14. John XXII, *Lettres communes*, digested by G. Mollat, 16 vols. (Paris, 1904–47), 2:418–19 nos. 9851 and 9860.

15. *Summa aurea*, Book 5, *De poenitentiis*, no. 25 (cited in n. 11 above);

Commentaria on *Decretales* 1. 9. 3: *Ex transmissa*, ad v. *abbatis* (1:87a): "scilicet saecularis, iuxta consuetudinem metropolitanae civitatis in qua rectores saecularium ecclesiarum vocantur abbates . . . vel secundum consuetudinem aliarum ecclesiarum in quibus abbates saeculares reperiuntur . . . et in Hispania sunt multi tales."

16. Emilio Sáez, José Trenchs, et al., *Diplomatario del cardenal Gil de Albornoz*: [vol. 1,] *Cancillería pontificia (1351–1353)* (Barcelona, 1976), pp. 329–31 nos. 357–58. For more on Juan Rodríguez de Cisneros, whom Sáez and Trenchs identify as Juan Ruiz, Archpriest of Hita and author of the *Libro de buen amor*, see section 4 below. One of the benefices that became vacant on the death of Cardinal Gutierre Gómez in 1391 was the "abbatia saecularis et collegiatae ecclesiae sanctae Mariae de Valleoleti" in the diocese of Palencia; the post is described as a "dignitas principalis electiva et curata." See Beltrán, *Bulario* (above, Chap. 1 n. 13), 1:483–84, no. 211. 1. The abbacy of Lavanca in the same diocese, mentioned in no. 211. 37–38 (p. 488) is probably also a secular curacy.

17. For an English archpriest of this sort, see n. 95 below.

18. According to Alfonso García-Gallo, "Nuevas observaciones sobre la obra legislativa de Alfonso X," *Anuario de historia del derecho español* 46 (1976): 609–70, the *Siete partidas* was first compiled ca. 1290, with a second redaction produced ca. 1300. But later studies restore the basic work to Alfonso X; see Aquilino Iglesias Ferreirós, "Alfonso X el Sabio y su obra legislativa: Algunas reflexiones," ibid. 50 (1980): 531–61, esp. 560, and Jerry R. Craddock, "La cronología de las obras legislativas de Alfonso X el Sabio," ibid. 51 (1981): 365–418. Craddock dates the long chronological note cited above, Chap. 1 at n. 112, to between 1272 and 1284 (pp. 396–98). García-Gallo says that the expanded version of the *Siete partidas*, represented by the Silos manuscript, which he dates ca. 1300, was the version that was preferred by Gregorio López (see next note), but for a more informed statement of the nature of López's edition, see Craddock's 1974 article (above, Chap. 1 n. 112), pp. 365–66 and n. 14.

19. *Siete partidas* 1. 6. 3–7, ed. Gregorio López (above, Chap. 1 n. 112), vol. 1, fols. 53–54v; ed. Martínez, *Códigos antiguos* (above, Chap. 1 n. 98), pp. 224–25. I also use the edition of Pedro Gómez de la Serna, vols. 2–5 of *Los códigos españoles* (Madrid, 1848), which includes the glosses of Gregorio López and provides a massive index.

20. *Siete partidas* 1. 6. 8. López's gloss, to the words *segund la costumbre usada* (given in Gómez's edition as n. 2, in vol. 2, p. 114) reads: "Statur ut hic vides in hoc consuetudini ecclesiarum. Et communiter videmus in his regnis non esse in ecclesiis cathedralibus, nisi in paucis, istam

dignitatem archipresbyteratus." There may have been an archpriest of Toledo at the end of the twelfth century; see n. 69 below.

21. *Siete partidas* 1. 6. 8.

22. See n. 5 above.

23. See n. 33 below. I take up the question at n. 57 below.

24. *Siete partidas* 1. 6. 8 (ed. Martínez, p. 225): "E las cosas que aquestos han de fazer son estas: deven requerir e visitar todas las eglesias de sus arciprestados, tambien las de las villas, como las de las aldeas; e saber como biven los clerigos, e como fazen su oficio; e otrosi, de que vida son los legos; e si fallaren que algunos destos han fecho algun yerro, deven gelo fazer enmendar, e castigarlos, que lo non fagan dende en adelante; e si los yerros fueren a tales que ellos non los puedan castigar nin fazer enmendar, develo dezir a los arcedianos, o a los obispos, que los castiguen; e pueden descomulgar (e vedar segund que dize en la quarta ley ante desta, que lo pueden fazer los arcedianos)."

25. The chapter *Ut singulae, Decretals* 1. 24. 4, in the shortened form that Raymond of Peñafort received from Bernard of Pavia, reads: "Ut singulae plebes archipresbyterum habeant, propter assiduam erga populum Dei curam; [. . .] qui non solum imperiti vulgi sollicitudinem gerant, verum etiam [. . .] presbyterorum qui per minores titulos habitant vitam iugi circumspectione custodiant; et qua unusquisque industria divinum opus exerceat, episcopo suo renuntie[n]t. Nec contendat episcopus, non egere plebem archipresbytero, quasi ipse eam gubernare valeat; quia, etsi valde idoneus sit, decet tamen ut sua onera partiatur; et sicut ipse matrici ecclesiae praeest, ita archipresbyteri praesint plebibus, ut in nullo titubet ecclesiastica sollicitudo. Cuncta tamen referant ad episcopum, nec aliquid contra eius decretum ordinare praesumant" (Friedberg, 2:154–55).

26. Above, Chap. 1 at n. 88.

27. Demetrio Mansilla, *La documentación pontificia hasta Inocencio III (965–1216)*, Monumenta Hispaniae vaticana: Registros 1 (Rome, 1955), p. 562 no. 524 (20 May 1215). The other two judges named are "R.," archdeacon of Toledo, and the sacrist (treasurer) of Toledo.

28. Hostiensis, *Summa*, Book 1, *De officio archipresbyteri* (cols. 272–73): "Cognoscit etiam archipresbyter de causis matrimonialibus"; he gives the argument that in the decretal *Ex literis* (4. 14. 1) there is an example of such a case being heard before an archpriest. He goes on to give arguments against the practice: "Sed contra, quia hoc magnum est sacramentum in ecclesia Dei. . . . Ergo magnum iudicem requirit, scilicet episcopum. . . . Item, archidiaconus non audit nisi vilia; maiora enim episcopo referre debet. . . ; multo minus archipresbyter, qui minor est. . . . Solutio: ad episcopum pertinet, et non ad inferiorem, nisi inferior hanc iurisdictionem habeat de consuetudine vel privilegio speciali."

29. Given in Demetrio Mansilla, *Iglesia castellano-leonesa y curia romana en los tiempos del rey San Fernando* (Madrid, 1945), pp. 321–30, esp. 328–29; the document is also edited by Beltrán, *Bulario* (above, Chap. 1 n. 13), 1:310–17, and by Ángel Riesco Terrero, "Constitución pontificia de Inocencio IV dada a la iglesia de Salamanca el año 1245," *Ius canonicum* 47 (1977): 244–56, at 244–50.

30. Rivera (above, Chap. 1 n. 100), p. 53; Konrad Eubel, *Hierarchia catholica*, vol. 1, 2d ed. (Münster, 1913), p. 5.

31. Peter Linehan, *The Spanish Church and the Papacy in the Thirteenth Century* (Cambridge, 1971), pp. 268–77.

32. Mansilla, *Iglesia*, pp. 371–77; 358–69.

33. Ibid., p. 365: "Cum autem archipresbyteri eligendi fuerint, vel rationabiliter ammovendi, per episcopum et archidiaconum loci (vel abbatem, ad quem in abbatia sua iurisdictio super hoc de consuetudine pertinere dinoscitur), quorum commune gerunt officium, communiter eligant[ur] et ammoveantur si fuerint ammovendi." Notice the similarity of Torres's language to that of Innocent III in the decretal *Ad haec* (n. 5 above); but Innocent was talking of temporary archpriests, or rural deans, rather than of permanent archpriests like those in Spain. See above at n. 23. Torres is probably drawing also on the decretal *Dilecto filio* of Honorius III (*Decretals* 1.23.10, Friedberg, 2:152–53), which states that archdeacons do not have jurisdiction in monasteries, except as obtained by local custom. The implication of Torres's clause is that monasteries in the diocese of Burgos have, or should have, their own archpriests to carry out archipresbyteral functions in the parishes that fall within the monastic exemption. In England, the four major abbeys had archdeacons to supervise their areas, of which the largest, that of St. Alban's, consisted of only fifteen parishes. See Jane Sayers, "Monastic Archdeacons," in *Church and Government in the Middle Ages: Essays Presented to C. R. Cheney*, ed. C. N. L. Brooke et al. (Cambridge, 1976), pp. 177–203. In one such jurisdiction, that of Bury St. Edmund's, consisting of two parishes, there was a dean as well as an archdeacon (or a sacrist exercising archidiaconal functions); ibid., pp. 179, 190, 200–201. For similar jurisdictions in France, Belgium, Germany, Switzerland, and Italy, see Ursmer Berlière, "Les archidiaconés ou exemptions privilégiées de monastères," *Revue Benedictine* 40 (1928): 116–22.

34. Mansilla, *Iglesia*, pp. 344–57. From p. 355, beginning "Ad reprimendam Archipresbyterorum insolentiam," to the end, the text corresponds fairly closely to that of the Salamanca constitutions, pp. 328–30. But in the Ávila document the licence of the archdeacons is not said to be necessary in assigning benefices; and at the end of the Salamanca text, provision is made for the replacement of negligent bishops and archdeacons,

whereas in the Ávila text only bishops are named.

35. Ibid., p. 322.

36. Edited by Peter Linehan, "Segovia: A 'Frontier' Diocese in the Thirteenth Century," *English Historical Review* 96 (1981): 481–508, at 507–8, with variants from the Salamanca and Ávila texts. The Segovia instruction stops short at the point after the penalty of expelling any delinquent archpriest from office has been threatened (that is, the instruction to bishops and archdeacons to be diligent against concubinary clerics is omitted).

37. Linehan, pp. 483–85.

38. Antonio García y García, "Primeros reflejos del Concilio IV Lateranense en Castilla," in *Studia historico-ecclesiastica: Festgabe für Prof. Luchesius G. Spätling O.F.M.*, ed. Isaac Vázquez, Bibliotheca Pontificii Athenaei Antoniani 19 (Rome, 1977), pp. 249–82, esp. 274–77 (canons 13 and 21).

39. Ibid., p. 272, statement no. 19 of the bishop (in which he rejects the constitution made by the clerics of Segovia to the injury of bishop, archdeacon, and archpriest).

40. Ibid., p. 274, canon 13 no. 1; approved on p. 277.

41. Ibid., p. 276, canon 21 no. 1: "Quod nullus canonicus de cetero fiat archipresbyter nisi in cathedrali ecclesia," approved on p. 278.

42. Ibid., p. 274, canon 13 no. 3; cf. no. 5: "Item pro redecimatione archidiaconus non vadat nisi unus solus eques archidiaconus [*lege* archidiaconi?] et unus solus pedes archipresbyteri."

43. Canon 4 of the Third Lateran Council, given in *Decretals of Gregory IX* 3. 39. 6 (Friedberg, 2:623): "Decani [*Ordinary Gloss*: id est, archipresbyteri rurales] constituti sub episcopis duabus equis contenti consistant." This canon was reaffirmed in canon 33 of the Fourth Lateran Council, given in *Decretals* 3. 39. 23 (Friedberg, 2:632).

44. García (n. 38 above), p. 271, no. 3; p. 277, re canon 13 no. 4.

45. Ibid., p. 271, no. 14.

46. Gratian, *Decretum* 1. 60. 1: *Nullus episcopus*; 1. 60. 2: *Nullus in praepositum* (Friedberg, 1:226); *Decretals of Gregory IX* 1. 14. 1: *Ut abbates* (2:125).

47. *Decretals* 1. 6. 7: *Cum in cunctis* (2:51–52).

48. *Ordinary Gloss* to *Cum in cunctis*, ad v. *a canonibus* (col. 117).

49. Gratian, *Decretum* 1. 77. 3–7; 1. 78. 1, 4 (Friedberg, 1: 272–76). But one canon, *Si triginta* (1. 78. 5), while maintaining the ideal of thirty as the proper age, lowers the limit to twenty-five in cases of necessity, and the *Ordinary Gloss* (col. 376) admits utility as another reason, and states that the age of twenty-five also seems to be allowed by law, namely, the decretal *Cum in cunctis*, which permits one to rule a church at that age.

50. Edwards (n. 13 above), p. 253.

51. García (n. 38 above), p. 257.

52. Most of the texts are given by Sánchez Herrero, *Concilios provinciales y sínodos toledanos* (above, Chap. 1 n. 12); for some omissions, see below, Chap. 3 n. 70.

53. Sánchez Herrero, p. 176, repeated in 1356 (pp. 227–28): "Nedum canones, sed et stilus curiae matrimoniales causas, cum solis committat episcopis, maioribus annumerare videntur [1356: videtur]; quae cum compositionis seu dispensationis non admittant remedium, sed secundum iuris rigorem debeant iudicari, non expedit earum iudices (ne caecus caeco ducatum praebeat), ut iam factum novimus, statuta canonum ignorare. Ideoque praecipimus ne aliquis archipresbyter vel quivis alius ius ignorans canonicum de praedictis causis se ullatenus intromittat." Cf. the language of the council held at Trèves in 1310, cited by Thompson (n. 4 above), p. 188: "Item cum causae matrimoniales tractari debent per discretos iudices, qui potestatem habeant iudicandi, et statuta canonum non ignorent, firmiter inhibemus ne decani rurales, seu forenses archipresbyteri, ecclesiarum pastores, seu vicarii, de causis matrimonialibus cognoscere vel iudicare praesumant" (Mansi, 25:256).

54. Sánchez Herrero, p. 193, repeated in 1356 (pp. 228–29): "Quia causae criminales maiores requirunt iudices qui multum [1356: merum] habeant imperium, grave est quod aliqui archidiaconi, archipresbyteri, et alii minores praelati et eorum vicarii de talibus causis se intromittere non verentur."

55. Ibid., pp. 193–94: "Idcirco nos, dictus vicarius, et Rodericus Gutterii ac Fernandus Primi (canonici toletani, praecatores capituli toletani), ac archipresbyteri, vicarii, et reliqui clerici in praedicta synodo congregati, statuimus quod de cetero tales praelati vel eorum vicarii de talibus causis se nullatenus intromittant; quod si fecerint, quidquid in eis egerint vel coram eis actum fuerit, pro irrito habeatur, nisi sint iurgia vel modica aut levia crimina, quorum examinatio et castigatio modica vel levis a iure talibus est concessa, vel nisi sit aliquis cui aliud competat ex statuto, consuetudine, vel privilegio speciali. Haec autem constitutio intelligatur de criminalibus criminaliter interpretatis, et de arduis, licet civiliter interpretentur; 'ardua' autem intelligimus quod de sui natura ad depositionem intendunt. Per hoc tamen non excludimus quin archidiaconus, archipresbyter, vicarius, vel praecator aut quicumque alius iudex, qui fuerit praesens ubi fuerit malefactor, eum capiat seu capi faciat et tradat seu tradi faciat ad carcerem domini archiepiscopi, etiam si oporteat violenter." In the 1356 text, the passage "ac Fernandus Primi, canonici Toletani, precatores Capituli Toletani" is omitted, and, later on, *procurator* is put for *precator*. According to the synod of 1354, the dean and chapter of Toledo were to be

represented at synods by their *procuratores* (see below, Chap. 3 at n. 36). We will see an example of the dean of Toledo serving as a judge (below, Chap. 3 n. 29); but it seems from these texts that the chapter proctors could also serve in this capacity. See Edwards (n. 13 above), pp. 125–26, 146–58, for practices in England.

56. *Cortes de los antiguos reinos de León y de Castilla,* 5 vols. (Madrid, 1861–1903), 1:491: "Alo que nos pidieron merçed que por quanto los perlados e otros sus vicarios e arciprestes se entremeten de conosçer delos pleitos que son de librar de nos e delos nuestros alcaldes, e ponen senten-çia de descomunion contra aquellos que no quieren consentir en ellos." This text is referred to by Joseph O'Callaghan, *A History of Medieval Spain,* (Ithaca, 1975), p. 494. I wish to thank Professor O'Callaghan for discussing the passage with me, and for giving me other valuable references.

57. R. A. Fletcher, *The Episcopate in the Kingdom of León in the Twelfth Century* (Oxford, 1978), p. 155, finds this subordination well established in León in the twelfth century.

58. Minguella, *Historia de Sigüenza* (above, Chap. 1 n. 12), 2:363: "Et quod collatio archipresbyteratuum tantum expectet [i.e., spectet] ad col-lationem domini episcopi Segontini et successorem eiusdem, secundum antiquam consuetudinem ipsius ecclesiae Segontinae; et quod eos [i.e., archipresbyteros] ammoveat cum viderit expedire; et quod [archipresbyteri] sint oboedientes et subditis [*lege* subditi] suis archidiaconis, sicut praeci-piunt canonicae sanctiones."

59. Beltrán, *Bulario* (above, Chap. 1 n. 13), 1:433–52 no. 162. 68, 235–42, 245 (Juan Rodríguez de Medina de Pomar), 335, 339.

60. Ibid., 1:449 no. 162. 282; and see Sánchez Herrero, p. 255: Men-tion is made of the conferral of benefices "per archidiaconos vel eorum vicarios"; and at the end we read: "Nota: Quod archidiaconi Toletanae ecclesiae conferunt beneficia" (this note sounds like a later scribal addition).

61. See below at n. 171.

62. G. Mollat, "La collation de bénéfices ecclésiastiques à l'époque des papes d'Avignon (1305–78)" = Introduction to *Lettres communes de Jean XXII* (n. 14 above), p. 34; Geoffrey Barraclough, *Papal Provisions* (Ox-ford, 1935), p. 10.

63. For the six archdeacons in the year 1310, see Fidel Fita y Colomé, *Actas ineditas de siete concilios españoles celebrados desde el año 1282 hasta el de 1314* (Madrid, 1882), pp. 54–60.

64. Juan Francisco Rivera Recio, *La iglesia de Toledo en el siglo XII (1086–1208),* vol. 1, Publicaciones del Instituto español de historia eclesiástica: Monografías, 10 (Rome, 1966); vol. 2, Publicaciones del In-stituto provincial de investigaciones y estudios toledanos, ser. 1: Monografías, 6 (Toledo, 1976), 1:112, 2:34–39.

65. Ángel González Palencia, *Los mozárabes de Toledo en los siglos XII y XIII*, 4 vols. (Madrid, 1926–30), 4:168. (N.B.: I designate the *volumen preliminar*, published in 1930, as vol. 4. I should note that the indexes and cross-references in this volume are haphazard and incomplete.)

66. Sánchez Herrero, pp. 255–78: schedules of archipresbyteral chanceries grouped by archdeaconry (though such grouping is not explicitly indicated). The schedule for the chancery of the archbishop and the schedule for the chancery of the archdeacons are given on pp. 252–55.

67. Louisa Guadalupe Beraza, *Diezmos de la sede toledana y rentas de la mesa arzobispal (siglo XV)*, Acta salmanticensia: Filosofía y letras, 69 (Salamanca, 1972), pp. 25–27.

68. Briheuga, a vicariate in the fifteenth century (see Guadalupe) is called an archipresbyterate in the 1379 schedule (Sánchez Herrero, p. 275), but probably mistakenly so, since there are earlier references to more than one *vicaria* (see n. 111 below), while only La Puebla is named such in the schedules (p. 264). More specific evidence is given by Balthasar Porreño, *Vida y hechos hazaños del gran cardenal don Gil de Albornoz* (Cuenca, 1626), fols. 33v–34v, who describes a letter dated 19 September 1348 that Archbishop Albornoz sent to the vicar of Briheuga.

69. For Servando, archpriest of Montalbán in A.D. 1230, see González Palencia (n. 65 above), 3:39–40 no. 768. Simeno Cayetano was "toletanus archipresbyter" in 1190 (3:318 no. 978), 1197 (3:552 no. 1126), and 1199 (1:239 no. 298). The head of the Toledo chapter was called "praepositus" in 1189 (1:155 no. 206), 1191 (1:163 no. 215), and 1197 (3:552 no. 1126), but "decanus" in 1193 (1:182 no. 237) and 1194 (1:197–98 no. 255; cf. 3:552 no. 1127), and "prior" in 1230 (3:39–40 no. 768). The usual title in later times came to be "decanus" (4:175). Rivera (n. 64 above), 2:132–36, claims to have found references to four other archpriests of Toledo in the twelfth century, but he does not document three of them, namely Nicolás, Bernardo, and Pedro Micael. Pedro Micael is presumably Pedro de Talavera (see below, Chap. 3 n. 44), who appears as archpriest (without further qualification) in a document of the year 1178 along with an archpriest named Nicolás: see González Palencia (n. 65 above), 1:102 no. 141. Rivera does document the fourth: Domingo ben Abdalá el Polichení, identified in an instrument of A.D. 1179 as "Dominicus Alpollichen, toletanus archipresbyter," who is probably the Toledan archpriest "D." who was quarrelling with the cathedral chapter, as reported to Pope Alexander III (1159–81); but in a related letter the pope seems to identify the archpriest in question as "B." See Rivera, 2:135, notes 56 and 55 respectively. Rivera states that Domingo was archpriest of Toledo from 1164 to 1180 (2.133). For the first date he cites González Palencia, 1:51 no. 73, where however only the signature "Dominicus

archipresbyter" appears. He may not be the same Domingo; for in 1170 Domingo ben Abdalá, whose brother is Nicolás the archpriest, is not himself said to be an archpriest (González Palencia, 1:65–66 no. 91). The documents collected by González Palencia have references to the archpriest Domingo ben Abdalá el Polichení only from circa A.D. 1173 onwards: 1:74 no. 104 (1173?); cf. 1:86 no. 120 (1175); 1:90 no. 126 (1176); 1:96 no. 134 (1177); 1:107 no. 147 (1180). He is first referred to as archdeacon (of Madrid) in 1181 (1:115 no. 157), but is named again as archpriest in 1182 (1:120 no. 163; cf. 3:173 no. 902). There are frequent references to him as archdeacon from 1184 (1:127 no. 171) until 1209, when his testament is mentioned (1:309 no. 369); he is also identified as such (as someone's uncle) in 1219 (2:53 no. 449). In 1191, his name is given as Domingo Alpolichén (4:57 n. 1). None of the references to Domingo as archpriest identify his archipresbyterate. González Palencia says he was an archdeacon from 1181 to 1209, and calls him *archpriest* of Madrid (4:176). This presumably is a mistake on González Palencia's part for *archdeacon* of Madrid; on the same page he refers to "F." and "D.," *archdeacons* in 1178, as the *archpriests* of Calatrava and Cuéllar (in the diocese of Segovia), respectively; but a document of 1178 (1:103 no. 141) identifies F. and D. as *archdeacons* of Calatrava and Cuéllar. (On Toledo's annexation of the diocese of Segovia, see Rivera, 2:39.) González Palencia gives a document of the year 1241 (2:137–38 no. 545) which refers to "don Martín Chofré, arcipreste de la Catedral Santa María," but this means nothing more than that Chofré was an archpriest who was also a member of the cathedral chapter; he signs himself, "Ego M. Gaufredi, canonicus toletanus, archipresbyter de Rodellis."

In short, according to the evidence of the documents given by González Palencia, only Simeno Cayetano is definitely said to be a "Toledan archpriest," and even this may mean nothing more than that he was an archpriest of one of the archipresbyterates of the diocese of Toledo. This is all that can be said of Domingo ben Abdalá el Polichení as an archpriest, before he became archdeacon of Madrid. Angus MacKay, *Spain in the Middle Ages* (London, 1977), p. 45, calls him "archpriest of the cathedral," but does not provide documentation.

70. I am not clear on how the city of Toledo was ruled. Perhaps it was in charge of a vicar appointed by the archdeacon of Toledo, with headquarters in the chancery of the archdeacons; or perhaps it fell to the chancery of the archbishop; or it may be that there was a "city dean" or "dean of Christianity" with archipresbyteral functions, who was not connected to the cathedral or any other specific church (for an example, see n. 90 below). Such an official may have been the successor to the twelfth-century archpriest of Toledo (if there was one). Other possibilities

suggest themselves from the ways in which some of the cathedral cities in England were governed, where the dean of the cathedral chapter was *ex officio* archdeacon of the cathedral city and its suburbs; in most of these churches the dean's authority in this sphere was carried out by the subdean, whether or not the dean was present. See Edwards (n. 13 above), pp. 146–47, 153. In the diocese of Sigüenza, there was an archpriest of Sigüenza who had jurisdiction over part of the city and also over the rural areas surrounding the city, which formed the archipresbyterate of Sigüenza. See below at nn. 148 and 181. On taxation of the clergy of the city and diocese of Toledo, see the document quoted in n. 106 below.

71. Sánchez Herrero, pp. 274–75. For some districts, in contrast to the Hita schedule (where arrest *in speciali* is indicated), no qualification is given to actions of arresting; but in the Almoguera schedule, a distinction is made between arrest *in genere* (for which no fee is to be charged) and arrest *in specie* (p. 278). Cf. the reference in the synod of 1326 to the archpriest's power to arrest persons whose offences were so great that they exceeded their jurisdiction (above at n. 55).

72. Manuel Criado de Val, "La tierra de Hita," in *Arcipreste de Hita* (above, Chap. 1 n. 74), pp. 447–55; and *Historia de Hita y su Arcipreste* (Madrid, 1976), pp. 78–82.

73. Guadalupe (n. 67 above), pp. 135–39, esp. nn. 193–97. On Mohernando as the home of Juan Ruiz's country mouse (stanza 1370), see Joset.

74. García (n. 38 above), p. 274, canon 13 no. 4.

75. *The Register of William Wickwane*, ed. William Brown, Surtees Society 114 (Durham, 1907), pp. 248–49 no. 606 (cf. pp. xi–xii); the relevant text is given by Thompson (n. 4 above), p. 155 n. 2. Of the limitation placed on the entourage of the distributor of tithes for the archdeacons of Toledo and Talavera, see below at n. 105.

76. Thompson (n. 4 above), p. 168 n. 2 and p. 185.

77. William Dansey, *Horae decanicae rurales: An Attempt to Illustrate . . . the Name and Title, the Origin, Appointment, and Functions, Personal and Capitular, of Rural Deans*, ed. 2, 2 vols. (London, 1844), 1:336–37; 2:5–12, 17–25; Paul Hinschius, *System des katholischen Kirchenrechts mit besonderer Rücksicht auf Deutschland*, 6 vols. (Berlin, 1869–97; repr. Graz, 1959), 2:275 n. 6.

78. Fletcher (n. 57 above), p. 157.

79. F. S. Pearson, "Records of a Ruridecanal Court of 1300," *Collectanea*, ed. Sidney Graves Hamilton for the Worcestershire Historical Society (London, 1912), pp. 69–80. The roll, given as the frontispiece, is transcribed on pp. 73–80; it is discussed by Pearson on pp. 70–72 and by Hamilton on p. iii.

80. Ibid., p. 74. The man confessed and was ordered to be whipped.

81. Ibid., p. 80: The record of the acts is brief, and reads in full as

follows: "Cum constaret nobis [i.e., the archdeacon?] per certificatorium decani de Wych omnes rectores et vicarios totius archidiaconatus ad dictos diem et locum super inquisitione tam de Hadesor quam etiam Oddingel vacatione et articulis consuetis faciendis, legitime omnibus et singulis vocatis et expectatis, infrascripti continuatim contraxerunt: rector ecclesiae de Doderhull; vicarius eiusdem; rector de Salwarp; rector de Opton; rector de Stok" (that is, these five priests formed a committee to complete the business).

82. Iohannes de Athon (= Acton), *In constitutiones legitimas Angliae glossemata*, commenting on the *Constitutions* of the papal legate Cardinal Otto of Tonengo, no. 6: *Quod in quodam concilio*, ad v. *erubescunt*: "Talis decanus saltem de consuetudine vice archidiaconi iurisdictionem habet cognitionalem quoad effectum corrigendi": p. 15 of the edition of the *Glossemata* and the *Constitutiones legatinae* of Otto and of Ottobono Fieschi published at Oxford in 1679 along with William Lyndwood's *Provinciale* (repr. Farnborough, Hants., 1968). Otto was legate to England from 1237 to 1241, and Cardinal Fieschi from 1265 to 1268. On Lyndwood, who completed his commentary on English ecclesiastical statutes in 1430, see C. R. Cheney, "William Lyndwood's *Provinciale*," *The Jurist* 21 (1961): 405–34, reprinted in Cheney's *Medieval Texts and Studies* (Oxford, 1973), pp. 158–84.

83. Lyndwood (see previous note), *Provinciale* 5. 17. 4: *Item contra gravamina*, ad v. *apparitores seu bedelli archidiaconorum vel decanorum* (p. 352): "sive [decanorum] ecclesiarum cathedralium sive ruralium; nam et decani rurales in quibusdam partibus habent iurisdictionem et apparitores sive bedellos sibi intendentes."

84. Dansey (n. 77 above), 2:73, 110–11; Jean Scammell, "The Rural Chapter in England from the Eleventh to the Fourteenth Century," *English Historical Review* 88 (1971): 1–21. Scammell does not make the distinction between deanery-wide and archdeaconry-wide chapters. She points out on p. 15 that Chaucer is quite accurate in using "chapter" and "court" interchangeably to designate the place where charges were tried. See also G. R. Owst, *Literature and Pulpit in Medieval England*, 2d ed. (Oxford, 1961), p. 282.

85. Acton (n. 82 above) on the *Constitutions* of Otto, no. 23: *Cum non solum*, ad v. *decani* (p. 59); Lyndwood, *Provinciale* 2. 1. 1: *In causis* (pp. 79–81).

86. Scammell, p. 11.

87. Chaucer, *Friar's Tale* 1317–18.

88. See Michael M. Sheehan, "The Formation and Stability of Marriage in Fourteenth-Century England: Evidence of an Ely Register," *Mediaeval Studies* 33 (1971): 228–63, esp. 232–33.

89. Acton (n. 82 above) on the *Constitutions* of Otto, no. 26: *Tanto calliditatis*, ad v. *rescribere* (p. 65); Lyndwood, *Provinciale* 2. 1. 2: *Quidam ruralium*, ad v. *decani rurales* (p. 81).

90. Lyndwood, *Provinciale* 3. 22. 7: *Cum apparitorum*, ad v. *dumtaxat* (pp. 225–26): "Et sic quantum est ad episcopum, intelligi potest quod hic dicitur ut viz. ipsi decani sint eius apparitores." In the 1431 trial of Joan of Arc in Rouen, the summoner was the "rural archpriest of the city," that is, the dean of Christianity; see Pierre Tisset, *Procès de condamnation de Jeanne d'Arc*, 3 vols. (Paris, 1960–71), 1:22.

91. *Ludus Coventriae; or, The Plaie Called Corpus Christi*, ed. K. S. Block, Early English Text Society, extra series, vol. 120 (London, 1922), pp. 123–31; R. T. Davies, *The Corpus Christi Play of the English Middle Ages* (London, 1972), pp. 147–56 and 451–52 (n. 32). Neither of these editors understand the meaning of "den." See the facsimile edition, *The N-Town Plays*, ed. Peter Meredith and Stanley J. Kahrl (Leeds, 1977), fols. 74–81v.

92. Pecham, constitution *Quia incontinentiae*, Powicke and Cheney (above, Chap. 1 n. 43), 2:837, given by Lyndwood in *Provinciale* 1. 2. 1 (pp. 10–16); see his comment on the word *decanus* (p. 15).

93. See especially Scammell (n. 84 above), p. 2.

94. See Edmund Hobhouse, *Calendar of the Register of John de Drokensford, Bishop of Bath and Wells (A.D. 1309–29)*, Somerset Record Society, vol. 1 (London, 1887), p. 236: In 1328 reference is made to the "laudable and immemorial custom of Bath Archdeaconry" of the clergy electing the dean in each deanery every year, and one such election, in 1319, is recalled. Bishop Hobhouse seems to assume that the same procedure was followed also in the deaneries of the other two archdeaconries (see p. xix). In the fifteenth century rural deans throughout the diocese were *appointed* for a year at a time. The candidates were recommended by the archdeacon's official and approved by the bishop's official. See Robert W. Dunning, "Rural Deans in England in the Fifteenth Century," *Bulletin of the Institute of Historical Research* 40 (1967): 207–13. Lyndwood appears to take it for granted that all rural deans in England have one-year terms. See *Provinciale* 2. 1. 2: *Quidam ruralium*, ad v. *omni anno* (p. 85): "Quolibet anno mutantur decani et fiunt novi."

95. Dansey, 1:151 n. 1, citing an excerpt from the register of Bishop Droxford (Drokensford): "MCCCXXV. 13 Kal. Oct., Joh. de Roulesham ad officium archipresbyteratus in ecclesia de Pokyngton secundum formam ordinationis dicti archipresbyteratus qui penes d'num remanet ad present. d'nae Aliciae de Knovil dictae ecclesiae et archipresbyteratus patronae." Hobhouse, *Calendar*, p. 248, summarizes the action thus: "John de Roulesham admitted to office of Archpresbyter in Puckington Church in the settled form of Installing. Patron of the Church and Archpriestship,

Alice de Knovill. Yatton, 12 Kal. Oct. Ind. Archd. Taunt." (that is, the Archdeacon of Taunton was to induct him.) Cf. also p. 49: In March, 1312, the archipresbyter John de Taleford was to induct a chaplain in the church of Puckington. The patron at this time is said to be Sir Gilbert de Knovill (i.e., Knowle), though, as Hobhouse points out, he must have been dead at this time, since the chaplaincies seem to have been established (endowed) under the terms of his will, after his death, in 1300 or 1301. In an entry of 1324 (p. 223), Lady Alice is said to be patron "on this occasion" (*hac vice*); but she may well have been "acting patron" from the beginning. This secular college of Puckington escaped the notice of David Knowles and R. Neville Hadcock, *Medieval Religious Houses: England and Wales*, 2d ed. (London, 1971).

96. Dansey (n. 77 above), 1:149–50. Thompson (n. 4 above), p. 190, speaks of the office of rural dean in the diocese of Norwich as "a freehold benefice which, freed from the responsibility of the cure of souls, was subject to the ordinary vicissitudes of vacancy by death, resignation, or exchange."

97. García (n. 38 above), p. 276, canon 21 no. 4; approved, p. 278.

98. Sánchez Herrero (n. 52 above), pp. 248–49: "At quod displicenter referimus, tam in habita pridem per nos visitatione quam in synodali etiam nuper congregatione strepentibus querelis, luculenter agnovimus tantam invaluisse archidiaconorum et archipresbyterorum quorundam et eorum loca tenentium ambitionis inordinatam licentiam, quod ultra fas et iustum ac antiquae consuetudinis institutum cancellariis suis adiectitiis exactionibus cumulatur; in tantum modestiae terminos excedebant quod triplum fere eius quod cancellariae nostrae litera solvebat ipsi, [in] animarum suarum periculum et contra caritatis vinculum, in multorum iacturam et dispendium, extorquebant."

99. Ibid., p. 279. Archpriests were also able to issue their own citatory letters (p. 247).

100. Ibid., p. 252; see nn. 54, 98 above. Below at n. 118 I discuss a letter addressed to "los arçiprestes, vicarios, o sus logares tenientes."

101. Ibid., p. 244.

102. Ibid., p. 245.

103. Cf. *Clementine Constitutions* 5. 11. 2: *Saepe* (Friedberg, 2:1200): "simpliciter et de plano ac sine strepitu et figura iudicii." In the synod of 1347, Archbishop Albornoz speaks of the *summaria cognitio* of persons accused of injuring or seizing ecclesiastics: Sánchez Herrero, pp. 211–12.

104. Sánchez Herrero, pp. 245–48.

105. Sánchez Herrero, p. 179. I do not understand the passage, "praesente nostro homine, vel habentis partem nostram post lapsum diei

assignandi capitulo admittendum, si voluerit, nuntium," which does not seem to make grammatical sense.

106. Sánchez Herrero, pp. 207–8: "Synodo approbante, archidiaconis ecclesiae nostrae, et archipresbyteris, et quibusvis aliis districte inhibemus ne exactiones sive tallias ab eisdem presbyteris et clericis civitatis et dioecesis toletanae vel ab aliquo eorum quovis modo sine licentia nostra exigant vel recipiant. Quod si quisquam presbyterorum aut clericorum eorum praetextu aliquid eis exsolverit, poenam quadrupli nobis et successoribus nostris applicandam irremissibiliter incurrat."

107. Ibid., p. 208: "Et nihilominus archipresbyteri et vicarii, qui ad hoc assensum praebuerint, fructibus omnium beneficiorum qui in civitate et dioecesi toletana obtinuerint illo anno eo ipso noverint se privatos, quorum medietas ecclesiis in quibus illa beneficia obtinent, alia vero medietas mensae nostrae applicetur."

108. Ibid.: "Si tamen archipresbyteros et clericos veniendo ad synodum vel alias pro utilitate communi expensas aliquis [*lege* aliquas] facere contigerit, volumus quod tales expensae non per eos sed per nos et successores nostros vel deputandos a nobis vel ab eis taxentur, et tunc colligantur, et non antea."

109. Ibid., p. 218. Bishop Giraldo in the synod of Segovia in 1216–17 stipulated that archpriests as well as archdeacons were to share in the *cathedraticum* (Garcia [n. 38 above], p. 276, canon 21 no. 2), but this provision was rejected by the arbiters (p. 278); only the bishop, according to written law (they said), was to receive a *cathedraticum* consisting of two *solidi*; archdeacons and archpriests were to receive nothing (p. 271, nos. 4–5).

110. Sánchez Herrero, pp. 183–84.

111. Ibid., pp. 197–98: "Statuimus quod synodus secunda dominica post festum Resurrectionis dominicae, videlicet quando legitur evangelium *Ego sum pastor bonus*, singulis annis apud Toletum celebretur, nisi aliter per nostras literas duxerimus ordinandum; ad quam diem omnes archipresbyteri et vicarii nostrae dioecesis, et de quolibet archipresbyteratu et vicaria duo clerici, de statu suorum archipresbyteratuum et vicariarum ac ecclesiarum informati, venire teneantur, et non vocati, et constitutiones provinciales et synodales afferre secum non postponant, ac synodo intersint superpelliciis induti. Non venientes autem [vel] de synodo sine speciali archiepiscopi vel eius locum tenentis licentia ante finem synodi recedentes tanquam inoboedientes ad eius arbitrium puniantur."

112. Sánchez Herrero, p. 218: "Ceterum cum in dicta constitutione contineatur quod omnes archipresbyteri et vicarii nostrae dioecesis, et de quolibet archipresbyteratu et vicaria duo clerici, de statu suorum archipresbyteratuum et vicariarum informati, venire teneantur, volumus

quod isti habeant procuratoria sufficientia a clericis suorum archipresbyteratuum et vicariarum ad tractandum, ordinandum, et conceden-
dum omnia et singula quae in synodo tractanda, concedenda fuerint, seu
etiam ordinanda." It is possible that he means that the archpriests and
vicars as well as the other clerics are to be so empowered; but it was
no doubt assumed that their official rank conveyed with it sufficient powers.
For the other clerics who were to attend the synod, see below, Chap.
3 at n. 36.

113. Sánchez Herrero, p. 218.

114. See below, Chap. 3 at n. 70.

115. Sánchez Herrero, pp. 298–99 (the text reads *archipresbyteratus*,
but the plural is clearly called for).

116. Fita (n. 63 above), pp. 59–60. Similar responses were received
from the archipresbyterates of Uceda and Buitrago on July 1 and July
23, respectively. These documents in the Archivo Histórico Nacional
are now gathered in the section *Ordenes militares*, carpeta no. 567, as
was discovered for me by Teofilo F. Ruiz at the intercession of Elizabeth
A. R. Brown (to both of whom I express my gratitude). This collection
of thirty documents dealing with the Templars is largely (but not entirely) treated by Fita, and it includes the two reports he mentions from
the archdeaconry of Calatrava, dated July 1 and July 6, but not, unfortunately, that of the archdeaconry of Talavera, dated July 16 (which if
found could perhaps tell us if there was an archpriest of Talavera in the
early part of the century; see below, Chap. 3 n. 44). Fita's work and
material he drew upon have not been utilized by historians of the Templars.
See, for example, Malcolm Barber, *The Trial of the Templars* (Cambridge,
1978), who gives just a short paragraph on Castile–León and Portugal
(p. 273). Fita says that the Archivo possessed other documents dealing
with the Templars which he had not yet studied and which were still
unregistered. They had been taken from the archiepiscopal archive at
Toledo and put into a seperate series in the Archivo under the title *Sec-
ción de diplomas: Templarios, procedencia de Toledo* (p. 26). But Professor
Ruiz was unable to locate them.

117. Fita, pp. 26–46.

118. Sánchez Herrero, p. 215. Sánchez calendars the document here
as a synodal constitution, but elsewhere (p. 50) admits that it is not. I
agree. Unlike the synodal constitutions of the time, this letter is in Spanish,
and it does not refer to a synod. Furthermore, it is dated June 24, which
was Friday of the eighth week after Easter (the week after Trinity Sunday), long after the standard time for the annual synod.

119. Ibid., p. 215. The text is obscure at this point: "Mandamos a
vos los dichos arçiprestes e vicarios o sus lugares tenientes do acaesçiere

sentençia de excomunion que lo fagades asi guardar cada uno en su arçi-
prestadgo o vicaria do sus constituçiones [some illegible words follow]
por sentençia de sancta iglesia de los rebelles contradictores. Et si por
esta rason los han tomado alguna cosa a todos o algunos dellos sus com-
paññeros o renteros o otros quales quier, mandamos vos que los apremiedes
que los tornen en guisa que los non menguen ende alguna cosa."
    120. Ibid.: "E mandamos que cumplades esta nuestra carta e guardedes
lo que en ella se contiene, segun que guardastes los usos e las costumbres
en tiempo de los otros arçobispos nuestros anteçesores."
    121. Ibid., p. 189 (cf. p. 89).
    122. Juan Tejada y Ramiro, *Colección de canones y de todos los concilios
de la iglesia española, traducida al castellano*, vol. 3 (Madrid, 1851), pp.
324–29, esp. pp. 325–26: "Item establecemos et mandamos . . . que los
deanes de las iglesias en sos cabildos, et los arcedianos et los arciprestes
en sus oficios diligientemiente demanden, et trabaien, se fallaran a tales
concubinarios despues que fue fecha la denunciación en el synodo, et
luego denúncienlos nombradamente por suspensos de oficio et de
beneficio, et fáganlo saber al obispo." For Torres, see above at n. 29.
For Halgrin, see Edwin B. Place, review of Mario Penna, ed., *Arcipreste
de Talavera* (1955) in *Speculum* 31 (1956): 396–99.
    123. Mansi, *Sacra concilia*, 25:695–724, esp. 702.
    124. Tejada, 3:610–19, esp. 615. Another text, faultily edited, of the
constitution can be found in Luis Suárez Fernández, *Castilla, el cisma,
y la crisis conciliar (1378-1440)* (Madrid, 1960), pp. 172–79.
    125. Sánchez Herrero, pp. 304–5, synod of 1480. On the parishioners
of the archpriests, see below at n. 137.
    126. Sánchez Herrero, pp. 307, 323–24.
    127. Ibid., p. 318; cf. p. 126.
    128. Vasco Ramírez de Rivera was the last owner of many canonical
works earlier owned by the brothers Diego and Vasco Ramírez de Guzmán: Diego was canon of Toledo and died in 1415, and Vasco was archdeacon of Toledo and died ca. 1439. Juan Ruiz, secretary of the cathedral
chapter in 1491, mistakenly attributed the donation of the books to the
"archdeacons Diego and Vasco Ramírez de Guzmán." See Antonio García y García, "Candalabrum iuris," *Revue de droit canonique* 28. 2–4 (1978):
167–79, esp. 169–70, as informed by Ramón Gonzálvez; this corrects
the account in their *Catálogo* (above, Chap. 1 n. 47).
    129. Sánchez Herrero, pp. 330, 336, 337.
    130. Ibid., p. 341.
    131. Sánchez Herrero (p. 339) classifies the meeting as a congregation
of parish priests, but it looks like an ordinary synod to me.
    132. Sánchez Herrero, p. 342.

133. Ibid., p. 346.

134. Tejada (n. 122 above), 3:326: "Item establecemos que los obispos, et los deanes, los arcedianos, et los arceprestes fagan todas estas cosas bien guardar, poniendo pena contra los que lo non fecieren; et si los deanes, los arcedianos, et los arceprestes fueren en esto negligentes, castiguelos el obispo."

135. Sánchez Herrero, pp. 326–27: "Todos los suso dichos en las dichas cibdades, villas, e logares, e sus arciprestes, los quales fueron nombrados et diputados en la dicha santa sinodo como personas en quien concurren las calidades de honestidad e suficiencia e buena fama que los derechos requieren e nuestra humana fragilidad nos da a conocer, de los quales, los que estan presentes, juraron en forma. . . ." (It could be, however, that this commendation is directed not only at the three archpriests, but at all of the appointed *testes*.)

136. Ibid., pp. 326–27.

137. Above at n. 125.

138. Sánchez Herrero, p. 304.

139. The document containing this reference has been variously described and partially quoted by Manuel Criado de Val in three publications: A) *Teoría de Castilla la Nueva*, 2d ed. (Madrid, 1969), p. 155; B) "El Cardenal Albornoz y el Arcipreste de Hita," in *Cardenal Albornoz y el Colegio de España* (above, Chap. 1 n. 80), 1:91–97 (1972) on p. 95; and C) *Historia de Hita* (n. 72 above), p. 91 (1976). He does not say what archive he is dealing with when he speaks of "significativo testimonio" found "en el Catastro del Marqués de la Ensenada, en la declaración del municipio del Trijueque" (A); that is, it is contained in "la declaración del Ayuntamiento de Trijueque," which is in turn to be found "en el Catastro, ordenado por el marqués de la Ensenada hacia el año 1751," and it deals with "la relación de cargas principales que seguían en vigor en la fecha de la declaración" (B); finally, it is "unas mandas 'inmemoriales,' que había encontrado reseñadas en el catastro correspondiente a Trijueque, ordenado por Ensenada, y que se mantenían todavía vigentes en el año 1751, 'del Arzobispo Don Gil al Arcipreste de Santa María de la villa de Hita' " (C). The text that Criado gives of the pertinent part of the Trijueque declaration is as follows in A (the significant variant in B that I note is presumably erroneous, rather than the other way round):

Primicia en virtud de gracia concedida al Monasterio de Sopetrán por Don Gil de Albornoz, Arzobispo de Toledo, y confirmada por el Sumo Pontífice que en la ocasión gobernaba la Silla Apostólica: El Arcipreste de Santa María de la Villa de Hita percibe de este Pontifical dos fanegas de trigo y otras dos de cebada y cinco reales por la venta de corderos por la conducción de los Santos Oleos. —Y del [B: de] Pontifical de dicha villa de Hita percibe por otro inmemorial veinte y cuatro fanegas de trigo y otras veinte y cuatro de cebada.

Criado adds: "La parte correspondiente al monasterio de Sopetrán, dice la declaración, 'corresponde al senor Arzobispo de Toledo,' pero no se sabe el título por que la percibe" (A; cf. B: "por el que la percibe").

The *pontifical* is the *tertia pontificalis* or bishop's third; see, for example, Minguella (n. 58 above), 2:376 no. 6. The original meaning of the provision may have been (if in fact it does reflect a grant by Albornoz) that the archpriest of Hita was to receive the stipulated fee *from* the church of Santa María of Hita for delivering the holy oils; we saw above at n. 133 that Cardinal Ximénez objected against this sort of fee, but perhaps it was condoned in Albornoz's time.

I should note that on p. 152 n. 1 of *Teoría* Criado cites the *Soledad laureada* of Gregorio de Argáiz (1675), vol. 1, Chap. 134, to the effect that on September 1, "year of 1372," the "Arcipreste de la Villa de Hita" gave the Benedictines possession of the church and sanctuary of Our Lady of Sopetrán.

140. Rivera, *Iglesia* (n. 64 above), 1:101.

141. See n. 7 above.

142. Vicente Beltrán de Heredia, *Cartulario de la Universidad de Salamanca (1218–1600)*, 6 vols., Acta salmanticensia: Historia de la Universidad, vols. 17, 19–20, 22–24 (Salamanca, 1970–72) 1:633–34 no. 52. The archbishop authorizes the bishop of Salamanca to proceed against the council of the town of Alba, the archpriest of the said town, and all the clergy, parishioners, collectors, tertiaries, and majordomos responsible for refusing to collect for the University of Salamanca a third of the tithes of the churches existing within the archipresbyterate.

143. John XXII, *Lettres communes* (n. 14 above), no. 22722, letter of 1 July 1325 (cf. nos. 1561, 3603, 13531, 18921). He is required to give up his expectative grace to a dignity in Albi.

144. For French practices, see Thompson (n. 4 above), p. 172 n. 1; John XXII, *Lettres communes* nos. 4593, 7584, 47749, 48115, etc. For Bergamo, see ibid., no. 57364. The prior of the secular church of Santa María de Daroca had authority to confer benefices both with and without cure of souls (John XXII, no. 25621, A.D. 1326), and we hear of a canonry in the church as early as 1316 (no. 2360). It is puzzling, then, when the priorate is conferred by the pope on Cardinal Pedro Gómez in 1328, to find the church described as noncollegiate: "collatio prioratus saecularis ecclesiae non collegiatae Sanctae Mariae de Darocha, Caesaraugustan.

dioces." (no. 41877). We might think that *non* is a mistake for *necnon*; but in 1338 we hear of the priorate of a *saecularis non collegiata ecclesia* in the diocese of Rodez: Benedict XII, *Lettres communes*, digested by J. M. Vidal, 3 vols. (Paris, 1902–11), no. 5430; and in 1431 the papal chancery distinguished between collegiate churches and lesser churches ruled by deans and possessing chapters; see n. 172 below.

145. John XXII, no. 57703. Raymond is provided with a canonry in the church of Laon in spite of holding the archipresbyterate of Daroca and a canonry and prebend in the church of Toulouse. He has clearly relinquished the canonry and prebend in Toledo, but is still a canon of Albi and Lavaur and still has higher expectations in both chapters.

146. Ibid., nos. 54587, 55282, 55515.

147. Ibid., nos. 27313, 50638. On the question of the ordinary collator of archipresbyterates, see above at n. 58.

148. Minguella (n. 58 above), 1:511–15 no. 149 (1207); 2:374–76 no. 5 (1302); 2:399–400 no. 25 (1309); 2:440–41 no. 48 (1317). One of the clerics of Santiago named in the 1309 document is Johan Rodriguez.

149. Ibid., 2:430–32 no. 42 (1315); 2:441–48 no. 49 (1318). In the survey of church income commissioned by the king of Castile in 1353, the archpriest of Sigüenza is identified as Diego Abbat, canon of Sigüenza (2:318). But we hear at the same time of Diego Abbat, canon of Sigüenza and archpriest of Medina, that is, Medinaceli (2:324). Perhaps it is another person of the same name, or a mistake for Domingo Abbat, a canon of Sigüenza named elsewhere: 2:504–6 no. 80 (1332); 2:518–20 nos. 88–89 (1337) 2:537–40 no. 103 (1348); cf. 2:548–51 no. 110 (1354) naming the portioner Juan Martínez de Domingo Abbat. The archpriest of Sigüenza is the only one of the archpriests who is mentioned at the beginning of the report as having been given a date for assembling all the clergy of his archipresbyterate for establishing the value of the benefices contained in it; but here he is referred to as the "said Abbat": "amonestamos a dicho abbat arcipreste de siguença" (2:316). *Dicho* must be a mistake for *diego* or *domingo*, for the archpriest is not mentioned previously. There is mentioned only "don diego Abbat de sant fagund" (2:315), that is, Didacus Alberti, abbot since 1329 of the Benedictine monastery of Sahagún in León (John XXII, no. 46822); but he is one of the commissioners of the king who ordered the report. The report lists the two parochial churches of Santiago and San Vicente as having only *beneficiados servideros* (2:318); on this point see below at n. 180. Minguella is puzzled by the status of the two churches: "Está muy obscura la parroquialidad de Santiago y San Vicente y hasta la diversidad de una y otra." He notes that some documents of the fifteenth century are signed by the curate (*cura*) of Santiago, whereas in 1315 there is mentioned only the archpriest and

clerics of the two churches (3:574; cf. 2:13–14). Minguella does not mention the document of 1318 identifying the archpriest as the archpriest of Sigüenza.

150. *Extravagants of John XXII* 3. 1: *Execrabilis* (Friedberg, 2:1207–9).

151. *Decretals of Gregory IX* 3. 5. 28: *De multa* (Friedberg, 2:477–78).

152. Hostiensis, *Commentaria* (n. 11 above) to *De multa*, ad v. *curam habens animarum* (3:23 no. 2): "Qualitercumque; hic enim verba haec generaliter intelliguntur: sive in foro poenitentiali curam animarum habeat sive alias; sive sit ecclesia cathedralis sive parochialis, sive capella habens parochianos et curam eorum de iure vel de facto, dummodo parochiam habeat in qua ius parochiale exerceat . . .; sive sit dignitas vel officium sine ecclesia, sicut sunt multi archidiaconi, decani, et archipresbyteri [qui] nullam habent specialem ecclesiam cui praesint – habent tamen iurisdictionem super multa loca."

153. *Execrabilis* (n. 150 above), col. 1209: "Illa duntaxat, et non alia, beneficia ecclesiastica, quocumque nomine nuncupentur, curam animarum habere censemus quae parochias habent in quibus est animarum cura, non per vicarios perpetuos, sed per rectores aut ministros beneficiorum ipsorum, vel illorum temporales vicarios, exercenda; necnon et illa quorum ministris ratione beneficiorum huiusmodi competit visitare, inquirere, procurationes recipere, suspendere, excommunicare, seu ab excommunicationis et suspensionis sententiis absolvere de consuetudine vel de iure."

154. John XXII, letter of 8 October (1318?), ed. Auguste Coulon, *Lettres secrètes et curiales du Pape Jean XXII (1316–1334) relatives à la France*, vol. 1 (Paris, 1900), pp. 628–29 no. 732. Cf. Mollat (n. 62 above), p. 27.

155. John XXII, *Lettres communes* no. 28925 (10 June 1327).

156. Ibid., nos. 17502, 27772, 50980, 60776.

157. Jesselin de Cassagnes, *Ordinary Gloss* (see above, Chap. 1, n. 1) to *Execrabilis*, ad v. *curam animarum* (col. 26). See Jacqueline Tarrant, "The Life and Works of Jesselin de Cassagnes," *Bulletin of Medieval Canon Law* 9 (1979): 37–64, esp. 56.

158. John XXII, no. 51498.

159. Ibid., no. 48125 (15 January 1330).

160. The letters digested in *Lettres communes* are numbered to 64,421, but not all are common letters (and some are by the antipope Nicholas V); and through a fault of counting, 30999 is followed by 40000 (omitting 31000–39999).

161. Above, n. 144.

162. John XXII, *Lettres communes* no. 26186; cf. no. 19031. This Alfonso Fernández is not to be confused with the Alfonso Fernández who was the illegitimate grandson of the Infante Juan, and likewise a canon of Zamora (ibid., nos. 11913–15; cf. 41233, 60704).

163. See Barraclough (n. 62 above), pp. 27–30.

164. Sáez and Trenchs, *Diplomatario* (n. 16 above), pp. 27–28 no. 28: "Canonicatum et praebendam . . . providemus . . . non obstantibus . . . quod in toletana quandam portionem et in caesaraugustana quandam capellaniam perpetuas, et in de Fluentlenzina quoddam beneficium ecclesiasticum 'servitorium' vulgariter nuncupatum, et in Alvalat ac de Laguardia ecclesiis quasdam praestimoniales portiones, et ruralem archipresbyteratum de Corita toletanae dioecesis nosceris obtinere."

165. Ibid., p. 169 no. 184 and pp. 197–98 no. 213.

166. Beltrán, *Bulario* (above, Chap. 1, n. 13), 1:406 no. 125.20.

167. Berte M. Marti, "1372: The Spanish College Versus the Executors of Cardinal Albornoz's Testament," in *Cardenal Albornoz y el Colegio de España* (above, Chap. 1 n. 80), 2:93–129, esp. 105.

168. Berte M. Marti, *The Spanish College at Bologna in the Fourteenth Century* (Philadelphia, 1966), pp. 342–44.

169. Ibid., pp. 93–94.

170. See above at n. 59.

171. Emil von Ottenthal, *Regulae cancellariae apostolicae: Die päpstliche Kanzleiregeln von Johannes XXII bis Nicholas V* (Innsbruck, 1888; repr. Aalen, 1968), p. 94 no. 22; p. 97 no. 34.

172. Ibid., p. 106 no. 64. In 1431 the chancery of Eugene IV ordered that in ultramontane regions where there are rectors who preside over chapters and have cures of them, apart from deans of cathedrals and heads of collegiate churches, such nonmajor dignities are to be given only to graduates. See ibid., p. 241 no. 10.

173. Ibid., p. 107 no. 67.

174. See Jesselin de Cassagnes, loc cit. (n. 157 above) ad v. *dignitates*. He first refers to another authority who attempted to make distinctions, and then he says: "Vel dic quod ista discernuntur ex institutione vel consuetudine cuiuslibet ecclesiae, nam dignitas in una aliquando in alia est personatus, vel officium; and he refers to Hostiensis's commentary on *De multa* (cf. n. 152 above). See also Edwards (n. 13 above), p. 135 n. 1.

175. García (n. 38 above), pp. 274–75, canon 13 nos. 2 and 7.

176. Minguella (n. 58 above), 2:315–56. The destination of the rent is made clear in the case of Atienza: "E primerament el arciprestadgo de Atienza vale al arcipreste seyscientos mrs., la decima xl mrs." (p. 347).

177. See above at nn. 109, 97, and 44, respectively.

178. *Common Extravagants* 10.1: *Vas electionis Paulus* (Friedberg, 2:1280–84).

179. Sánchez Herrero, p. 232.

180. See above at n. 73.

181. See n. 149 above.

182. See Barraclough (n. 62 above), p. 44.

183. Ibid., pp. 121–25.

184. Criado de Val, *Historia de Hita* (n. 72 above), p. 93. For the statement of Sáez and Trenchs, see below at n. 190.

185. On this point, see Mollat (n. 62 above), p. 25

186. Sáez and Trenchs, *Diplomatario* (n. 16 above), pp. 543–44.

187. Beltrán, *Bulario* (above, Chap. 1 n. 13), 1:483–89 no. 211. See n. 16 above.

188. Emilio Sáez and José Trenchs, "Juan Ruiz de Cisneros (1295/96–1351/52): Autor del *Buen amor*," in *Arcipreste de Hita* (above, Chap. 1 n. 74), pp. 365–68. The date "1351/52" in their title is presumably a mistake for "1353," for they are able to trace Cisneros to 1353, as will appear below.

189. Ibid., p. 367: "En la documentación pontificia no se hallan referencias a este cargo eclesiástico; y ello es lógico, puesto que se trata de un oficio de provisión episcopal."

190. Ibid., p. 367.

191. Sáez and Trenchs, *Diplomatario*, pp. 130–32 nos. 141–42. According to the first letter, Pedro has attained his thirteenth year; in the second letter, he is said to be in his thirteenth year. Criado (n. 184 above) makes Pedro eighteen years old.

192. Sáez and Trenchs, *Diplomatario*, pp. 155–56 no. 168.

193. Ibid., pp. 220–21 no. 238.

194. Ibid., nos. 238–45, 249, 269–70, 435–36.

195. Criado, *Historia*, p. 93. See Sáez and Trenchs, art. cit., p. 367: "No hay que confundir al arcipreste de Hita con el mayordomo o administrador de los bienes de don Gil en España y también en Hita, cargo que ostentaba Pedro Fernández, que aparece como tal en un documento de don Gil conservado en Osma."

196. The letter is faultily transcribed by Juan Loperráez Corvalán, *Descripción histórica del obispado de Osma*, 3 vols. (Madrid, 1788–90; repr. Madrid, 1978), 3:262 no. 107: "Nobitque [*lege* Noveritis quod] Petrus Ferrandi Archipresbyter, et Majordomus noster in Archipresbyteratu de Fita, emit de pecunia nostra, et pro nobis, quandam domum quae vulgariter vocatur la Casa de Heras."

197. Ibid., 3:261–62 no. 106. *Onera* is my conjectural emendation of Loperráez's reading, *Osna*. Here is part of the text: "Ceterorum [*lege* Ceterum] Archipresbiterorum [*lege* Archipresbytero] de Fita, vel ejus locum tenenti tenore praesentium conmitimus, et mandamus, quas [*lege* quod] Sacristam, vel procuratorem ipsius incorporalem [*lege* in corporalem] posesionem dictarum praestimonialium porcionum . . . inducat." Lucius Gaston

Moffat, "The Evidence of Early Mentions of the Archpriest of Hita or of His Work," *Modern Language Notes* 75 (1960): 33–44, esp. 36, is mistaken in interpreting the *locum tenens* of the archpriest to signify someone "acting" in the office during a vacancy; it refers rather to the archpriest's vicar. See above at n. 118.

198. See the Appendix below, nos. 1, 4, and 8.

199. John XXII, *Lettres communes* no. 45657, letter of 8 July 1329. See Appendix, no. 1.

200. Minguella (n. 58 above), 2:507 no. 82, document of 28 March 1334, referring to "casas de Don Johan Rodriguez arcidiano de Siguença." Cf. 2:504–6 no. 80, document of 30 June 1332, where Johan Rodriguez signs as archdeacon of Sigüenza. Another witness who does not know how to write has his name signed by Johan Royz. Another witness signs as Johannes Roderici.

201. Ibid., 2:510–12 no. 84. Simón appears as dean as early as 1 March 1327 (John XXII, nos. 28045, 28048).

202. Minguella, 2:529–30 no. 96. This document mentions the *racionero* or portioner of Sigüenza John Royz (of Medinaceli), notary public, who appears elsewhere in the records; see 2:48; 2:537–40 no. 103 (1348).

203. See Minguella, 2:47–48. The vicar of Archbishop Albornoz on 18 June 1342 referred to "Don Simón de Rodrigo, Arcediano," and other members of the church of Sigüenza, according to a document cited by Mariano Juárez. Simón is still archdeacon of Sigüenza in 1348 (2:537 no. 103). In 1354 we hear of Simón Royz, canon of Sigüenza (2:548–51 no. 110), and again in 1356 (2:555–56 no. 113).

204. Sáez and Trenchs, art. cit., p. 367.

205. Sáez and Trenchs, *Diplomatario*, pp. 329–31 nos. 357–58.

206. Ibid., pp. 332–35 nos. 360–61.

207. Ibid., pp. 412–14 nos. 441–43.

208. Ibid., pp. 414–15 no. 444.

209. I should note that the archpriests' income from the archipresbyterates of the diocese of Sigüenza in 1353 (see n. 176 above) far exceeded the set income for archdeacons established in 1301, that is 150 maravedís, when they were also told that they were not entitled to any tithes or "retithes" from the bishop or chapter (Minguella, 2:363, 365). The archpriest of Sigüenza, for instance, received 300m., with tithes of 20m. (ibid., 2:318). The income from other archipresbyterates ranged from 180m. to 1000m. But archdeacons must have had supplemental income, even apart from other benefices that they might have held. We find indications of such in the 1353 census; e.g., "las fanegas del arciprestadgo [de Caracena] del arcediano de Siguença" amount to 72m. (2:323), and "el prestamo de las fanegas del arcediano de Siguença" from the archi-

presbyterate of Ayllón come to 270m. (2:330). We must remember too that Simón Rodríguez de Cisneros exchanged the deanship (given an income of 300m. in 1301) for the archidiaconate of Sigüenza.

210. Above at n. 45.

211. Below, Chap. 3 at n. 15.

Notes to Chapter Three

The Archpriest at Talavera

1. Beltrán, *Cartulario* (above, Chap. 2 n. 142), 1:551–80. Beltrán corrects many misconceptions that have been harbored about Martínez de Toledo. For instance, he absolves him of the charges of immorality (and *a fortiori* concubinage) and neglect of duty, and shows that there is no reason for believing that he was ever archdeacon of Toledo. For documents concerning him, see the Index of Beltrán's *Bulario* (above. Chap. 1, n. 13), 3:484.

2. Beltrán, *Cartulario*, 1:554.

3. Alfonso Martínez de Toledo, *Arcipreste de Talavera* 3. 8, ed. Marcella Ciceri, 2 vols. (Modena, 1975), 1:223.

4. John Andreae, *Ordinary Gloss* to the *Prooemium* of the *Clementines*, ad. v. *silentio* (Lyons, 1606, col. 4). See above, Chap. 1 at n. 14.

5. E. Michael Gerli, *Alfonso Martínez de Toledo*, Twayne World Authors Series, vol. 398 (Boston, 1976), pp. 64–65. Moffatt (above, Chap. 2 n. 197), p. 39, suggests instead stanzas 553, 569, and 722. However, in his recent edition of the *Arcipreste de Talavera* (Madrid, 1979), pp. 220–21, Gerli follows Ciceri in thinking that the reference is to Martínez de Toledo himself, and says that the whole passage, including the *Clementines* citation, is "without doubt" (Ciceri, 2:149, says "perhaps") an interpolation from a marginal gloss, since it appears in the manuscript but not in the printed versions of the text. The same is true of the citation from Hostiensis's *Summa* in 3. 9 (1:229), according to Gerli's edition (pp. 225–26), but Ciceri in her table of variants (2:105) indicates that three-fourths of the chapter (viz., pp. 227–32) is missing from the printed texts; she does single out the particular passage in which the reference to Hostiensis occurs as a possible interpolation (2:149), but gives no reason for so thinking. There is a vague reference to canon law which occurs in 2.5 (1:155–56) which I have not attempted to trace. The text reads: "E como dize la *Decretal*: "Al aflicto non deve ser dada aflición; mas dévese onbre doler de su miseria e mal.' " It is noteworthy that in 2. 1 (1:134), when

there is question of getting a letter of excommunication, one is urged to go not to the archpriest but to the archbishop's vicar: "Ve en un salto al vicario del arçobispo; que te dé una carta de descomunión, que muera maldido e descomulgado el traydor malo que me la comió."

6. Beltrán, *Cartulario*, 1:567–70. See above, Chap. 2 at n. 40 for various reasons accepted as early as the beginning of the thirteenth century for absences from the post of archpriest.

7. Beltrán, *Cartulario*, 1:566–67; *Bulario* (above, Chap. 1 n. 13), 2:304–5 no. 762; 308–9 no. 768. See above, Chap. 2 at n. 47 for time-limits on ordination.

8. Beltrán, *Bulario*, 2:310–11 no. 771.

9. See below at n. 21.

10. Beltrán, *Bulario*, 2:13 no. 426. The archidiaconate of Talavera would have been reserved to the pope as early as 1329, when it was vacated by the death of Cardinal Bernard de Garves at the Holy See. See John XXII, *Lettres communes* no. 45611.

11. Beltrán, *Bulario* 2:109 no. 559.

12. Ibid., 2:156–57 nos. 619–·20.

13. John XXII, *Lettres communes* no. 9540.

14. See *Calendar of Entries in the Papal Registers, Relating to Great Britain and Ireland: Papal Letters*, ed. W. H. Bliss et al. (London, 1893–   ), vols. 4–7. For the example of the canonist Juan Alfonso de Madrid, who was allowed by Benedict XIII in 1409 to be both dean of Santiago and archdeacon of Briviesca, see above, Chap. 1, n. 13.

15. Beltrán, *Cartulario*, 1:563.

16. Ibid., 1:569

17. Beltrán, *Bulario*, 2:359–60 no. 840. On the terms dignity and personate, see above, Chap. 2 at n. 174.

18. Ibid., 3:130 no. 1218a. See Beltrán's discussion in *Cartulario*, 1:564.

19. Beltrán, *Bulario*, 3: 132 no. 1218b: "qui ruralis est et ab aliquibus dignitas reputatur, cuique cura iurisdictionalis imminet animarum." The major duty, of course, if things had not changed since 1379, would have been the operation of the chancery of the archipresbyterate. See above, Chap. 2 at n. 71.

20. Beltrán, *Bulario*, 2:383–84 no. 866.

21. Beltrán, *Bulario*, 2:374–75 no. 856; *Cartulario*, 1:573.

22. Beltrán, *Bulario*, 2:415 no. 910.

23. Ibid., 2:375 no. 856.

24. Ibid., 2:383 no. 866.

25. Ibid., 3:130 no. 1218a.

26. See above at n. 7. His second guess was 100 Aragonese florins. Beltrán considers the first estimate to be a miscalculation.

27. Beltrán, *Bulario*, 2:255 no. 694.

28. See above, Chap. 2 at n. 58.

29. Beltrán, *Bulario*, 2:255 no. 694. Perhaps Medina del Campo or Medinaceli is meant. Some years later, in a dispute over a benefice in the Toledo cathedral church, Martínez de Toledo appealed to the dean of the chapter for adjudication; the dean, after dealing with the case for a while, decided to submit it to Rome. See *Bulario*, 2:347–48 no. 828: letter of 11 September 1431 from Pope Eugene IV.

30. Beltrán, *Cartulario*, 1:183.

31. In England, where rural archpriests were called deans and their regions deaneries, we hear of subdeans performing archipresbyteral duties for their deans. Dansey (above, Chap. 2 n. 77), 1:373–74, tells of the rural subdean of Wodesdon in the diocese of Lincoln; the subdean himself was vicar of Wynchendon. On pp. 426–27, he reports on the dean of the deanery of the city of Norwich, who was answerable to the archdeacon for a certain tax; he deputed his subdean to collect it. Norwich was a cathedral city, but the cathedral chapter was monastic and headed by a prior. In Toledo, in the time of Archbishop Albornoz, there was, or could be, a subdean in the cathedral chapter. According to a capitular constitution dated *pridie Kalendas Ianuarii, anno nativitis Domini* 1339, issued by Albornoz in consultation with the dean of the chapter, Blas Fernández, the dean or the subdean had the duty of disciplining the members of the choir in the chanting of the Office (Sánchez Herrero, pp. 205–6). Perhaps a subdean was appointed when there was an absentee dean, as there was in 1343; see Beltrán, *Bulario*, 1:351 no. 45, 353 no. 48. Sánchez Herrero classifies the above-mentioned constitution as synodal, but there is no reference in it to a synod, and it comes at the wrong time of year. The date for the annual synod was set in 1336 by Archbishop Ximeno de Luna, who also ordered the year to begin on the Calends of January (loc. cit. above, Chap. 2 n. 111). But Albornoz, who was Ximeno's nephew, here dates the year from Christmas, and Sánchez Herrero is no doubt correct in translating the date cited above as 31 December 1338. On the various practices in use, see Santos A. García Larragueta, "El comienzo del año en dataciones de documentos hispánicos," in *Homenaje a Don Agustín Millares Carlo*, 2 vols. (Madrid, 1975), 1:125–46.

32. Beltrán, *Cartulario*, 1:565; *Bulario*, 2:87 no. 523.

33. Beltrán, *Bulario*, 1:373 no. 83.

34. See above, Chap. 2 at n. 206. According to Beltrán, *Bulario*, 1:52, Sierra was a doctor of canon law and held the chair in that subject at the University of Salamanca in 1351. He was an auditor of Cardinal Albornoz in 1355, and later dean of Salamanca, bishop of Orense, and finally bishop of Segovia. He died in 1374. Cf. *Bulario*, 3:535.

35. John XXII, *Lettres communes* nos. 42786, 48467–68.
36. See above, Chap. 2 n. 55.
37. Sánchez Herrero, p. 226. In the 1354 document the collegiate church of Talavera is mistakenly designated as that of Calatrava (p. 218; cf. p. 123).
38. See above, Chap. 2 at n. 112.
39. Beltrán, *Cartulario*, 1:183.
40. Beltrán, *Bulario*, 1:475–76 no. 195.
41. Ibid., 1:500 no. 220.39.
42. Beltrán, *Cartulario*, 1:184, citing J. de Sigüenza, *Historia de la Orden de San Jerónimo*, part 2, chapter 23 (Madrid, 1600), pp. 158–59.
43. Beltrán, *Bulario*, 1:417 no. 139; Sánchez Herrero, p. 260. Earlier (see above, Chap. 2 n. 68) we found reason to suspect that the district of Brihuega, also called an archipresbyterate in the constitutions of 1379, was in fact a vicariate, as in later times. But in the case of Talavera, the designation was no doubt accurate, since there was an archpriest of Talavera in 1369.
44. On the question of an archpriest of Talavera early in the fourteenth century, see above, Chap. 2 n. 116. In the twelfth century a person from Talavera is designated as archpriest, but there is no reason to suppose that he was archpriest of Talavera. See González Palencia (above, Chap. 2 n. 65), 1:102 no. 141, a document of A.D. 1178, where reference is made to "arcipreste don Pedro, hijo de Micael," who is "imam en la iglesia de Santa María de Talavera." In 1192, he appears as "arcipreste don Pedro, hijo de Micael ben Amor" (1:171 no. 224), and in 1199 as "arcipreste don Pedro de Talavera" (1:237 no. 295). In 1202, "Pedro ben Amir" is archdeacon of Guadalajara, and "Pedro, hijo de Micael ben Amir," is simply called archdeacon in 1206 (1:257 no. 318 and 3:83 no. 807). the term *imam*, which in Muslim circles normally refers to a prayer leader, was used by the Christians in a variety of ways. For instance, the priest Don Yago, "imam en la alquería" (3:280 no. 961, A.D. 1271), seems to have been in charge of a rural estate. It was sometimes used of the *capiscol* or *caput scholae* in the cathedral church of Toledo: "capiscol don Raimundo, imam en la catedral Santa María" (3:517 no. 1098, Dec. 1169); "capiscol don Raimundo, imam de la Catedral Santa María la Mayor" (3:517 no. 1099, March, 1170); cf. "el imam don Pedro Chelabert (1:51 no. 73, A.D. 1164). In a confused paragraph (4:178), González Palencia interprets the term in these last instances to refer to the cantor or precentor, that is, the head of the choir, and to be equivalent to the "capellán del coro de la Catedral," a title applied to the priest Don Esteban in December, 1170 (1:68–69 no. 96). Perhaps, however, *imam* refers to the *maestrescuela* or *magister scholarum*. But what it could refer to in the church of Santa

María of Talavera in the twelfth century is not clear, since the church was not made a collegiate church with a secular chapter until 1211: so Rivera, *Iglesia* (above, Chap. 2 n. 64), 1:100. Rivera says that a Pedro Micael was archpriest of Toledo in the second half of the twelfth century, but he gives no documentation (2:132). See above, Chap. 2 n. 69.

45. See Joset, 2:303; Anthony N. Zahareas, *The Art of Juan Ruiz, Archpriest of Hita* (Madrid, 1965), pp. 105–6, and Zahareas's edition, with translation by Saralyn R. Daly, *The Book of True Love* (University Park, Pennsylvania, 1978), esp. pp. 441–42.

46. Beltrán, *Bulario*, 1:417 no. 139. The "Collector of the Apostolic Camera for Castile" sent a letter to Archbishop Manrique through his subcollector Diego Martínez concerning the gathering of *mediae procurationes* that were due from the diocese. The archbishop responded that he would depute trustworthy and trained men "qui, consideratis facultatibus ecclesiarum singularium, ordinarent quod mediae procurationes possent levari a civitate Toletan. et a singulis archipresbyteratibus et vicariis dictae dio."

47. Beltrán, *Cartulario*, 1:555.

48. Sánchez Herrero (above, Chap. 1 n. 12), pp. 177, 189. See above, Chap. 2 at n. 121.

49. Ibid., p. 177. Rules for tonsure and dress of married clerics were repeated in the council of 1388: Tejada (above, Chap. 2 n. 122), 3:615–16, and the council of 1474: Sánchez Herrero, p. 292.

50. Guadalupe (above, Chap. 2 n. 67), pp. 69–74.

51. See Lecoy (above, Chap. 1 n. 4), pp. 229–32.

52. Thomas Wright, *The Latin Poems Commonly Attributed to Walter Mapes* (London, 1841), pp. 174–79.

53. The cantor is named as Sancho Muñoz (stanza 1705). There was a well-known Gil Sancho Muñoz, doctor of laws and provost of Valencia, who in 1374–76 represented the pope in negotiations with the English (John Wycliff was one of Edward III's delegates). See Mollat (above, Chap. 2 n. 62) p. 110; Édouard Perroy, *L'Angleterre et la grande schisme d'Occident* (Paris, 1933), pp. 35–41. He was elected as Pope Clement VIII in 1423 to succeed Pedro de Luna (Benedict XIII). I should note that when the treasurer says that he will leave Talavera and go to Oropesa (stanza 1702), he must surely not mean Oropesa in the diocese of Tortosa (province of Tarracona), but Oropesa in the diocese of Plasencia (province of Santiago), which is only a few miles to the west of Talavera.

54. The council began in Palencia in 1321. See José Goñi Gaztambide, "Una bula de Juan XXII sobre reforma del episcopado castellano (4 junio 1318)," *Hispania sacra* 8 (1955): 409–13, at 410.

55. Godin, Council of Valladolid, chap. 7: *Quia clericorum* (Mansi,

25:703): "Sicut iure divino et humano iustum dignoscitur quod iuxta mensuram delicti culpabiles puniantur, ita pium et sanctum est quod rigori detrahatur iustitiae, ut occurratur insurgentibus periculis animarum. Hoc sane felicis recordationis Alexander papa IV [1254–61], pii more patris considerans, suspensionis et excommunicationis poenas quas recolendae memoriae dominus Ioannes, episcopus sabinensis, apostolicae sedis legatus, contra clericos concubinarios publicos ac concubinas eorum per suum statutum vel constitutiones tulerat [in 1228], voluit et commisit praelatis aliquibus quod poenas praedictas, maxime propter irregularitatum quae ex hoc saepius sequebantur periculum, in poenas alias rationabiles permutarent. Quia igitur per aliam constitutionem nostram, sacro approbante concilio, per condignam inflictionem poenarum contra delinquentes huiusmodi providimus, congruenter, dicto approbante concilio, statuimus quod antedicti legati constitutiones praedictae, [quoad] suspensionis et excommunicationis poenas, non ligent de cetero."

56. Tejada 3:325.

57. *Decretals of Gregory IX* 5. 39. 55: *Si concubinae* (Friedberg, 2:912).

58. Sánchez Herrero, pp. 165–66.

59. Godin, *Quia clericorum* (col. 703).

60. Ibid. (col. 702); for the text, see above, Chap. 1 n. 118.

61. Godin, chap. 22, *Lex continentiae* (col. 720). In my correction, *ipsae* refers to Christian concubines of married men; the reading is confirmed by the constitution of Pedro de Luna in 1388, cited in n. 63 below.

62. To yield 1301, the expression "enl" must be taken to mean "en el," but the usual abbreviation mark is missing (Criado and Naylor, p. 630). Corominas in his edition reads "ent" for "enl" and emends it to "*ochenta*," reading the date as 1381 E.S. = A.D. 1343. However, other emendations along this line would be equally possible, e.g., "sesenta" and "setenta."

63. Pedro de Luna, Council of Palencia, chap. 7: *In paradiso* (Tejada, 3:618–19):

In paradiso voluptatis, ubi primum parentem creaverat Creator omnium gloriosus, matrimonium hac lege instituit ut sic vir per consensum legitimum feminae iungeretur, quod, duobus existentibus in carne una, aliam personam quae unitatem divideret superaddere non licerit.

Hanc unitatem nonnulli coniugati, Dei timore posposito, deturbantes, "sicut equus et mulus, quibus non est intellectus," concubinis se commiscere in suarum animarum damnationem publice non verentur. Contra quos praefatus Guillelmus, episcopus sabinensis, sanctae romanae ecclesiae cardinalis, statuit et ordinavit ut quicumque coniugatus concubinam publice detinere praesumeret, et insuper non coniugatus qui concubinam infidelem praesumeret detinere, tam ipsi quam ipsae eo ipso sententiam excommunicationis incurrerent.

Nos vero dictam constitutionem innovantes, tam praedictos, quam coniugat[a]s qu[ae] cum adulteris publice commiscentur, et ipsos adulteros, praedictae excommunicationis sententiae decernimus subiacere; volentes insuper quod nisi adulteri et alii suprascripti praefatas concubinas, vel coniugatae dictos adulteros, per duos menses ante eorum vel earum obitum dimiserint et se ab eisdem sine fraude separaverint, etiam si tempore obitus sui vel antea fuerint a dicta excommuncationis sententia absoluti, nihilominus tam ipsi quam ipsae careant ecclesiastica sepultura.

64. Sánchez Herrero, p. 87, mistakenly says that he increased the penalties. In fact, Pedro reduced from five months to two months the time of ineligibility after one was deprived of one's benefices.

65. Pedro de Luna, chap. 2: *Speciosus*(Tejada, 3:614-15).

66. Ibid. (p. 613): "Guillelmus . . . quandam constitutionem provide edidit, quae antiqui hostis procurante versutia usquequaque non exstitit observata."

67. See above, Chap. 2 at n. 111. Lecoy, pp. 234-35, suggests that it was meetings held in anticipation of this synod that inspired Juan Ruiz to write the *Cántica de los clérigos de Talavera*. But the constitution issued at the synod (which Lecoy did not see) suggests no such anticipated meetings as having been held. We have concluded that meetings of the clergy of each archipresbyterate must have been held before each synod, if only to choose delegates for the synod (see above, Chap. 2 at n. 112). But we have found no indication that draft constitutions or lists of *agenda* were circulated before the synods met.

68. J. Beneyto Pérez, *El Cardenal Albornoz, canciller de Castilla y caudillo de Italia* (Madrid, 1950), p. 89.

69. The four letters are calendared in Benedict XII, *Lettres communes* (above, Chap. 2 n. 144), no. 9358, and the copy addressed to the archbishop of Seville and his suffragan bishops is given in full in Cesare Baronio et al., *Annales ecclesiastici*, ad annum 1342, nos. 1-2, ed. Augustinus Theiner, 37 vols. (Bar-le-Duc, 1864-83), 25:275-76. Cf. the letter that John XXII sent in 1318 to the archbishop and bishops of the province of Toledo (ed. Goñi, n. 54 above), where concubinage is only one of the faults mentioned.

70. Sánchez Herrero, pp. 208-9, compared with and corrected by the version published by F. Filippini, "Costituzioni inedite di Egidio Albornoz," *Studi storici* 5 (Leghorn, 1896): 211-28, esp. 219-20. Some of the constitutions published by Filippini are unknown to Sánchez Herrero, including those of the synod of Alcalá, 11 April 1345 (pp. 222-24); those of the provincial council of Alcalá, 22 April 1345 (pp. 224-26; also pub-

lished by Tejada and by Hefele); and a synodal constitution that Filippini dates to 1347 (pp. 227–28).

71. Sánchez Herrero, p. 47, notes a similar penalty imposed by the synod of León in 1267, but reduced by the synod of 1303.

72. Mansilla, *Iglesia* (above, Chap. 2 n. 29), pp. 322, 345.

73. Rivera, *Arzobispos* (above, Chap. 1 n. 100), p. 87, says he was made cardinal of St. Praxedes. The title of St. Clement is specified by Adalbert Erler, *Aegidius Albornoz als Gesetzgeber des Kirchenstaates* (Berlin, 1970), pp. 16–17, and Eubel (above, Chap. 2 n. 30). Beneyto (n. 68 above) on p. 181 cites Zurita (writing in 1579) as calling Albornoz cardinal of St. Praxedes, and on p. 184 he cites Daumet (writing in 1914), who names him cardinal of St. Clement. The difficulty arose from the fact that another Giles (Aegidius Regaudi, abbot of Saint-Denis in France) was made cardinal (of St. Praxedes) on the same day as Gil de Albornoz, viz., December 17, 1350; see Eubel, 1:45.

Notes to Chapter Four

Procedure in the Court of Don Ximio

1. See above, Chap. 2 at n. 56.

2. See William Durantis, *Speculum iudicale*, Lib. 2, Partic. 2, rubr. *De disputationibus et allegationibus advocatorum*, par. 5: *Porro*, no. 4; vol. 1, p. 753 of the edition of Venice, 1585. This edition includes the *Additiones* by John Andreae. Andreae was still working on the *Additiones* in 1346, when he was in his late seventies, two years before his death in 1348 (Kuttner, *Jurist* 24:398; see above, Chap. 1 n. 77). This edition of the *Speculum* also contains the commentary of the civil-law jurist Baldo degli Ubaldi (ca. 1320–1400).

3. See especially Martín Elizaga y Gondra, *Un proceso en el Libro de buen amor*, a pamphlet of 56 pages (Bilbao, 1942), and Lorenzo Polaino Ortega, *El derecho procesal en el Libro de buen amor*, a pamphlet of 45 pages (Madrid [1948]). According to Steven D. Kirby, "Juan Ruiz and Don Ximio: The Archpriest's Art of Declamation," *Bulletin of Hispanic Studies* 55 (1978): 283–87, p. 286 n. 6, Polaino's piece is a reprinting of an article that appeared in the *Revista de derecho procesal* 3(1947): 581–621. Professor Kirby himself has treated the subject of the bearing of the *Libro de buen amor* on Spanish law in "Juan Ruiz, Don Ximio, and the Law," *Studies in Language and Literature: The Proceedings of the Twenty-Third Moun-*

tain Interstate Foreign Language Conference, ed. Charles L. Nelson (Richmond, Kentucky, 1976), pp. 295–300, a copy of which he kindly sent to me. See also his essay, "Legal Doctrine and Procedure as Approaches to Medieval Hispanic Literature," *Corónica* 8 (1979–80): 164–71.

4. See R. Naz, "Inquisition," *Dictionnaire de droit canonique,* 6:1418–26. A somewhat similar method of public prosecution of crime had been introduced into the "Romanizing" Spanish law codes, culminating in the *Siete partidas,* and it came to overshadow the accusatory procedure after the *Partidas* was officially accepted in 1348. See Joaquín Cerdá Ruiz-Funes, "En torno a la pesquisa y procedimiento inquisitivo en el derecho castellano-leonés de la edad media," *Anuario de historia del derecho español* 32 (1962): 483–515, and Evelyn S. Procter, *The Judicial Use of Pesquisa (Inquisition) in León and Castille, 1157–1369, English Historical Review* Supplement 2 (London, 1966). But the *pesquisa* was a formal investigation that preceded the levying of charges, whereas in canon law the *ex officio* inquisition was the trial itself: on the basis of public infamy (which was often not formally established), the judge summoned the suspect to inquire into the truth of the reports.

5. *Costituzioni egidiane* 4. 1–2, ed. Pietro Sella (Rome, 1912), pp. 138–41. For an early Italian translation of the constitutions, see Paolo Colliva, *Il cardinale Albornoz, lo Stato della Chiesa, le "Constitutiones aegidianae" (1353–1357),* Studia albornotiana 32 (Bologna, 1977), pp. 533–735. See Charles Lefebvre, "Le droit romain dans les *Constitutiones aegidianae,*" *Cardenal Albornoz y el colegio de España* (above, Chap. 1 n. 80) 3:47–65, esp. 51–54.

6. Durantis, *Speculum* (n. 2 above), Lib. 4, Partic. 4, rubr. *De accusationibus et inquisitionibus et denuntiationibus,* par. 1: *Est ergo,* no. 1 (p. 483).

7. Ibid., no. 2 (p. 483).

8. Gratian, *Decretum,* 2. 2. 8. 3: *Quisquis* (Friedberg, 1:503) and 2. 4. 4. 2: *Nullus,* par. 1: *Inscriptio* (1:541–42); *Justinian Digest* 48. 2. 3: *Libellorum; Justinian Code* 9. 1. 3: *Qui crimen;* 9. 2. 16: *In causis;* 9. 2. 17: *Accusationibus.*

9. *Siete partidas* (SP) 7. 1. 14. I will use the edition by Pedro Gómez de la Serna, *Códigos españoles,* vols. 2–5 (Madrid, 1848), which contains the glosses of Gregorio López from his edition of 1555.

10. On the year given in this stanza, see above, Chap. 3 n. 62.

11. Gregorio López, n. 8 to SP 7. 1. 14 (4:270) and n. 3 to SP 4. 9. 13 (3:452). See Durantis, *Speculum,* Lib. 1, Partic. 2, rubr. *De accusatore,* no. 34 (p. 196): "Hodie tamen de consuetudine multorum regionum non fiunt inscriptiones"; and see John Andreae's discussion (pp. 196–97); he cites an authority against the abolition of the *inscriptio* and another in favor of it.

12. SP 7. 1. 1 describes the sort of accusation "quando alguno acusa a otro de yerro que es de tal natura que si lo non pudiere provar, que deve aver el acusador la pena que deve aver el acusado, si le fuesse provado." SP 7. 1. 26 directs the judge on what to do when the accusation is not proved: "Si por su conoscencia, nin por las pruevas que fueron aduchas contra el, non lo fallare en culpa de aquel yerro sobre que fue acusado, develo dar por quito, e dar al acusador aquella mesma pena que daria al acusado."

13. SP 4. 9. 13.

14. *Decretals of Gregory IX* 1. 38. 5: *Tuae fraternitati* (Friedberg, 2:214).

15. See E. Martínez Marcos, "Fuentes de la doctrina canónica de la IV Partida del código del Rey Alfonso el Sabio," *Revista española de derecho canónico* 18 (1963): 897–926, esp. 921, referring to Peñafort's *Summa de casibus* 4. 22. 1.

16. SP 4. 9. 13, with a reference to SP 7. 17. 1.

17. SP 4. 9. 2. Martínez Marcos (n. 15 above), p. 921, traces this law to Goffredo da Trani's commentary on the *Decretals* (Goffredo died in 1245).

18. See above, Chap. 2 at n. 53.

19. *Justinian Novels* 53. 3: *Illud quoque*, par. 1: *Sancimus*.

20. Gratian, *Decretum* 2. 3. 3, dictum post 4, par. 5: *Offeratur* (Friedberg, 1: 511).

21. *Ordinary Gloss* to *Decretum* 2. 3. 2, dictum ante 1: *De induciis* (Lyons, 1606, col. 718): "In civili autem causa sunt induciae deliberativae viginti dierum, ut infra" (referring to the text cited in the previous note).

22. Azzo, *Summa* (Venice, 1581), col. 884 no. 8, on *Justinian Code* 9. 1: *De accusationibus et inscriptionibus*: "Oblato autem libello, dabitur dilatio ad deliberandum, forte viginti dierum, ut in pecuniaria causa."

23. SP 7. 1. 14; cited by Kirby 1976 (n. 3 above), p. 296.

24. Gregorio López, n. 9 to SP 7. 1. 14 (4:270).

25. For the text of the second exception, see above, Chap. 3 at n. 62. In my quotations from the *Libro de buen amor*, I will use the form *exepçión* (favored by the Salamanca MS) rather than *esençión*.

26. Durantis, *Speculum* 1. 2, *De accusatore*, no. 21 (p. 194): Item [excipi potest] quod est infamis"; no. 25 (p. 195): "Item excipitur quod fuit de publico crimine damnatus"; no. 30 (p. 196): "Item quod est anathematizatus vel excommunicatus"; no. 31: "Item quod est publice concubinarius."

27. *Ordinary Gloss* to *Decretals* 5. 1. 1: *Si legitimus*, ad v. *legitimus* (col. 1573): " 'Legitimus' ideo dicit quia si sit criminosus non potest alium accusare," etc.

28. Azzo, *Summa* on *Code* 8. 35: *De exceptionibus sive praescriptionibus*,

col. 843 no. 2: "Dividuntur autem exceptiones, quia aliae sunt perpetuae et peremptoriae, aliae temporales et dilatoriae. Perpetuae sunt et peremptoriae quae semper agentibus obstant, et rem de qua agitur perimunt"; col. 844 no. 8: "Perpetuae autem et peremptoriae exceptiones . . . opponuntur a reo quandocumque ante sententiam, sed non postea, nisi in casibus specialibus."

29. Durantis, *Speculum* 2. 1, *De exceptionibus et replicationibus*, par. 4: *Viso*, no. 29 (p. 529): "Validis autem exceptionibus admissis, statim praefigat terminum congruentem peremptorium suo arbitrio reo intra quem probet eas (et actor pro expensis protestetur, si forte reus, qui in exceptione sit actor, deficeret in probando)"; no. 30: "Praefixo igitur termino ad probandum, reus postulet statim actorem per iuramentum super ipsis exceptionibus interrogari."

30. Baldo degli Ubaldi, commenting on the title *De incidentibus quaestionibus et de ordine cognitionum*, Durantis, *Speculum* 2. 1 (p. 556): "Quando incidens est talis quae non patitur litem contestari nec procedi, prius est cognoscendum de incidenti." However, John Andreae, *Novella* to *Decretals of Gregory IX* 2. 10 .1: *Intelleximus* (2:57 no. 1), notes that if a peremptory exception is entered after the *contestatio*, the *cognitio* of the exception must occur before the principal matter can proceed, but it need not be pronounced upon until the time comes to give sentence on the principal matter.

31. See Durantis, *Speculum* 2. 1, *De exceptionibus*, par. 3: *Dicto de dilatorio*, no. 48 (p. 523), for a sample form of sentence: since the judge finds the peremptory exception to be proved, he declares that so-and-so (the accuser) "non esse ulterius audiendum, sibi super hoc perpetuum silentium imponendo." For forms of interlocutory sentences on exceptions of excommunication see par. 4 nos. 30–31 (p. 529).

32. Durantis, *Speculum* 2. 1, *De exceptionibus*, par. 4 no. 31 (p. 529): "Et si lis fuerit contestata et ordo iudiciarius servatus in huiusmodi exceptionis cognitione, fiat de hoc mentio in ipsa pronuntiatione."

33. See, for example, the sample verdict given in SP 3. 18. 109.

34. See Baldo's comment on the rubric *De disputationibus et allegationibus* in Durantis, *Speculum* 2. 2 (p. 756): he speaks of the "allegationes seu rationes" that are urged by both parties in a case.

35. Durantis, *Speculum* 2. 1, *De exceptionibus et replicationibus*, par. 5: *Nunc dicendum* (p. 533): "Et est replicatio exceptio competens actori contra exceptionem rei"; no. 1: "Replicationes autem post fundatam intentionem rei sunt probandae." Baldo, commenting on the title *De incidentibus* (n. 30 above), p. 556, says that if an accuser responds to the accused's exception with a replication, the reaccusation must be considered as an exception: "Item incidit criminalis criminali, ut si accusas me de

vulnere, ego excipio quod prius illum occideras, immo et si tu reaccuso, habet etiam vim exceptionis reaccusatio."

36. Durantis, loc. cit. (p. 533), ante no. 1: "Quandoque tamen 'replicatio' ponitur pro 'responsione,' " citing Gratian, *Decretum* 2. 9. 3. 14: *Aliorum* (Friedberg, 1:610).

37. This is the reading of the Salamanca manuscript. The Gayoso text reads "costytuçion" for "conclusyon" in the second line, and "mester es" for "menester" in the last line. The Toledo text has "confision" for "conclusion" in the last line and could make sense if it referred to Wolf's confession.

38. SP 7. 1. 22.

39. Hostiensis, *Summa* (above, chap. 2 n. 11), Lib. 1, rubr. *De transactionibus*, par. 1: *Quid sit transactio* (col. 373).

40. Ibid., par. 3: *Super quibus rebus* (cols. 374–75).

41. Ibid., par. 4: *Et in quibus cessat* (col. 375): "Si tamen super actione iniuriarum vel furti fiat transactio, auctoritate iudicis tenet."

42. See n. 86 below.

43. Durantis, *Speculum* 2. 2, *De renuntiatione et conclusione*, no. 3 (p. 758).

44. Ibid.

45. Andreae, *Additiones* ad loc. cit. (n. 43 above) note k (p. 758): "Item quaestio eius minus esset dubia quando super aliquo emergenti esset facta illa renuntiatio. Et scias ad utrumque dictum quod in talibus renuntiationibus ponderanda sunt verba, et status causae, et consuetudo fori."

46. Durantis, *Speculum* 2. 3, *De sententia*, par. 4 no. 2 (p. 784): "Nam eo quod ab initio consensit in terminum, talis terminus vicem obtinet peremptorii, adeo ut etiam conclusionis loco censeatur."

47. John Andreae, *Ordinary Gloss* to *Clementines* 2. 12. 7: *Cum a repulsione* (cols. 149–50), makes this point.

48. See the medieval authorities cited by Gregorio López in n. 4 to SP 3. 22. 2 (3:279–80), and also Andreae's admission at the end of the gloss cited in n. 47: "In effectu tamen fatetur quod sententia lata super peremptorio quod obstet habet vim definitivae."

49. See the *Ordinary Gloss* to the *Decretals of Gregory IX* 1. 6. 32: *Cum dilectus* ad v. *infra dicendium* (col. 164) and 2. 20. 36: *Significaverunt* ad v. *infra decem dies* (col. 734).

50. Durantis, *Speculum* 2. 2, *De petitione sententiae et eius cautela*, no. 2 (p. 770): "Quae autem praemissa sunt, etiam in interlocutionibus observentur"; *De requisitione consilii*, no. 12 (p. 768): "Nota quod non solum super decisione quaestionis principalis eliguntur huiusmodi sapientes, quinimmo et super quolibet litis ambiguo casu. Porro huiusmodi dato consilio, iudex secundum illud sententiam definitivam seu interlocutoriam formare curabit, sicut dixi supra de exceptionibus." He is speaking here

of the Italian system of having counsellors for the judge chosen by the parties to the case, whereas outside Italy the judge selects his own counsellors (no. 15).

51. See above, chap. 2 at n. 104, and cf. the schedule of charges for judicial documents, chap. 2 at n. 71.

52. Sánchez Herrero (above, chap. 1 n. 12), p. 245: "Ita et taliter quod infra quinque dies in ipsis, in aliis autem maioris summae vel aestimationis excedentibus quantitatem, infra novem a die libelli vel petitionis oblatae in iudicio, adversa parte praevente [*lege* praesente], die qua oblata fuerit computata, lis pure et sine conditione contestetur legitime." For the usual term of twenty days, see n. 22 above.

53. On the exception of *spoliatio*, see *Decretals*, 2. 10. 1: *Cum dilectus*, and the *Ordinary Gloss*'s commentary. The ordinary term set for proving this exception was sixteen days, using Tenorio's inclusive method of counting (see preceding note). See Durantis, *Speculum* 2. 1, *De exceptionibus*, par. 4 no. 29 (p. 529): "Item in exceptione spoliationis probanda statuuntur quindecim dies, die in qua proponitur non computata," citing *Sextus* 2. 5. 1: *Frequens* (Friedberg, 2:999).

54. Sánchez Herrero, p. 245: "Etiam, si recusationis in iudicem, expoliationis, vel excommunicationis in partem, aut alterius cuiuslibet exceptionis dirigere velit obiectum—de quibus tamen vel earum quacumque post contestationem ipsam [si excipiat litigator], iuxta traditiones canonicas prius et ante omnia legitime cognoscatur—verum si de re iudicata, transacta, vel finita ante litem contestatam excipiat litigator, et ad probandum admissus non probaverit quod obiecit, calumniantem ipsum haberi volumus pro confesso, nisi eundem a labe calumniae causa manifesta et probabilis excusaret; quo casu, pronuntiato iudice supra illo, infra novem dies immediatos sequentes teneatur, uti praefertur, litem ipsam legitime contestari." This confusing text could be read as forbidding all exceptions but that of *res iudicata* to be entered before the contestation; but this would go against the canonical traditions, especially as treated in the title *De ordine cognitionum* (on the order in which points are to be heard) in the *Decretals of Gregory IX* 2. 10 and Innocent IV's decretal *Pia consideratione*, *Sextus* 2. 12. 1 (see below at n. 70). Furthermore, Clement V's decretal *Saepe* on summary procedure (*Clementines* 5. 11. 2) could hardly be taken as authorizing the mandatory postponement of such exceptions. On the subject of admitting or rejecting exceptions, John Andreae in his *Ordinary Gloss* on *Saepe* (ad v. *dilatorias*, col. 336) professes ignorance of any dilatory exception that could be repelled by a judge using summary procedure, but which a judge not using summary procedure would be forced to admit, and he rhetorically asks to be instructed on the point: "Sed quaero quam exceptionem vel appellationem per haec verba, non dico per hanc

constitutionem, possit talis iudex repellere quam alter iudex teneatur admittere; hoc vellem doceri." On the question of hearing exceptions entered after the contestation, see n. 30 above.

55. Sánchez Herrero, p. 245: "Porro lite ipsa, ut praemittitur, legitime contestata, in causis praetaxatam summam non excedentibus infra decem, in aliis autem dictam excedentibus quantitatem infra viginti dies, [qui] a dictae contestationis tempore numerantur, omnes exceptiones peremptorias sibi competentes proponere teneantur; quibus elapsis, nequaquam ulterius super non propositis audiantur, nisi forte aliqua de novo sibi competens exceptio postea sit exorta, vel de novo ad eius dicat notitiam pervenisse, de quo fidem faciat proprio iuramento."

56. Ibid.: "Plane petitione ipsa vel libello simpliciter et absolute negatis, actor ad probandum eam vel eum illico et ante omnia, omnibus exclusis allegationibus, rationibus, et aliis quibuscumque anfractibus, admittatur infra competentis et moderatae dilationis terminum ei per iudicem assignandum; qua dilatione pendente, si per reum aliqua exceptio peremptoria proponatur, ad eam probandam arbitrio iudicis terminus praefigatur. Quod si priusquam super eadem exceptione ad ipsius termini assignationem a iudice sit processum, actor contra eam duxerit replicandum, utique ad probationem earum idem et moderatus terminus assignetur."

57. Ibid., pp. 245–46: "At si dictae contestationis tempore ipse alicuius peremptoriae exceptionis proponat obiectum, ad petita et obiecta probandum idem utrique parti competens et moderatus terminus a iudice statuatur, post cuius exceptionis obiectum , etiamsi ad eam probandam sit terminus assignatus per iudicem et pendeat probationis dilatio super ea, si actor crediderit replicandum, usque ad decem dies, a die exceptionis propositae numerandos, competere sibi noverit facultatem, quibus elapsis cuiuscumque replicationis diffugium sibi sciat penitus interdictum, nisi de novo replicandi facultas emerserit vel proponens iuramento firmaverit ad eius ipsam de novo notitiam pervenisse, quam, si iudex viderit admittendam, moderato termino de ipsius veritate cognoscat."

58. Durantis, *Speculum* 2. 1, *De exceptionibus et replicationibus*, par. 5 (p. 533), says that a defendant's exception can be opposed by the plaintiff's replication, and then the defendant can respond with a duplication, which can be opposed by the plaintiff's triplication. But later, 2. 2, *De allegationibus*, par. 2 (p. 746), though he refers back to this treatment, he gives a different vocabulary: the plaintiff's replication is answered by the defendant's triplication, and the plaintiff can respond with a quadruplication.

59. Sánchez Herrero, p. 246: "Potiores autem replicationes ultra istas, sive sint triplicationes vel aliae ulteriores, quibuscumque nominibus nuncupentur (quae 'implicationes' potius sunt censendae, et quas ad prorogan-

dum lites et confundendum veritatem advocatorum calliditas saepius adinvenit), iudicantis perita discretio diligenter advertat, ut eas si urgens casus exegerit (quod raro contingit) admittat, vel (quod magis expedit) iustitia suadente repellat."

60. Ibid.: "Sciturus quod si per malitiam vel negligentiam, ignorantiam, aut per gratiam vel per sordes male versatus fuerit in praemissis, frustratorias videlicet et superfluas involutiones aut cavillationes indebite admittendo, praeter expensas et damna de quibus partem querulam servare sua iactura oportebit indemnem, nostrae animadversionis condignam non effugiet ultionem."

61. Ibid.: "Ceterum si super principali aut exceptionibus vel replicationibus partes ipsae, vel earum altera, positiones vel articulos ad intentiones suas facili compendio comprobandas obtulerint, cogatur pars diversa personaliter et absque diminiculo advocati singulariter et clare eis sacramento prius ab utraque parte praestito respondere; si vero articulos vel positiones ipsas hinc et inde duxerint offerendum, respondere cogantur vicissim mutuis positionibus et articulis, uti praefertur, singulariter et clare, sacramento hinc inde praestito per easdem. Quod si quis a iudice interrogatur [*lege* interrogatus] et iussus super aliqua positione vel articulo contumaciter respondere contempserit, ipsum iudex habeat pro confesso super tali exceptione vel articulo, et tanquam contra confessum procedere non omittat, probationibus autem litis receptis et suo tempore publicatis, ceterisque peractis quae qualitati causae crediderit convenire."

62. Ibid.: "Iudex ad renuntiandum et concludendum terminum assignet partibus competentem, cui etiamsi altera partium parere contumaciter (iusto cessante impedimento) distulerit, elapso termino, iudex pro renuntiato habeat et concluso, eius contumacia non obstante. Post quam quidem renuntiationem et conclusionem legitime et debito more factam, in causis ducentorum morabetinorum excedentibus quantitatem usque ad viginti [dies post huiusmodi terminum] renuntiationis et conclusionis modo praedicto factae proximii immediati sequentis [*lege* proximos immediate sequentes], in aliis vero citerioris quantitatis et summae infra quindecim dies, definitivam sententiam proferat, prout iustitiae viderit convenire."

63. Ibid., pp. 246–47: "Quod si neglecta hac salubri iussione non fecerit, praeter damna, sumptus, et interesse in quibus eum teneri volumus parti quae se propter hoc docuerit esse laesam, centum morabetinorum poenam, nostrae toletanae ecclesiae fabricae applicandum, incurrere volumus ipso facto."

64. Ibid., p. 247: "In causis autem beneficialibus et matrimonialibus, in quibus maius noscitur versari periculum et maior est cautela et sollertia adhibenda, praefatum ordinem nolumus observari, sed in ipsis iuxta sacrorum statuta canonum procedatur."

65. Durantis, *Speculum* 2. 2, *De disputationibus*, par. 6 (p. 754): "Nec motum animi sui multum aperiat, sed dissimulet, nunc pro hac parte, nunc pro illa allegando et respondendo."

66. See Hostiensis, *Summa* (above, chap. 2 n. 11), Lib. 2, rubr. *De sententia*, par. 5: *Qualiter proferri debeat* (col. 764), citing *Justinian Digest* 38. 15. 2: *Utile tempus*, par. 1: *Dies*, and *Novels* 71. 1: *Sancimus*. The same requirement is in SP 3. 22. 5 and 3. 22. 12, cited by Kirby 1976 (n. 3 above), p. 297. When summary procedure is used (see above, chap. 2 at n. 103), the judge is allowed to stand. See John Andreae's *Ordinary Gloss* on *Clementines* 5. 11. 2: *Saepe*, ad v. *stans* (col. 340).

67. Durantis, *Speculum* 2. 3, *De sententia*, par. 6: *Ut autem* (pp. 788–93); e.g., nos. 18, 20, 26: "In Dei nomine, Amen." Other forms begin, "In nomine Domini" (no. 6), and "In Christi nomine" (no. 26, second form).

68. Ibid., par 5: *Qualiter*, no. 13 (p. 787): "Ceterum in sententiae prolatione iudex exprimere debet actoris petitionem et rei responsionem et eius exceptionem, et generaliter quidquid in causa utriusque petitum vel allegatum seu actum est sub epilogo referat."

69. Cf. ibid., par. 6, no. 6 (p. 789), a sample sentence delivered by an ordinary judge in a personal action: "Et deliberatione insuper nobiscum et cum peritis praehabita diligenti . . . Dei nomine invocato."

70. *Sextus* 2. 12. 1: *Pia consideratione* (Friedberg, 2:1004–6, esp. 1005): "Dum enim in causis ecclesiasticis frequentius haec exceptio per malitiam opponitur, contingit interdum differri negotia, et partes fatigari laboribus et expensis. . . . Si quis igitur excommunicationem opponit, speciem illius et nomen excommunicatoris exprimat, sciturus eam rem se deferre debere in publicam notionem, quam infra octo dierum spatium (die in quo proponitur minime computato) probare valeat apertissimis documentis." This requirement to prove the exception within eight days is stated by Durantis, *Speculum* 2. 1, *De exceptionibus*, par. 2 no. 8 (p. 513). The decretal goes on to say: "Quod si non probaverit, iudex in causa procedere non omittat, reum in expensis quas actor ob hoc diebus illis se fecisse docuerit, praehabita taxatione, condemnans." See below at n. 75.

71. See n. 52 above.

72. *Sextus* 5. 11. 8: *Decernimus* (Friedberg, 2:1101); see Durantis, loc. cit. in n. 70 above, no. 10 (p. 513).

73. *Clementines* 2. 10. 1: *Excommunicationis exceptio* (Friedberg, 2:1150).

74. This is the reading of the Gayoso manuscript; the Salamanca text omits the crucial word "mas."

75. Though the language of *Pia consideratione* indicates that the plaintiff is to know about the short term for proof beforehand, it also indicates that a definite pronouncement from the judge is in order when no proof is forthcoming: the judge shall not omit to proceed in the case. For the

text, see n. 70 above. The question of whether the term is in force without being assigned by the judge is discussed by Durantis, *Speculum* 2. 1, *De dilationibus*, par. 1 no. 14 (p. 496): "Sed numquid currunt isti octo dies ipso iure, licet eos iudex excipienti non praefigat, adeo ut ipsis elapsis procedi possit in causa? Et videtur quod non, quia talis terminus est a iudice assignandus. . . . Dic contra, quia terminus iste a iure statutus est. Unde licet iudex eum non assignet, tamen ex quo exceptionem admittit, debet statim excipiens suas probationes inducere, et hoc satis innuit praedicta constitutio *Pia consideratione*." John Andreae in the *Additiones* notes that even holidays are counted in such continuances or delays (note c).

76. See the first passage cited from Durantis in n. 29 above; also, *Speculum* 2. 2, *De petitione sententiae*, no. 4 (p. 770): "Illud autem tibi sit memoriae, ut semper adversarium petas in expensis tibi legitimis condemnari." He gives sample forms of this request for the plaintiff and the defendant, earlier, *De disputationibus*, par. 3 no. 7 (p. 747) and par. 4 no. 23 (p. 752).

77. Durantis, *Speculum* 2. 2, *De disputationibus*, par. 6 no. 12 (p. 755): "Tunc supplebit in expensis omissis . . . quod intellige de factis post litem contestatam, etiam non petitis; . . . in factis autem ante litem contestatam non, nisi petitae fuerint." See the long commentary on this subject in the *Ordinary Gloss* to *Decretals of Gregory IX* 2. 14. 5: *Finem litibus*, ad v. *expensas* (cols. 653–54).

78. Durantis, *Speculum* 1. 4, *De salariis*, par. 3: *De salario advocatorum*, nos. 1–5 (pp. 347–48).

79. Ibid., par. 1: *De salariis iudicum*, nos. 3, 5, 9, 14 (pp. 344–45). The modest payments assigned in Archbishop Tenorio's schedules (see above, chap. 2 at n. 71) are mostly for the expense of producing documents. For instance, there is no charge for an interlocutory or definitive sentence in a case heard *sine scriptis*.

80. John Andreae in the *Ordinary Gloss* to *Sextus* 2. 12. 1: *Pia consideratione* (Lyons, 1606, col. 361) says that the obligation to submit proof within eight days comes into effect when the plaintiff denies the charge: "Sed quid si actor negat se excommunicatum maiore excommunicatione? Respondet quod reus tenebitur probare illam excommunicationem infra octo dies per literas vel testes vel per alia manifesta documenta." This perhaps assumes that a confession of the charge would be sufficient proof. Or it may be that such a confession is sufficient in the case of an excommunication incurred by judicial sentence (*lata sententia*) and not for one incurred *ipso facto* because of infringing a law, as in our case, where the terms of a legatine constitution are at issue. But in the *Novella in Sextum*, written some forty years later, Andreae agrees with Durantis (n. 75 above) in saying that the eight days run from the time that the judge admits

the exception. See the edition of Venice, 1499 (repr. Graz, 1963), p. 134. In the same work, p. 137, in commenting on his gloss *Hoc ideo* in the *Ordinary Gloss* ad v. *speciem* (col. 363), he discusses whether the name of the excommunicator is enough without specifying the canon. He agrees with Hostiensis and Guido of Baysio that the canon (or in our case constitution) must be named or at least described in sufficient detail to be identified: "Patet ergo quod requiritur quod specificetur canon, vel nomine proprio vel competentibus indiciis quae aequipolleant nomine proprio."

81. Durantis, *Speculum* 2. 1, *De exceptionibus*, par. 2 no. 11 (p. 513): "Quandoque tamen haec exceptio est vere peremptoria, puta cum contra electum opponitur; tunc enim in totum perimit ius electi." John Andreae, *Ordinary Gloss* to *Clementines* 2. 10. 1: *Excommunicationis exceptio*, ad v. *dilatoriae* (col. 125), gives the same example: "Opponitur enim interdum in vim peremptoriae, puta ad perimendam electionem propter excommunicationem eligentium vel electi; quo casu locum non habet decretalis *Pia consideratione*." I should think, however, that the electors or the candidate could have another try at the matter once the excommunication is absolved. Cf. the decretal *Ad probandum* (n. 83 below), where an excommunicated judge's confirmation of an election is considered void, but the matter can be heard again before a different judge.

82. This is also covered by Durantis, *Speculum* 2. 1, *De exceptionibus*, par. 2 no. 17 (p. 514), and by the *Ordinary Gloss* to the *Decretals of Gregory IX* 2. 25. 12: *Exceptionem excommunicationis* ad v. *condemnandus* (Lyons, 1606, col. 851).

83. The *Ordinary Gloss* (loc. cit. in n. 82) speaks "de illa exceptione quae proponitur contra iudicem publice excommunicatum, in quem nulla cadit iurisdictio; unde dum sic est excommunicatus, non tenet processus illius." Innocent III in his decretal *Ad probandum*, *Decretals of Gregory IX* 2. 27. 24 (Friedberg, 2:409), notes that a sentence is void if the judge were publicly excommunicated ("excommunicationis vinculo esset publice innodatus") at the time he delivered it. See also John Andreae, *Novella in Sextum* (no. 80 above) on 2. 12. 1: *Pia consideratione* (p. 135): "Et haec vera quo ad actorem vel ad reum excommunicatum; secus in iudice, qui, si publicus sit excommunicatus, ipsius sententia non valet, si postea derogatur excommunicatus."

84. *Ordinary Gloss* (loc. cit. in n. 82), ad v. *in dilatoriis:* "Et est alia dilatoria quae partim accedit ad naturam verae dilatoriae et partim ad naturam peremptoriae, sicut est exceptio excommunicationis, quia proponi potest quandocumque, et ante litem contestatam et post sententiam, et etiam si non appellaretur: quia quandoque facit retro iudicium nullum, ut hic, et infra, *De re iudicata*, *Ad probandum*; et vere dilatoria est quia ea probata iudicium sive processus est nullus, sed actio remanet salva,

ut in praedicta decretali *Ad probandum* [see nn. 81 and 83 above]; quandoque temen non facit iudicium nullum."

85. Durantis, *Speculum* 2. 1, *De exceptionibus*, par. 2 no. 8, and cf. no. 12 (p. 513).

86. Ibid., no. 13: "Idem etiam in teste, ut ei possit quandocumque opponi, et idem in denuntiatore, et in accusatore, et impetratore inquisitionis. . . . Item, potest opponi excommunicatio post conclusionem, et etiam post sententiam contra executionem, ut in praedicto capitulo *Pia consideratione*."

87. John Andreae, *Novella in Sextum* (n. 80 above), p. 136, commenting on his *Ordinary Gloss* entry *Intelligas* on 2. 12. 1: *Pia consideratione*, ad v. *opponit* (col. 363), where he interpreted the pope's words, "Si quis igitur excommunicationem opponit," to mean "in vim dilatoriae." He now adds: "Et dicebat Abbas hoc patere ex eo, quia in vim peremptoriae non potest quandocumque proponi." (For Abbas Antiquus, see above, Chap. 1 n. 86.) And to the end of his original gloss he adds: "Item nec locum habet quando excipitur de excommunicatione iudicis vel testis: tunc enim assignabitur dilatio congrua, ponderatis circumstantiis, secundum Archidiaconum." Both of these additions are reproduced in the sixteenth-century Roman edition of the *Liber sextus* (col. 363 of the reprint of Lyons, 1606).

88. *Decretals of Gregory IX* 2. 25. 2: *Denique* (Friedberg, 2:374), and *Ordinary Gloss* ad v. *per sententiam* (col. 834).

89. I follow the Salamanca text.

90. *Decretals of Gregory IX* 2. 4. 1: *Ex literis* (Friedberg, 2:256–57).

91. *Ordinary Gloss* to *Ex literis* (see preceding note), ad v. *super suis quaestionibus* (col. 564) and also to *Decretals* 2. 1. 4: *At si clerici*, ad v. *non tenet* (col. 523), citing Gratian, *Decretum* 2. 3. 11. 1: *Neganda* (Friedberg, 1:535), and *Justinian Digest* 48. 1. 5: *Si quis* (which may have been confused with 48. 2. 4: *Is qui*).

92. John Andreae, *Novella* on *Decretals* 2. 4. 1 (2:33a, no. 3): "Quamvis ex illis legibus dici posset locum habere reconventionem, cum ibi dicit quod deponere debet inscriptionem accusatus contra accusatorem, etiam pendente accusatione. . . . Item quod de maiori potest reaccusare." This edition of Andreae's commentary must be faulty, for it omits the reference to the law on which he is clearly drawing, namely, *Justinian Code* 9. 1. 19: *Neganda*, which reads: "Neganda est accusatis, qui non suas suorumque iniurias exsequantur, licentia criminandi in pari vel minori crimine, priusquam se crimine quo premuntur exuerint, secundum scita veterum iuris conditorum; ita tamen ut et ipsi inscriptiones contra eos, etiam pendente accusatione, deponere possint."

93. SP 7. 1. 4.

94. SP 3. 10. 4.

95. See Gregorio López, n. 4 to SP 7. 1. 4 (4:260), citing the *Ordinary Gloss* to *Justinian Code* 9. 1. 1: *Prius est*.

96. Durantis, *Speculum* 2. 1, *De incidentibus quaestionibus*, par. 1 no. 15 (p. 555).

97. *Ordinary Gloss* to *Decretals of Gregory IX* 5. 1. 16: *Super his*, ad v. *accusatione* (col. 1584): "Potest accusator repelli obiecto sibi maiori crimine, pari, vel etiam minori in modum exceptionis: quia criminosus criminosum accusare non debet." See also Durantis, loc. cit. in n. 96.

98. *Decretals of Gregory IX* 2. 25. 1: *Denique*: "Ceterum si de criminibus ad solam exceptionem obiectis testes convicti fuerint sive confessi, poena ordinaria mulctari non debent, cum accusatio in ipsos secundum iuris ordinem non procedat. Sufficit ergo si a perhibendo testimonio repellantur." Similar language is found in *Decretals* 2. 10. 2: *Cum dilectus* (see below at n. 101).

99. *Ordinary Gloss* to Gratian, *Decretum* 2. 15. 6, dictum ante 1, ad v. *Quod vero* (col. 1080), citing *Justinian Digest* 48. 18. 15: *Ex libero*.

100. SP 3. 16. 42: "Otorgamos por esta ley lleno poderio a todos los judgadores que han poder de fazer justicia que quando entendieren que los testigos que aduzen ante ellos van desvariando sus palabras e cambiandolas, si fueren viles omes aquellos que esto fizieren, que los pueden tormentar, de guisa que pueden sacar la verdad dellos. Otrosi dezimos que si ellos pudieren saber que los testigos que fueren aduchos ante ellos dixeren o dizen falso testimonio, o que encubren a sabiendas la verdad, que maguer otro non los acusasse sobre esto que los juezes de su officio los pueden escarmentar e darles pena, secund entendieren que merecen."

101. See *Decretals of Gregory IX* 2. 10. 2: *Cum dilectus* (Friedberg, 2: 273–74), and John Andreae, *Novella* on the last gloss (2:60, no. 38) following Hostiensis.

102. *Decretals of Gregory IX* 5. 41. 6: *Cum in contemplatione* (Friedberg, 2:928): "In ipso causae initio non est a quaestionibus inchoandum." The *Ordinary Gloss* (cols. 1963–64) explains: "Iudices a principio causae non debent incipere a tormentis, nisi primo aliquae praesumptiones praecedant."

103. L. Chevailler, "Torture," *Dictionnaire de droit canonique*, 7:1293–1314, esp. 1297–1300.

104. *Clementine Constitutions* 5. 3. 1: *Multorum querela* (Friedberg, 2:1181). The pope also prohibits the opposite occurrence: the bishop must not torture suspected heretics unless the papal inquisitor is present. (These provisions only applied, of course, to regions where papal inquisitors had been appointed.) The one who wishes to use torture must request the other's presence, and must wait for eight days for him to appear or give consent. If he does not respond, the torture can presumably proceed on the single authority's command.

105. Andreae, *Novella* on *Decretals* 5. 41. 6: *Cum in contemplatione* (5:161 no. 3): "Et quod praedixi, quaestionem esse debere moderatam, declarabat Hugutio, dicens quod in ecclesiastico foro non debent fieri tormenta quae quandoque fiunt in saeculari, cum scilicet subiicitur equuleis, ungulis, fidiculis, et huiusmodi severioribus, sed virgis et scuticis (quas 'scorezatas' vocamus) subiici poterunt," citing Gratian, *Decretum* 2. 23. 5. 1: *Circumcelliones* (Friedberg, 1:928–29), where Augustine speaks of such things.

106. See Lyndwood (above, chap. 2 n. 82), *Provinciale* 5. 5. 4: *Finaliter*, ad v. *testium receptionem* (p. 304), citing Gratian, *Decretum* 2. 23. 8. 30: *His a quibus* (Friedberg, 1:964), and *Decretals of Gregory IX* 5. 17. 4: *In archiepiscopatu* (Friedberg, 2:809).

107. For examples, see H. A. Kelly, *Love and Marriage in the Age of Chaucer* (Ithaca, 1975), pp. 170–71. It is allowed by *In archiepiscopatu* (see note above).

108. See above, chap. 1 n. 118.

109. Lyndwood (loc. cit. in n. 106), ad v. *non obstante* (p. 305), justifies the torture of a defendant in a heresy inquisition (conducted by the bishop) when a single witness of good repute has testified against him and he fails to confess; he not only cites Clement V's *Multorum querela* (n. 104 above) and Gratian, *Decretum* 2. 2. 1. 7: *Imprimis* (Friedberg, 1:442), which refers to the Roman civil laws urging all vile witnesses to be tortured, but also to *Decretum* 1. 35. 9: *Ante omnia* (Friedberg, 1:133), which provides for corporal punishment for drunken clerics. John Andreae in his *Ordinary Gloss* to *Clementines* 5. 3. 1: *Multorum querela*, ad v. *tormenta* (col. 264) classifies the fasts that inquisitors often impose upon suspected heretics as a form of torture, which therefore cannot be used without the consent of the bishop.

110. *Costituzioni egidiane* (n. 5 above) 2. 15 (Sella, p. 72). In 6. 24 (p. 232), we hear of *indicia* that are sufficient to call for torture.

111. "Desechar e aun tachar": this is the reading of the Gayoso manuscript, while the Salamanca text has "tachar e retachar."

Notes to the Appendix

1. I use the following abbreviations:

B = Benedict XII (1334–42), *Lettres communes*, 3 vols. (Paris, 1902–1911)

C = Clement V (1305–14), *Registrum*, 9 vols. (Rome, 1885–88)

E = Konrad Eubel, *Hierarchia catholica*, ed. 2, vol. 1 (Münster, 1913)

J = John XXII (1316–34), *Lettres communes*, 16 vols. (Paris, 1904–1947)

2. The archdeaconry of Medinaceli was created as a fourth archdeaconry in 1301, by re-zoning those of Sigüenza, Molina, and Almazán. See Minguella, *Historia de Sigüenza* (above, chap. 1 n. 12), 2:3, 363, 366.

3. Minguella, 2:450–54 nos. 52–53, documents of 6 March 1320. He is named here as "Johan Rodriguez," whereas his brother, the archdeacon of Almazán, is "Simon Royz." But in a document of 1324 (2:471 no. 64) it is "Johan Royz Arcidiano de Siguença."

4. According to *Decretals of Gregory IX* 1. 6. 7: *Cum in cunctis* (Friedberg, 2:51–52), bishops had to be aged thirty and legitimate.

5. The archdeacon of Campos is one of the executors of letter no. 6774, dated 16 October 1339. He is doubtless the Juan Rodríguez mentioned in the letter as having resigned a portion at Palencia on becoming canon of Palencia, since in letter no. 7689, dated 16 January 1340, Juan Rodríguez is named as having resigned the sacristy of Valladolid on becoming archdeacon of Campos.

Bibliographical Index

to the Notes

References are to chapter and note; for example, "3.8" means "Chapter 3, note 8." Full bibliographical details are normally given in the first place cited.

In the notes, a cross reference in the form, "See above, Chap. 2 at n. 27," means, "See above in the text of Chapter 2, near superscript 27."

The following abbreviations are used in the notes or in the entries of this index:

DDC	*Dictionnaire de droit canonique*, 7 vols. (1935–65)
DNB	*Dictionary of National Biography*
DTC	*Dictionnaire de théologie catholique*, 16 vols. (1903–72)
NCE	*New Catholic Encyclopedia*, 15 vols. (1967)
PL	*Patrologia latina*, ed. J. P. Migne
SP	*Siete partidas*

Acton, J. *In constitutiones legitimas Angliae glossemata* (ca. 1335, ed. 1679), 2.82, 85, 89
Aguado, J. M. *Glosario sobre Juan Ruiz* (1929), 2.1
Albornoz, Gil de. *Costituzioni egidiane* (1357, ed. 1912; Ital. tr., ed. 1977), 4.5, 110
Amanieu, A. "Archiprêtre" (DDC), 2.4
Andreae, J. *Glossa ordinaria in Sextum* (1301, ed. 1606), 1.1, 89; 4.80, 87
———. *Glossa ordinaria in Clementinas* (1322, ed. 1606), 1.1, 13, 62, 81; 3.4; 4.47–48, 54, 66, 81, 109
———. *Novella in Decretales Gregorii IX* (1338, ed. 1581), 1.77, 87–88; 4.92, 101, 105
———. *Novella in Sextum* (1342–46, ed. 1499), 1.89; 4.80, 83, 87
———. *Additiones in Speculum* (1346–47, ed. 1585), 4.2, 11, 45, 75
Anesiac (or Ennezat), Nicholas of. *Tabula super Septimum* (or *Directorium*) (1319), 1.62
Aquinas, Thomas. *Summa theologiae*, 1.13
Argáiz, Gregorio de. *Soledad laureada*, vol. 1 (1675), 2.139
Arnold, H. H. Review of Lecoy, q.v. (1940), 1.101
Azaceta, J. M., ed. *Cancionero de Juan Alfonso de Baena*, 3 vols. (1966), 1.110
Azzo of Bologna. *Summa codicis* (before 1230, ed. 1581), 1.20–21; 4.21, 28

Baldo degli Ubaldis. *Commentum in Speculum* (before 1400, ed. 1585), 4.2, 30, 34–35
Barber, M. *The Trial of the Templars* (1978), 2.116

Baronio, C. et al. *Annales ecclesiastici*, 37 vols. (1864–83), 3.69

Barraclough, G. *Papal Provisions* (1935), 1.22; 2.62, 163, 182–83

Bartholomew of Brescia. *Glossa ordinaria in Decretum* (ca. 1245, ed. 1606), 1.1; 2.9, 49; 4.21, 99

Beltrán de Heredia, V. *Bulario de la Universidad de Salamanca*, 3 vols. (1966–67), 1.13, 95; 2.16, 29, 59–60, 166; 3.7–46 passim

———. *Cartulario de la Universidad de Salamanca*, 6 vols. (1970–72), 2.142; 3.1–47 passim

Benedict XII. *Lettres communes*, 3 vols. (1902–11), 2.144, 161; 3.69; app. 1, 5

Beneyto Pérez, J. *El Cardenal Albornoz, canciller de Castilla y caudillo de Italia* (1950), 3.68, 73

Berlière, U. "Les archidiaconés ou exemptions privilégiées de monastères" (1928), 2.33

Bermejo Cabrero, J. L. "El saber jurídico del Arcipreste" (1973), 1.74

Bernard of Pavia. *Compilatio prima antiqua* (ca. 1190, ed. 1882), 2.4, 25

Bernard of Parma. *Glossa ordinaria in Decretales Gregorii IX* (1266, ed. 1606), 1.1, 23, 25, 85; 2.10–12, 48; 4.27, 49, 53, 77, 82–84, 88, 91, 97, 102

Bertram, M. "Zur wissenschaftlichen Bearbeitung der Konstitutionen Gregors X" (1973), 1.75

Bliss, W. H., et al. *Calendar of Entries in the Papal Letters, Relating to Great Britain and Ireland: Papal Letters* (1893ff.), 3.14

Block, K. S., ed. *Ludus Coventriae* (1922), 2.91

Boniface VIII. *Liber sextus decretalium* (1298, ed. 1881), 1.1, 76; 4.53, 70, 72, 75

Brown, W. *The Register of William Wickwane* (1907), 2.75

Burchard of Worms. *Decreti* (ca. 1010, PL), 2.7

Burn, A. E. *The Athanasian Creed* (1896), 1.42

Cantini, J. A. "Sinibalde dei Fieschi" (DDC), 1.49

Cassagnes, Jesselin de. *Glossa ordinaria in Extravagantes Iohannis XXII* (1325, ed. 1606), 1.1; 2.157, 174

Catalán, D., ed. *Gran crónica de Alfonso XI*, 2 vols. (1976), 1.98

Cerdá Ruiz-Funes, J. "En torno a la pesquisa y procedimiento inquisitivo en el derecho castellano-leonés de la edad media" (1962), 4.4

Chaucer, Geoffrey. *Canterbury Tales*, 2.87

Cheney, C. R. *Handbook of Dates for Students of English History* (1961), 1.90

———. "William Lyndwood's *Provinciale*" (1961), 2.82

Chevailler, L. "Torture" (DDC), 4.103

Chiarini, G., ed. *Libro de buen amor* (1964), 1.2, 72, 91, 99

Ciceri, M., ed. *Arcipreste de Talavera*, 2 vols. (1975), 3.3, 5

Clement V. *Constitutiones clementinae* (1317, ed. 1881), 1.1, 13, 40, 62, 76; 2.103; 4.73, 104, 109

———. *Registrum*, 9 vols. (1885–88), app. 1

Colliva, P. *Il cardinale Albornoz, lo Stato della Chiesa, le "Constitutiones adgidianae"* (1977), 4.5

Corominas, J., ed. *Libro de buen amor* (1967), 1.2, 73

Corpus iuris canonici (1582, ed. 1606), 1.1; 4.87

Corpus iuris civilis, ed. P. Krueger et al., 3 vols. (repr. 1959 etc), 1.11, 13, 18

Cortes de los antiguos reinos de León y de Castilla, 5 vols. (1861–1903), 2.56

Craddock, J. R. "La nota cronológica inserta en el prólogo de las *Siete partidas*" (1974), 1.112

————. "La cronología de las obras legislativas de Alfonso X el Sabio" (1981), 2.18

Criado de Val, M. *Teoría de Castilla la Nueva*, 2d ed. (1969), 2.139

————. "El Cardenal Albornoz y el Arcipreste de Hita" (1972), 2.139

————, ed. *El Arcipreste de Hita* (1973), 1.74

————. "La tierra de Hita" (1973), 2.72

————. *Historia de Hita y su Arcipreste* (1976), 2.72, 139, 184, 191, 195

Criado de Val, M. and E. W. Naylor, eds. *Libro de buen amor*, parallel texts (1965), 1.2, 90, 97; 3.62

————. *Libro de buen amor*, Toledo MS, 3 vols. (1977), 1.2

Dansey, W. *Horae decanicae rurales*, 2d ed., 2 vols (1844), 2.77, 84, 95–96; 3.31

Dante Alighieri, *Comedy*, 1.13

Davies, R. T. *The Corpus Christi Play of the English Middle Ages* (1972), 2.91

Deyermond, A. D. Introduction to reprint of Lecoy (1973), 1.4, 96

Dondaine, A. "Le manuel de l'inquisiteur (1230–1330)" (1947), 1.76

Dunning, R. W. "Rural Deans in England in the Fifteenth Century" (1967), 2.94

Duparc, P., ed. *Procès en nullité de la condemnation de Jeanne d'Arc*, 2 vols. (1977–79), 1.13

Durantis, William de. *Repertorium* (ca. 1280, ed. 1513), 1.45

————. *Speculum iudiciale* (ca. 1289, ed. 1585), 1.19; 4.2, 6–7, 26–50 passim

Edwards, K. *The English Secular Cathedrals in the Middle Ages* 2d ed. (1967), 2.13, 50, 56, 70, 174

Eliaza y Gondra, M. *Un proceso en el Libro de buen amor* (1942), 4.3

Estienne, Raymond, O.P. *Directorium ad passagium faciendum* (1332, ed. 1906), 1.51

Eubel, K. *Hierarchia catholica*, vol. 1, 2d ed. (1913), 2.30; 3.73; app. 1

Extravagantes communes (ca. 1490, ed. 1881), 1.1, 76; 2.178

Eymeric, Nicholas, O.P. *Directorium inquisitorum* (1376), 1.51

Falletti, L. "Guillaume Durand" (DDC), 1.45

Fantini, C. "Il trattato ps.-agostiniano *De vera et falsa paenitentia*" (1954), 1.8

Filippini, F. "Costituzioni inedite di Egidio Albornoz" (1896), 3.70

Fita, F. *Actas ineditas de siete concilios españoles celebrados desde el año 1282 hasta el de 1314* (1882), 2.63, 116–17

Fletcher, R. A. *The Episcopate in the Kingdom of León in the Twelfth Century* (1978), 2.57, 78

Frere, W. H., and L. E. G. Brown, eds. *The Hereford Breviary*, 3 vols. (1904–15), 1.76

Friedberg, E., ed. *Corpus iuris canonici*, 2 vols. (1879–81), 1.1 and passim

————. *Quinque compilationes antiquae* (1882), 2.4

————. *Die Canones-Sammlungen zwischen Gratian und Bernhard von Pavia* (1897), 2.4

García Blanco, M. "D. Alonso de Paradinas, copista del *Libro de buen amor*" (1956), 1.92–94

García-Gallo, A. "Neuvas observaciones sobre la obra legislativa de Alfonso X" (1976), 2.18

García Larragueta, S. A. "El comienzo del año en dataciones de documentos hispanicos" (1975), 3.31

García y García, A. "La penetración del derecho clásico medieval en España" (1966), 1.79

————. "La canonística ibérica medieval posterior al *Decreto* de Graciano," part 3 (1976), 1.13

————. "Primeros reflejos del Concilio IV Lateranense en Castilla" (1977), 2.38–42, 44–45, 51, 74, 97, 109

————. "Candalabrum iuris" (1978), 2.128

————. and R. Gonzálvez, *Catálogo de los manuscritos jurídicos medievales de la catedral de Toledo* (1970), 1.47, 75, 82–84; 2.128

Gerli, E. M. *Alfonso Martínez de Toledo* (1976), 3.5

————, ed. *Arcipreste de Talavera* (1979), 3.5

Gerson, John, *De laude scriptorum* (1423, ed. 1973), 1.13

Gillmann, F. "Zur Frage der Abfassungszeit der Novelle des Johannes Andreä zu den Dekretalen Gregors IX" (1924), 1.78

Giménez y Martínez, J. "San Raimundo de Peñafort y las *Partidas* de Alfonso X" (1955), 2.2

Gimeno, J. Review of E. v. Kraemer, ed., *Disputa del alma* (1962–63), 1.111

Goffredo da Trani. *Commentum in Decretales* (ca. 1245), 4.17

Gómez de la Serna, P., ed. *Los códigos españoles*, vols. 2–5: *Siete partidas* (1848), 2.19–20; 4.9

Goñi Gaztambide, J. "Una bula de Juan XXII sobre reforma del episcopado castellano (4 junio 1318)" (1955), 3.54, 69

González Palencia, A. *Los mozárabes de Toledo en los siglos XII y XIII*, 4 vols. (1926–30), 2.65, 69; 3.44

Gratian of Bologna. *Decretum* (ca. 1140, ed. 1879), 1.1, 5–36 passim, 45; 2.7–8, 46, 49; 4.8, 20, 105–6, 109

Gregory IX. *Decretales* (1234, ed. 1881), 1.1, 22–23, 38, 45, 85, 88; 2.3–5, 33, 43, 46–47, 151; 3.57; 4.14, 53–54, 83, 88, 90, 98, 101–2, 105–7; app. 4

Guadalupe Beraza, L. *Diezmos de la sede toledana y rentas de la mesa aszobispal (siglo XV)* (1972), 2.67–68, 73; 3.50

Gui, Bernard. *Practica inquisitionis haereticae pravitatis* (ca. 1323, ed. 1886), 1.76

Hamilton, S. G., ed. *Collectanea* (1912), 2.79

Hobhouse, E. *Calendar of the Register of John de Drokensford, Bishop of Bath and Wells*, vol. 1 (1887), 2.94–95

Hostiensis. *Summa aurea* (1253, ed. 1537), 1.22

————. *Summa aurea* (ed. 1574), 1.22; 2.11–12, 15; 4.39–41, 66

————. *Commentaria in Decretales* (1271, ed. 1581), 2.11–12, 15, 152, 174

Iglesias Ferreirós, A. "Alfonso X el Sabio y su obra legislativa" (1980), 2.18

Innocent IV. *Commentaria in Decretales* (ca. 1251, ed. 1578), 2.10

————. *Novellae constitutiones* (1253), 4.54, 70, 75

Ivo of Chartres, St. *Decretum* (before 1115, PL), 2.7

John XXII. *Lettres communes*, 16 vols. (1904–47), 2.14, 143–62 passim, 199, 201; 3.10, 13, 35; app. 1

————. *Lettres secrètes et curiales ... relatives à la France*, vol. 1 (1900), 2.154

————. *Extravagantes* (1325, ed. 1881), 1.1; 2.150, 153

Johnson, C., ed. *Registrum Hamonis Hethe, diocesis Roffensis* (1948), 1.76

Joset, J., ed. *Libro de buen amor*, 2 vols. (1974), 1.2–3, 44, 102; 2.1, 73; 3.45

Justinian. *Codex*, 1.13, 18; 4.8, 92, 95

————. *Digestum*, 4.8, 66, 99

————. *La documentación pontificia hasta Inocencio III* (1955), 2.27
————. *Catálogo documental del archivo catedral de Burgos* (1971), 1.105–6, 108–9
Marti, B. M. *The Spanish College at Bologna in the Fourteenth Century* (1966), 2.168–69
————. "1372: The Spanish College versus the Executors of Cardinal Albornoz's Testament" (1972), 2.167
Martínez Alcubilla, M., ed. *Códigos antiguos de España* (1885), 1.98; 2.19, 24
Martínez de Toledo, Alfonso. *Arcipreste de Talavera* (1438), 3.3, 5
Martínez Marcos, E. "Fuentes de la doctrina canónica de la IV Partida" (1963), 4.15, 17
Menéndez Pidal, R. "Un copista ilustre del *Libro de buen amor* y dos redacciones de esta obra" (1941), 1.92
————. Review of J. Ducamin, ed., *Libro de buen amor* (1901), 1.92
Meredith, P., and S. J. Kahrl, eds. *The N-Town Plays* (1977), 2.91
Mesini, C. "Gli Spagnoli a Bologna prima della fondazione del collegio di Egidio d'Albornoz" (1972), 1.80
Minguella, T. *Historia de la diócesis de Sigüenza*, 3 vols. (1910–13), 1.12; 2.58, 139, 148–49, 176, 200–3, 209; app. 2–3
Moffat, L. G. "The Evidence of Early Mentions of the Archpriest of Hita or of His Work" (1960), 2.197; 3.5
Mollat, G., ed. *Lettres communes de Jean XXII*, 16 vols. (1904–47), 2.14
————. "La collation de bénéfices ecclésiastiques à l'époque des papes d'Avignon" (1921), 2.62, 154; 3.53
————. "Les Clémentines" (DDC), 1.39

Naz, R. "Inquisition" (DDC), 4.4
Nörr, K. W. "Guido de Baysio" (NCE), 1.50

O'Callaghan, J. *A History of Medieval Spain* (1975), 2.56
Olsen, M. A. "Three Observations on the *Zifar*" (1979–80), 1.117
Ottenthal, E. v. *Regulae cancellariae apostolicae* (1888) 2.171–73
Owst, G. R. *Literature and Pulpit in Medieval England*, 2d ed. (1961), 2.84

Pearson, F. S. "Records of a Ruridecanal Court of 1300" (1912), 2.79–81
Perarnau, J. "Tres nous tractats de Nicolau Eimeric" (1979), 1.51
Perroy, E. *L'Angleterre et la grande schisme d'Occident* (1933), 3.53
Place, E. B. Review of M. Penna, ed., *Arcipreste de Talavera* (1956), 2.122
Polaino Ortega, L. *El derecho procesal en el Libro de buen amor* (1948), 4.3
Porreño, B. *Vida y hechos hazaños del gran cardenal Gil de Albornoz* (1626), 2.68
Powicke, F. M. *The Medieval Books of Merton College* (1931), 1.56, 60
Powicke, F. M., and C. R. Cheney, *Councils and Synods ... Relating to the English Church*, vol. 2 (1964), 1.42; 2.92
Procter, E. S. *The Judicial Use of Pesquisa (Inquisition) in León and Castille* (1966), 4.4

Quétif, J., and J. Échard. *Scriptores ordinis praedicatorum* (1719–23), 1.51
Quesnel, Petrus. *Directorium iuris* (1322), 1.57–63, 65–67, 70–71

Real de la Riva, C., ed. Salamanca MS of *Libro de buen amor*, 2 vols. (1975), 1.2
Regino of Prüm. *De synodalibus causis* (before 915, ed. 1840), 2.7
Reynolds, R. E. "The 'Isidorian' *Epistula ad Leudefredum*" (1980), 2.3
Riesco Terrero, A. "Constitución pontificia de Inocencio IV dada a la iglesia de Salamanca el año 1245" (1977), 2.29

General Index

Persons are usually alphabetized under patronymics or toponymics, unless translated into an English form; thus, "Fonte, Bernard de," but "Bernard of Parma." The following abbreviations are used:

arbp	archbishop
ardn	archdeacon
ardny	archdeaconry
arpt	archpriest
arpbyt	archipresbyterate
bp	bishop
card.	cardinal
cath.	cathedral
chap.	chapter
dio.	diocese
k.	king
spec.	specifically

Canon Law and the Archpriest of Hita is a study of the great fourteenth-century poem, the *Libro de buen amor*, and its author, Juan Ruiz, Archpriest of Hita. Nothing is known about Ruiz or his office beyond what can be conjectured from the poem itself. In this careful and fully-researched study, Kelly approaches the problem by examining the poem's references, explicit or implicit, to canon law, the knowledge that Ruiz shows of the subject, and the canonical status he claims in calling himself an archpriest. Kelly's researches lead him to modify or reject previous conjectures and arrive at important new conclusions. Among other things, he establishes definitively that accepted dates for the *Libro* are untenable, showing that the work was most likely completed in the last quarter of the fourteenth century. While some of his conclusions are tentative and simply illustrate a new range of possibilities in areas previously considered certain, the greatest value of this study may well derive from the methodology developed and demonstrated.

Henry Ansgar Kelly is Professor of English and Medieval-Renaissance Studies at the University of California, Los Angeles. He was a Junior Fellow of the Society of Fellows of Harvard University and has held both a Guggenheim and a National Endowment for the Humanities Fellowship. His publications include *The Devil, Demonology, and Witchcraft* (Doubleday, 1968; rev. ed., 1974); *Divine Providence in the England of Shakespeare's Histories* (Harvard, 1970); *Love and Marriage in the Age of Chaucer* (Cornell, 1975), and *The Matrimonial Trials of Henry VIII* (Stanford, 1976).